From Reveille to Retreat

A Handbook for the Army Chaplain's Spouse

★

From Reveille to Retreat

★

The Journey of a Lifetime

FROM REVEILLE TO RETREAT:
THE JOURNEY OF A LIFETIME

ISBN: 978-0-692-37345-3

Bugle calls courtesy of www.music.army.mil.

15 16 17 18 19 20 21 22 23 24—10 9 8 7 6 5 4 3 2 1

MANUFACTURED IN THE UNITED STATES OF AMERICA

We dedicate this book to all our Army Chaplain Corps members and their Families who have served our great nation since 1775. Their journey of care, devotion, and sacrifice has made our Chaplain Corps strong and enduring, so that it may continue serving the Army Family with honor and compassion. May this book be an everlasting tribute to their love and service to our nation and our Army.

Chapelle Sainte-Anne
Varennes, Qu.

CONTENTS

FOREWORD

The Chief of Staff of the Army, General Raymond T. Odierno, often says that "the strength of our Soldiers is our Families." The Month of the Military Child (April), Military Spouse Day (May), Gold Star Mother's Day (September), and the Military Family Appreciation Month (November) are all reminders of the selfless service and sacrifices made by Soldiers and their Families every day.

Our Army Families exemplify the strength that sustains our Soldiers. Husbands and wives, parents and children, sisters and brothers have all risen to the challenge of multiple deployments, mobilizations, and frequent moves.

On behalf of the United States Army Chaplain Corps, I am honored to commend this handbook to you. Within these pages lay the collective wisdom and experience gleaned from decades of service by spouses of Army Chaplains. As you read their stories, I encourage you to add your story to the chapters of this book.

This book is also a practical guide to living and understanding the Army culture. It is designed to equip you with resources, support, and encouragement wherever you are in your journey as an Army Chaplain Spouse. These thoughtful contributions were researched and written by fellow Chaplain Spouses, for Chaplain Spouses. As you read these pages, I encourage you to discover your own unique path to living this life with confidence, contentment, and compassion. In so doing, you sustain the "Strength of the Nation."

Chaplain (Major General) Donald Rutherford
Chief of Chaplains, United States Army

PREFACE

At the March 2012 Senior Leadership Development Training, as Chaplain Spouses shared their best practices, one particular need stood out—the shared desire for a supportive, informative guide written specifically for Chaplain Spouses. The hope was to provide a quality resource to guide spouses through their "journeys of a lifetime." Quickly, this vision grew to include the desire for a comprehensive look at all aspects of Army life. The idea to consolidate this valuable information was born, and the Chaplain Corps' senior spouse, Karen Bailey, took on the task of organizing this unique project.

Soon, surveys and brainstorming sessions were underway, and spouses in every time zone in the world contributed their unique insights. Next, an evolving steering committee met in Washington, DC to compile data and help the contents of the book take shape. Volunteer authors stepped up to write each chapter. Under Mrs. Bailey's leadership, countless hours were spent over the next two years crafting every detail. The result is a comprehensive look at the nuts and bolts of life in the Army Chaplain Family.

ACKNOWLEDGMENTS

Over a hundred spouses and kids worldwide. You completed surveys, emailed ideas, met in brainstorming groups, compiled data, and offered encouragement throughout the process. Your honest, thoughtful remarks became the backbone of this book. You were so generous with advice, suggestions, cheerleading, and sharing must-know information. The final outcome of this book was determined by you.

The "DC Committee"—Sheryl Walker, Robin Stice, Karen Smith, Ilona Scott, Rayanne Moser, Linda Melvin, Amie Fisher, Holly Dunn, Wendy Brzezinski, Genie Brainerd, and Karen Bailey. For over a year, this core group of spouses met monthly, then bimonthly, then weekly, as they gathered information, sorted surveys, completed outlines, and discussed chapter titles. They hung in there throughout the laborious process of editing.

The Chapter and Tool Kit Authors. These folks took piles of raw material and created a heartfelt, organized product. Their creative efforts and investment of time were generous and invaluable.

The Artist. Lenore Hysom deftly blended the Army and Chaplain Corps in the beautiful inside art for this volume. Her inclusion of the flag, the chapel, and the bugle symbolize the rich traditions of the Corps.

The Chief of Chaplains. Major General Donald Rutherford fully supported this project. His staff, many of whom read and reread each chapter, helped us be certain that information was correct.

The Deputy Chief of Chaplains. Brigadier General Ray Bailey provided insight and encouragement throughout the process.

The Chief of Chaplains Project Advisor, CH (LTC) Charles Causey. This project could not have succeeded without his invaluable leadership and knowledge, wise counsel and constant support.

The Advisory Chaplains. These subject matter experts provided information on everything from history lessons to army regulations.

The Editor. Karen Bailey brought this project to life in response to many requests, and carefully saw it through the entire process. She created and distributed surveys, and read each response; assembled committees; researched and researched some more. She typed, compiled, edited and navigated the world of publishing on behalf of each Chaplain spouse, in order that the way ahead be smoother for those who follow.

The Proofreader. Wendy Brzezinski went through five manuscript drafts, four red pens, three highlighters, two pairs of reading glasses and a box of tissues as she polished our words for publication. No comma was safe from her scrutiny.

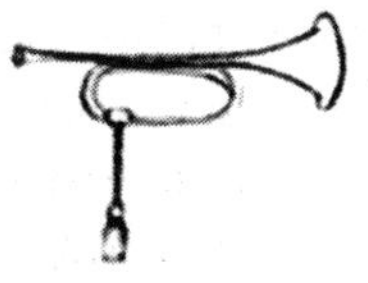

CHAPTER 1

FOR GOD AND COUNTRY

REVEILLE

Signals the troops to awaken for morning roll call. Used to accompany the raising of the National Colors.

The US Army Chaplain Corps provides religious support to America's Army while assisting commanders in ensuring the right of free exercise of religion for all Soldiers. In short, US Army Chaplains nurture the living, care for the wounded, and honor the fallen.

—US Army Chaplain Corps Mission Statement

HISTORY

As long as armies have existed, military Chaplains have served alongside Soldiers, providing for their religious needs, working to improve morale, and aiding the wounded. The Bible tells of the early Israelites bringing their priests into battle with them. Pagan priests accompanied the Roman legions during their conquests; as Christianity became the predominant religion of the Roman Empire, Christian Chaplains ministered to Roman soldiers. In fact, the word *Chaplain* is derived from *cappa,* the Latin word for "cloak."

The US Army Chaplain Corps is one of the oldest and smallest branches of the Army. The Chaplain Corps dates back to July 29, 1775, when the Continental Congress authorized one Chaplain for each regiment of the Continental Army, with pay equaling that of a captain, which was $20 per month plus forage for one horse. In addition to Chaplains serving in Continental regiments, many militia regiments counted Chaplains among their ranks. The Office of the Chief of Chaplains was created by the National Defense Act of 1920.

Since the War for Independence, Chaplains have served in every American war. Over that period of time, the US Army Chaplain Corps has evolved, with the addition of Roman Catholic Chaplains in the Mexican-American War, and Jewish and African American Chaplains during the Civil War. In 1909, the position of Chaplain Assistant was created to support the work of Army Chaplains. In January 1979, the Army commissioned its first female Chaplain. Muslim Chaplains were added in 1994, Buddhist in 2008, and Hindu in 2010. Currently, over 3,000 Chaplains including 1,600 active duty Army Chaplains and 1,200 in the reserve components are serving the total Army, representing over 140 different religious organizations.

While their duties are primarily focused on providing for the free exercise of religion for Soldiers, many Army Chaplains have also demonstrated tremendous bravery. Stories abound of Chaplains administering the last rites to fallen Soldiers, oblivious to the fire around them, or dashing out into the open to rescue the wounded without regard for their own lives. Seven Chaplains have earned the Medal of Honor for their bravery. Dozens of others have made the ultimate sacrifice, living up to the Chaplain Corps motto, Pro Deo Et Patria (For God and Country).

The importance of the Chaplain to the religious, moral, and spiritual health of the Soldiers has been noted throughout the history of the Army. Army Chaplains represent faith groups within the pluralistic religious culture in America and demonstrate the values of religious freedom of conscience and spiritual choice. In many nations of the world, religious beliefs influence perceptions of power, diplomacy, law, and social customs. Chaplains provide to commanders and staff invaluable insight into the impacts of religion when developing strategy, campaign plans, and conducting operations. Commanders continue to value the impact of the Chaplain Corps in its core commitment to the soul and spirit of the Army to nurture the living, care for the wounded, and honor the fallen across the full spectrum of military operations.

Chaplains, on behalf of their Commanders, provide and perform Religious Support (RS) in the Army to ensure the free exercise of religion. Chaplains are obligated to *provide* for those religious services or practices that they cannot personally *perform*. Chaplains perform religious support when their actions are in accordance with the tenets or beliefs of their faith group. Chaplain Assistants assist the Chaplain in providing or performing this religious support.

THE CHAPLAIN CORPS AND THE US CONSTITUTION

The First Amendment to the US Constitution says that Congress shall make no law respecting an establishing of religion or prohibiting the free exercise thereof. Congress recognizes the necessity of the Chaplain Corps in striking a balance between the Establishment and Free Exercise Clauses.

The Establishment Clause forbids any governmental authority from mandating a religion or way of prayer. In the pluralistic religious setting of the military, Unit Ministry Teams (UMTs) provide opportunities for religious support (worship services, religious classes, prayers, and so forth) for individuals from all religious backgrounds. Chaplains cooperate with each other without compromising their faith tradition or ecclesiastical endorsement requirements, to ensure the most comprehensive religious support opportunities possible within the unique military environment.

The Free Exercise Clause guarantees individuals the right to practice what their religion requires and conscience dictates. Soldiers, Family Members, and authorized Department of Defense (DOD) civilians are entitled to Chaplain support. Chaplains are expected to advise the Command on all matters pertaining to the free exercise of religion and to speak with a candor and urgency befitting the exercise of their religious duties. Chaplains assist the Commander in providing for the accommodation of religious practices.

The Chaplain Corps is an instrumentality of the US Government to ensure that the "free-exercise" rights of religion are not abridged. This constitutional principle is deeply imbedded in the statutory foundations of the Army. The Chaplain and Chaplain Assistant are core and essential manpower at every echelon of the force and are both inherently Governmental in Nature (GIN).

The Chaplain Corps and Public Law

It is helpful for spouses to understand that their Chaplain's primary responsibility is not to provide worship services and counseling, but to secure the Constitution-based free exercise rights of Soldiers and Family Members. When Chaplains don't do that, then the legitimacy of the Chaplaincy itself can be challenged in court. Once this is understood, then the Title 10, U.S. Code (Public Law) responsibilities for the Chaplain to provide worship services can be understood as having grounding in the Constitution.

Advising the Commander on Free Exercise rights and ensuring appropriate implementation is the *primary* responsibility of a Chaplain. His/her secondary responsibility is found in Title 10, US Code. By secondary, this does not mean less important; it means that the Constitutional responsibilities are foundational and all other mandates flow out of it. The US Code is the compilation of Federal law and Title 10 contains the laws that apply specifically to the military. Thus, Title 10 of the US Code, and the paragraphs that apply to Chaplains and Religious Support, are the *means* by which Free Exercise is fulfilled.

The rank on Chaplains' uniforms reminds them that they are government employees, paid with US tax dollars, and have a Constitutional responsibility. (This is referred to as being "inherently governmental," which means that these Constitutional functions are so critically related to the public interest that they can only be performed by federal employees.) The religious insignia indicates the capabilities Chaplains bring in providing for Title 10, predominantly those specific religious rites and services.

The Chaplain

Army Chaplains are members of the Army Chaplain Corps, as commissioned Army officers, with the Military Occupational Skill (MOS) of 56A. They accept their commissions from the President with a swearing-in ceremony and oath, swearing to defend the Constitution of the United States, and to obey the lawful orders of those appointed over them—as do all officers in the military. They serve as religious professionals in the Army Profession, members of a Special Branch (Chaplain Corps). Other professionals in the Chaplain Corps include Chaplain Assistants (56M); Chaplain Candidates (56X); and Directors of Religious Education (DRE). The three core competencies of the Army Chaplain Corps are: Nurture the Living, Care for the Wounded, and Honor the Fallen. The Army regulation which describes and governs the Army Chaplain Corps function is Army Regulation 165-1 "Religious Support: Army Chaplain Corps Activities." The Department of Defense respects the certification of religious organizations who endorse individuals to be Army Chaplains as qualified religious professionals.

There are special standards for individuals who apply to become Army Chaplains, and an Accessions Board is convened to ensure they meet the standards and qualifications established by the Department of Defense, and the Army—before they may join the Chaplain Corps as Army Chaplains (either on Active Duty, or in the United States Army Reserves, or the Army National Guard). The primary mission of the Army Chaplain Corps and therefore the basic duty of Army Chaplains is to provide Religious Support to Army Soldiers and Families and to advise the Commander. Those duties reflect the Army's obligation to provide for the Free Exercise of Religion of its members (a freedom secured in the US Constitution). In this regard, although Chaplains are endorsed as representatives of their specific religious organizations and faith groups, they serve to meet the needs of the service members.

Although Chaplains serve as commissioned officers with rank, they do not command. Chaplains are required in their official duties to perform religious services, pastoral care, counseling, training, and leadership to support the Garrison and Unit religious program. **Chaplains are expected to participate in chapel services and programs, even when assigned to troop units. The garrison religious program depends upon the collective support of all assigned Chaplains and Chaplain Assistants to provide the essential worship services and religious programs of the chapels—delivered to**

not only the resident population of an installation, but also the unit members who choose to worship and attend chapels on the installation.

Chaplains enter the Army with the knowledge that they are fully certified in their religious professional qualifications but will require leader development and training to function as Army officers and Chaplains in this dynamic environment. Leader development, training, and supervision help new Chaplains to understand the expectations of the Army Chaplain Corps, to serve the diverse needs of Soldiers and Families, advise the Commander, work on teams with professional colleagues, and perform the duties of a staff officer in a unit.

Each Army Chaplain is coupled with an enlisted Soldier known as a Chaplain Assistant. Together they form the Unit Ministry Team (UMT). To military types they're simply referred to as the UMT. The UMT is inseparable in duty. Due to the noncombatant status of a Chaplain, the Chaplain Assistant is responsible for the security of the team. Fully trained in Soldier tasks and religious support matters, the Chaplain Assistant rounds out the ministry of the UMT.

US Army Chaplain Center & School (USACHCS)

The US Army Chaplain Center & School is located at Fort Jackson, South Carolina, and is co-located with the Air Force and Navy Chaplains' Schools. USACHCS is led by the Commandant, a Chaplain Colonel. The USACHCS mission is to be the institutional means of educating and training Chaplains and Chaplain Assistants to provide Religious Support leadership with a full range of staff and advisement capabilities to the Army so that it can support Combatant Commanders in a joint, interagency, intergovernmental and multinational environment.

The facility contains the US Army Chaplain Center and School Library, a primary center for Army Chaplains. The school employs a branch historian and also houses the US Army Chaplain Museum, a repository for artifacts relating to the history of Chaplains and Chaplain Assistants.

USACHCS was created in 1917 to train Chaplains for service in World War I. The first session of the Chaplain School commenced March 3, 1918, at Fort Monroe, Virginia. Since then, the school has moved sixteen times. The last move was from Fort Monmouth, New Jersey.

The Center

The Center is comprised of the following: the Center for World Religion, which enables the Army to have the capability to assess the impact of religion on the mission; the Center for Spiritual Leadership, established to provide means for care to the caregivers; the Capabilities Development Integration Directorate, providing the Army with multi-functional religious support concepts, doctrine, force design, and material solutions to support the Warfighter.

The School

The US Army Chaplain School is the Chief of Chaplains's institutional means to educate and train Chaplains and Chaplain Assistants. The school is designed to safeguard the free exercise of religions and assist in the implementation of Title10 (US Code) as it relates to fulfilling the religious and spiritual needs of Soldiers and Family Members in all conditions and locations. Aligned with the Army Training and Doctrinal Command (TRADOC), USACHCS utilizes practical military and pastoral training objectives for the purpose of developing a well-rounded religious ministry professional capable of serving the needs of a highly dynamic and diverse force.

Training for the Chaplain

Throughout an Army Chaplain's entire career, there are requirements and opportunities for military training. The following is a listing of schools and courses offered by the Army Chaplain Corps.

Chaplain Basic Officer Leadership Course (CH-BOLC): Chaplains and Chaplain Candidates do not go through Basic Training. Instead, they attend the Chaplain Basic Officer Leadership Course (CH-BOLC), which is a twelve week course. CH-BOLC provides an introduction to the noncombatant common core skills, Army writing and Chaplain-specific training.

Chaplain Captain Career Course (C4): C4 provides mid-career Chaplains with the military common core to develop their staff officer skills and Chaplain Education to develop their proficiency as Chaplains.

Chaplain Captain Career Course/Reserve Component: Reserve Chaplains at the company grade level receive this training in a hybrid distance learning and residential course.

Brigade Chaplain Functional Qualification Course: Provides Chaplains selected for the rank of Major with the specific skills and knowledge needed for success as a Brigade Chaplain who will supervise the Battalion UMTs assigned to the Brigade.

Chaplain Lieutenant Colonel Course: Trains all new Chaplain Lieutenant Colonels.

Chaplain Colonel Course: Trains all new Chaplain Colonels.

Chaplain Resources Manager (CRM) Course: Selected Chaplains are trained in the skills and knowledge necessary to function as Chaplain Resources Managers.

Additional Chaplain Training (not necessarily at USACHCS)

Clinical Pastoral Education (CPE): This training is normally offered to select Chaplains between their third and sixth year of Active Duty. Selected Chaplains can opt to earn a Doctorate of

Ministry degree while attending this program of study. During this time they become fully qualified Chaplains for the institutional settings of prisons and hospitals.

Intermediate Level Education (ILE): The Army mandates that all Majors complete ILE either in-residence or through a variety of distance education options.

Advanced Civilian Education: Selected full-time Chaplains are sent to universities to obtain a graduate degree in areas such as Ethics, World Religions, Family Life and Resource Management. Afterward, they are employed in their area of training at key positions throughout the Army.

Senior Service Colleges: Colonel and Lieutenant Colonel attendees are chosen by a board approved by the Chief of Chaplains. A master's degree is awarded upon completion.

Training for the Reserve Component Chaplain

The Brigade Chaplain Functional Qualification Course, the Chaplain Lieutenant Colonel Course, and the Chaplain Colonel Course are optional for reservists and not necessary for advancement. However, it is imperative for Reserve Chaplains to be as well trained in Army Chaplain core skills as possible, and it is recommended that Reserve Chaplains attend each Chaplain course as promotions allow. Though some United States Army Reserve (USAR) Chaplains take the Clinical Pastoral Education (CPE) or Family Life training courses as opportunities and funding permits, these two courses are chiefly available to Active Duty Chaplains.

Training for the Chaplain Assistant

The Chaplain Assistant also receives training at USACHCS, which includes the following:

Chaplain Assistant Advanced Individual Training (AIT): Prepares enlisted Soldiers who have graduated from Basic Combat Training to perform or provide the religious support necessary to accomplish the Battalion level Unit Ministry Team mission in combat and in garrison.

Chaplain Assistant MOS-T Course (Reclassification Course): Provides Soldiers with basic Chaplain Assistant Military Occupational Skills training to transition from their current specialty to the 56M MOS.

Chaplain Assistant Senior Leader Course (SLC)

Chaplain Assistant Advanced Leader Course (ALC)

A Glance at the US Army Chaplain Corps

Regimental Crest

The sun and rays allude to the provision and presence of God in nature. The dove with olive branch, a traditional symbol of peace, embodies the Corps' mission in the Army to deter war and strive for peace. The pages of the open book represent the primacy of God's Word. The blue is representative of the heavens and alludes to the spiritual nature of the mission of the Chaplain Corps. The rays represent universal truth, and the surrounding palm branches represent spiritual victory. The shepherd's crook is emblematic of pastoral ministry. The numerals "1775" commemorate the date of the establishment of the Army Chaplain Corps. The motto *Pro Deo Et Patria* translates "for God and country." The regimental insignia was approved on June 4, 1986, and revised on February 11, 1993, to add the motto on the book in lieu of the Christian and Jewish insignia.

Branch Plaque

The plaque design has the emblem of the Office of the Chief of Chaplains.

Regimental Coat of Arms

A coat of arms is not authorized for the Chaplain Corps. The regimental flag consists of the regimental insignia on a dark blue background with yellow fringe. Below the insignia is a yellow scroll doubled and inscribed "Chaplain Corps" in oriental blue.

Branch Colors

Chaplains have used the color black since 1835. In regulations dated that year, a black coat was prescribed for Chaplains.

The "Shepherd's Crook"

This was the original insignia authorized for US Army Chaplains, 1880–1888, and is still included as part of the US Army Chaplain Corps regimental insignia.

Birthday Observance

The legal origin of the Chaplain Corps is found in a resolution of the Continental Congress, adopted July 29, 1775, which made provision for the pay of Chaplains. Every year on most Army Posts, the birthday of the Chaplain Corps is celebrated on this date.

A Rich Heritage

To give an example of the rich history and legacy of the Chaplain Corps, the story of the Four Chaplains is told below. This epitomizes what the Chaplain Corps is all about: service and sacrifice. It tells how four Chaplains of different faiths during a time of war served together in a common mission to bring religious care to Soldiers.

WASHINGTON (Jan. 28, 2014)—It was Feb. 3, 1943, and the U.S. Army Transport Dorchester was one of three ships in a convoy moving across the Atlantic from Newfoundland to an American base in Greenland. A converted luxury liner, the Dorchester was crowded to capacity, carrying 902 servicemen, merchant seamen, and civilian workers.

It was only 150 miles from its destination when shortly after midnight, an officer aboard the German submarine U2 spotted it. After identifying and targeting the ship, he gave orders to fire. The hit was decisive, striking the ship far below the water line. The initial blast killed scores of men and seriously wounded many more.

Others, stunned by the explosion, were groping in the darkness. Panic and chaos quickly set in! Men were screaming, others crying or frantically trying to get lifeboats off the ship. Through the pandemonium, four men spread out among the Soldiers, calming the frightened, tending the wounded, and guiding the disoriented toward safety. They were four Army chaplains, Lt. George Fox, a Methodist minister; Lt. Alexander Goode, a Jewish rabbi; Lt. John Washington, a Roman Catholic priest; and Lt. Clark Poling, a Dutch Reformed minister.

Quickly and quietly the four chaplains worked to bring calm to the men. As Soldiers began to find their way to the deck of the ship, many were still in their underwear, where they were confronted by the cold winds blowing down from the arctic.

Petty Officer John J. Mahoney, reeling from the cold, headed back towards his cabin. "Where are you going?" a voice of calm in the sea of distressed asked. "To get my gloves," Mahoney replied. "Here, take these," said Rabbi Goode as he handed a pair of gloves to the young officer. "I can't take those gloves," Mahoney replied. "Never mind," the rabbi responded. "I have two pairs." It was only long afterwards that Mahoney realized that the chaplain never intended to leave the ship.

Once topside, the chaplains opened a storage locker and began distributing life jackets. It was then that Engineer Grady Clark witnessed an astonishing sight. When there were no more life jackets in the storage room, the chaplains simultaneously removed theirs and gave them to four frightened young men. When giving their life jackets, Rabbi Goode did not call out for a Jew; Father Washington did not call out for a Catholic; nor did Fox or Poling call out for a Protestant. They simply gave their life jackets to the next man in line. One survivor would later say, "It was the finest thing I have seen or hope to see this side of heaven."

As the ship went down, survivors in nearby rafts could see the four chaplains—arms linked and braced against the slanting deck. Their voices could be heard offering prayers and singing hymns.

Of the 902 men aboard the U.S.A.T. Dorchester, only 230 survived. Before boarding the Dorchester back in January, Chaplain Poling had asked his father to pray for him, "Not for my safe return, that wouldn't be fair. Just pray that I shall do my duty . . . never be a coward . . . and have the strength, courage and understanding of men. Just pray that I shall be adequate."

Although the Distinguished Service Cross and Purple Heart were later awarded to each chaplain posthumously, Congress wished to confer the Medal of Honor but was blocked by the stringent requirements which required heroism performed under fire. So a posthumous Special Medal for Heroism, The Four Chaplains' Medal, was authorized by Congress and awarded by the President on January 18, 1961.

It was never given before and will never be given again.[1]

The US Army Chaplain Corps Medal of Honor Recipients

The Medal of Honor is our nation's highest honor bestowed on warriors. Seven Army Chaplains have been awarded the Medal of Honor through the years. Most of them earned it for acts related to caring for the wounded—one of the core competencies of the Chaplain Corps.

Four Army Chaplains earned the Medal of Honor during the Civil War. The first went to Chaplain John M. Whitehead of the 15th Indiana Infantry. At the Battle of Stone's River on December 31, 1862, Chaplain Whitehead went to the front under fire and, unaided, carried to the rear several wounded and helpless Soldiers. Chaplain Francis B. Hall of the 16th New York Infantry performed similar acts in rescuing wounded men a few months later at Salem Heights, Virginia. James Hill of the 21st Iowa Infantry earned the Medal of Honor in May 1863 for capturing enemy lookouts at the Battle of Champion Hill, although it should be noted that Hill was serving as an Infantry Lieutenant at that time; later during the war he became his Regiment's Chaplain. Milton L. Haney of the 55th Illinois was his Unit's Chaplain at the Battle of Atlanta in 1864, although his bravery was for acts outside the scope of a Chaplain's duties: he volunteered to serve as a rifleman in ranks and rendered heroic service in retaking a Federal position that the enemy had captured.

More recently, two Army Chaplains earned the Medal of Honor during the Vietnam War. Chaplain (Major) Charles J. Watters, assigned to the 173rd Airborne Brigade, earned the medal on November 19, 1967, in Dak To Province by selflessly moving under fire to carry wounded Soldiers to safety. Just a couple of weeks later, Chaplain (Captain) Angelo J. Liteky of the 199th Infantry Brigade earned the Medal of Honor in Bien Hoa Province. Similar to the actions of Watters, Liteky moved under fire with disregard for his own safety, recovered numerous wounded men from exposed positions, directed medical evacuations, and inspired his fellow Soldiers with his courage and calm demeanor. Unlike Watters, however, Liteky survived his ordeal. Watters was fatally injured while giving aid to the wounded.

On April 11, 2013, President Obama posthumously awarded Chaplain (Captain) Emil J. Kapaun the Medal of Honor for his extraordinary heroism. Chaplain Emil J. Kapaun distinguished himself by acts of gallantry and intrepidity above and beyond the call of duty while serving with the 3d Battalion, 8th Cavalry Regiment, 1st Cavalry Division during combat operations against an armed enemy at Unsan, Korea, and as a prisoner of war. At Unsan, as Chinese forces viciously attacked friendly elements, Chaplain Kapaun calmly walked through withering enemy fire in order to provide comfort and medical aid to his comrades and rescue friendly wounded from no-man's land. Though the Americans successfully repelled the assault, they found themselves surrounded by the enemy. Facing annihilation, the able-bodied men were ordered to evacuate. However, Chaplain Kapaun, fully aware of his certain capture, elected to stay behind with the wounded. After the enemy succeeded in breaking through the defense in the early morning hours of November 2, Chaplain Kapaun continually made rounds, as hand-to-hand combat ensued. Chaplain Kapaun, with unwavering resolve and with complete disregard for his personal safety, bravely pushed aside a Korean soldier preparing to execute Sergeant First Class Herbert A. Miller. Chaplain Kapaun hoisted the wounded soldier up, carried Sergeant Miller on his back to safety and assisted him for several days. As Korean and Chinese infantry approached the American position, Chaplain Kapaun noticed an injured Chinese officer amongst the wounded and convinced him to negotiate the safe surrender of the American forces. Not only did Chaplain Kapaun's gallantry save the life of Sergeant Miller, but also his unparalleled courage and leadership inspired all those present, and many men who might have otherwise fled in panic were encouraged by his presence and remained to fight the enemy.

NOTES

1. John Brinsfield, "Chaplain Corp History: The Four Chaplains," January 28, 2014, *U.S. Army*, http://www.army.mil/article/34090/Chaplain_Corps_History__The_Four_Chaplains/.

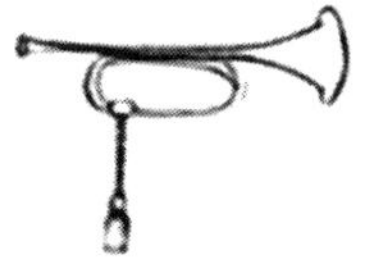

CHAPTER 2

HOOAH AND ALL THINGS ARMY

Becca Whitham

Assembly

Signals troops to assemble at a designated place.

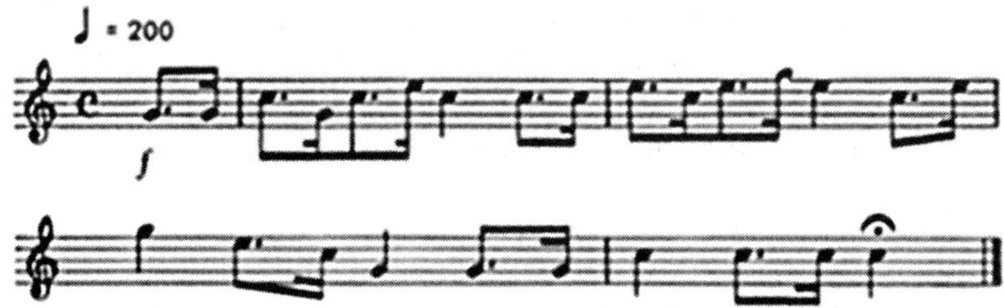

Hooah!" It's the Army version of "Amen, preach it!" The word *hooah* comes from the acronym "HUA," which is the abbreviation for "heard, understood, and acknowledged." It can also mean:

- "Roger," "solid copy," "good," "great," "message received," "understood," "acknowledged"
- "Glad to meet you," "welcome"
- "Thank you"
- "You've taken the correct action"
- "Outstanding!"

Often, *hooah* is used to

- motivate another Soldier
- indicate that one did not hear what was said, but is not going to ask you to repeat it
- anything and everything except "no"

Hooah can also be used

- as a call and response cheer, with one Soldier exclaiming, "Hooah!" and other Soldiers responding in kind

- at random and in a group in order to boost morale. One or a few Soldiers will begin chanting "Hooah!" and then others join in

Army 101

The History and Roles of the US Army

The Second Continental Congress founded the Army in 1775; it is the oldest service of the United States military. Originally formed to protect the freedom of the first thirteen colonies, the Army has evolved and grown from this small militia force into the world's premier fighting force. The Army exists to serve the American people, to defend the Nation, to protect vital national interests, and to fulfill national military responsibilities. The mission is enduring: to provide necessary forces and capabilities to the Combatant Commanders in support of the *National Security* and *Defense Strategies*. The Army recruits, organizes, trains, and equips Soldiers who, as vital members of their units and the Joint Team, conduct prompt, sustained combat and stability operations on land. The Army is also charged with providing logistics and support to enable the other Services to accomplish their missions, and supporting civil authorities in time of emergency, when directed.

The Army continues to provide Combatant Commanders with a wide range of forces and capabilities to prevail in the war on terror, to sustain our global commitments, and to build effective multinational coalitions. The Army's requirements, however, are far greater than those needed to support the war on terror (http://www.military.com/join-armed-forces/us-army-overview.html).

US Army Structure

The Army, as one of the three military departments (Army, Navy and Air Force) reporting to the Department of Defense, is composed of distinct and equally important components: the active component and the reserve components. The reserve components are the United States Army Reserve and the Army National Guard. Regardless of component, the Army conducts both operational and institutional missions. The operational Army consists of numbered armies, corps, divisions, brigades, and battalions that conduct full spectrum operations around the world. The institutional Army supports the operational Army. Institutional organizations provide the infrastructure necessary to raise, train, equip, deploy, and ensure the readiness of all Army forces. The training base provides military skills and professional education to every Soldier—as well as members of sister Services and allied forces. It also allows the Army to expand rapidly in time of war. The industrial base provides world-class equipment and logistics for the Army. Army installations provide the power-projection platforms required to deploy land forces promptly to support Combatant Commanders. Once those forces are deployed, the institutional Army provides the logistics needed to support them. Without the institutional Army, the operational Army cannot function. Without the operational Army, the institutional Army has no purpose.

The senior leader of the Army, the Chief of Staff of the Army (CSA), serves on the Joint Chiefs of Staff advisory board. This board is headed by the Chairman of the Joint Chiefs of Staff (CJCS), who reports directly to the Secretary of Defense and the Commander in Chief, the President of the United States (POTUS). Members of the Joint Chiefs of Staff come from all branches of the military.

Army Command Structure

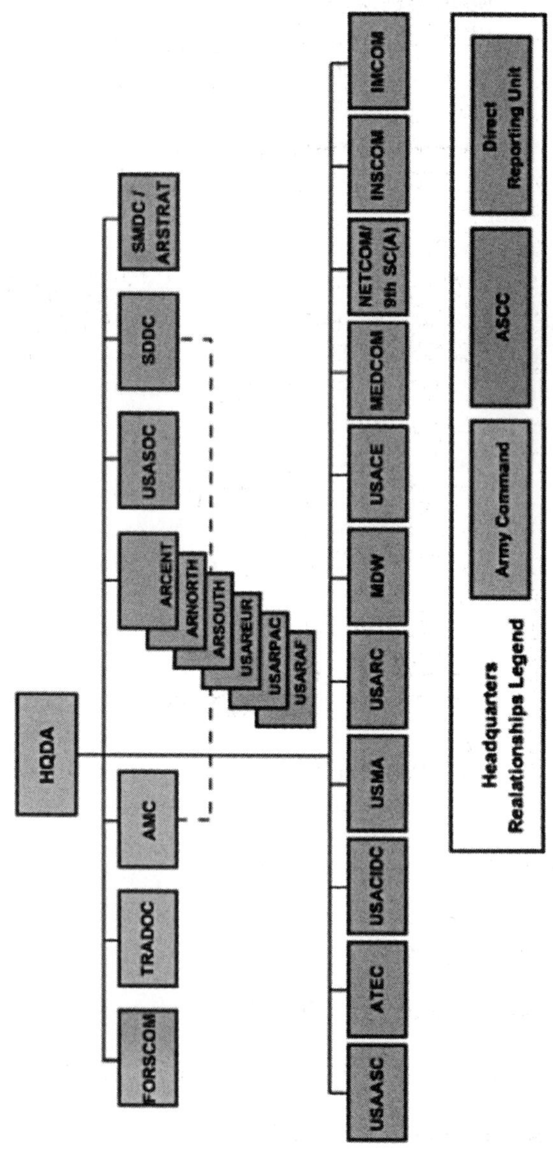

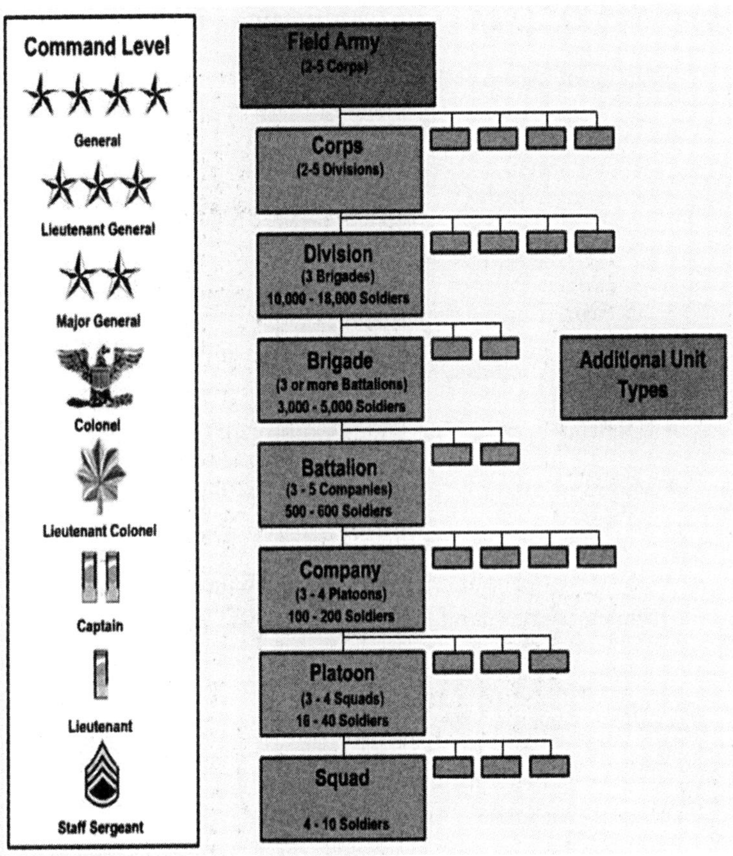

Headquarters Department of the Army (HQDA) Staff:

Army Commands (ACOM)

- US Army Forces Command (FORSCOM)
- US Army Training and Doctrine Command (TRADOC)
- US Army Materiel Command (AMC)

Army Service Component Commands (ASCC)

- US Army Africa (USARAF)
- US Army Central (USARCENT)
- US Army North (USARNORTH)
- US Army South (USARSO)
- US Army Europe (USAREUR)
- US Army Pacific (USARPAC)
- US Army Special Operations Command (USASOC)
- Military Surface Deployment and Distribution Command (SDDC)
- US Army Space and Missile Defense Command/Army Strategic Command (USASMDC/ARSTRAT)

Direct Reporting Units (DRU)

- US Army Network Enterprise Technology Command/9th Signal Command (Army) (NETCOM/9thSC(A))
- US Army Medical Command (MEDCOM)
- US Army Intelligence and Security Command (INSCOM)
- US Army Criminal Investigation Command (USACIDC)
- US Army Corps of Engineers (USACE)
- US Army Military District of Washington (MDW)
- US Army Test and Evaluation Command (ATEC)
- United States Military Academy (USMA)
- US Army Reserve Command (USARC)

- US Army Acquisition Support Center (USAASC)
- US Army Installation Management Command (IMCOM)

Unit Command/Leadership Structure

Unit	Composition	Unit Commander	Senior NCO
Corps The Corps HQ performs primarily as a war fighting headquarters. The Corps HQ is capable of rapid transitions to a Joint Task Force Headquarters for small scaled contingency.	Headquarters (HQ of about 400 Soldiers) Command and controls Divisions and other units (leads a total of approximately 50,000–120,000 forces)	Lieutenant General	Command Sergeant Major
Division Provides a modular command and control headquarters for Brigade Combat Teams (BCTs) during full spectrum operations to destroy enemy forces, seize and secure land area and terrain.	Headquarters (HQ of about 300) (about 750 Soldiers) 3 or more BCTs and Support Brigades (leads a total of between 16,000 and 25,000 forces)	Major General	Command Sergeant Major

Unit	Composition	Unit Commander	Senior NCO
Brigade (Group/ Regiment) Employed on independent or semi-independent operations.	Headquarters (HQ of about 120) 2–8 Battalions (leads a total of between 2,500 and 5,000 forces)	Colonel (Sometimes a Brigadier General)	Command Sergeant Major
Battalion (Squadron)	2–8 Companies (Batteries/ Troops) (leads 700–1,000)	Lieutenant Colonel	Command Sergeant Major
Company	Headquarters (HQ of about 60)	Captain	First Sergeant
(Battery/Troop)	2–8 Platoons (leads 100-200)	(Sometimes a Major or Warrant Officer)	or Detachment Sergeant
Platoon	2–6 Squads	Lieutenant	Platoon Sergeant
Squad (Section/Team)	2–8 Teams/ Sections	Staff Sergeant or Sergeant	N/A

Force Modernization and the Division

Our world changed dramatically after September 11, 2001, and that has caused many changes in the structure and operation of the US Army. Our Army is currently bigger now than ten years ago, and spread into almost eighty countries throughout the world. The Army is continually reshaping and transforming to meet future requirements.

In 2003, the Army began to move from a Divisional structure with large brigades to a modular force centered around Brigade Combat Teams. The Army recognized a need for smaller units that can deploy more easily with greater capabilities. Army brigades are now being organized with an expanded set of organic (permanent) capabilities to enhance unit cohesion, give them the greatest combat effectiveness, and the ability to respond to fleeting opportunities and unforeseen dangers.

Divisions are still present along with these modular brigades, and both are still named and numbered as "conventional" units, but with the advent of the Brigade Combat Team concept, both kinds of units have changed significantly.

A Division usually consists of three to ten brigade-sized elements (10,000 to 30,000 Soldiers) and is commanded by a Major General. Divisions are historically numbered and assigned to specific posts as senior Headquarters (HQs). Under Modularity, there is no standard division structure. Divisions no longer have a fixed structure and organic (permanent) brigades or division troops. Now only the Headquarters and its Special Troops Battalion are organic. The Division performs major tactical operations for its assigned higher headquarters and conducts sustained battles and engagements with a mission-tailored set of subordinate units. There are currently ten Divisions in the Active Army.

Brigade Combat Team (BCT) Modernization

BCTs form the basic block of the Army's tactical formation. They consist of 1,500–5,000 Soldiers and are normally commanded by a colonel with a command sergeant major as senior NCO. Brigades are organized as permanent combined arms teams (more like mini-divisions) and consequently are no longer primarily composed of all members of one branch. There are three types of Brigade Combat Teams:

- Heavy Brigade Combat Team (HBCT). Heavy BCTs are balanced combined arms units that execute operations with shock and speed. Their main battle tanks, self-propelled artillery, and fighting vehicle-mounted infantry provide tremendous striking power. They have the greatest firepower and protection of the BCTs.

- Infantry Brigade Combat Team (IBCT). Infantry BCTs are optimized for operations in restricted terrain and urban areas. They are more easily deployed than the other BCTs. The infantry Soldier is the centerpiece of the infantry BCT.

- Stryker Brigade Combat Team (SBCT). The Stryker BCT is more deployable than the heavy BCT and has greater tactical mobility, protection, and firepower than the infantry BCT. This design facilitates Stryker BCT operations in urban and other complex terrain against wide range opponents.

Modular Support Brigades complement the BCT by providing capabilities to deployed forces. More than one type of support brigade may be task-organized to a division or corps (except for sustainment brigades).

- Maneuver Enhancement consists of an organic support battalion, signal company, and headquarters company.

- Battlefield Surveillance conducts intelligence, surveillance, and reconnaissance (ISR) operations.

- Combat Aviation can contain four aviation battalions including support, attack, utility assault, and general support; also contains a headquarters and signal company.

- Fires: Assets include a Multiple Launch Rocket System battalion, headquarters, battery, and target acquisition battery.
- Sustainment consists of an organic Brigade Troops Battalion; provides direct or general support to division and brigades.

Basic Staff Structure

The battle staff's primary function is to assist the commander in the synchronization and integration of the unit's operations. A commander's staff is made up of two types of staff members: the primary staff and the special staff. Each primary staff position has a specific function and is designated by a letter. "S" stands for staff for brigade level and below. "G" stands for general staff because it is above brigade (division and higher) and has a general officer as the commander. When the Army staff is designated into a Joint Force, the letter "J" is used. This combines all three services, Army, Navy, Air Force, into one military force. There can be many more staff members beyond the normal army staff positions on a Joint Force staff.

To give you an idea of the functions of the primary staff, below are the functions of the primary staff for battalions and brigades, designated by the letter "S."

- The Executive Officer (XO). A Major (MAJ) at the Battalion (BN) and Brigade (BDE) level, the XO may serve as the second-in-command and as the principal assistant to the Commanding Officer. He usually directs, coordinates, and supervises the activities of the staff sections.
- The Command Sergeant Major (CSM). The CSM is the principal advisor to the Commander on all matters regarding enlisted personnel.
- The S1 (Adjutant). Captain (CPT) The S1 is charged with the staff responsibility of personnel management; matters

pertaining to unit strength, morale, discipline; and miscellaneous administrative tasks.

- The S2 (Military Intelligence). CPT or Lieutenant (LT) The S2 is responsible for the production and dissemination of combat intelligence and counterintelligence matters. Other duties include being responsible for physical security of the unit, producing combat intelligence and interpreting information of the enemy, weather, and terrain.

- The S3 (Operations). (MAJ) The S3 Staff has responsibility for planning the successive combat operations, organization, and training as directed by the Commanding Officer.

- The S4 (Internal Logistics). (CPT) The S4 is the battalion supply and logistic officer and has staff responsibility for the internal logistics services and facilities available to the battalion. These are supply, transportation, maintenance, logistics plans and records, and other matters in the field of logistical support.

- The S5 (Civil Affairs). (CPT or LT) The S5 is the principal staff officer for all matters concerning civil-military operations (CMO).

- The S6 (Communications). (CPT or LT) The S6 is the principal staff officer for all matters concerning command, control, communications, and computer operations.

- The S7 (Information Operations). (CPT or LT) The S7 is the principal staff officer for all matters concerning information operations, including current operations and plans.

The Special Staff is made up of officers with specific expertise and knowledge such as Chaplains, civil affairs, lawyers, and medical. The Chaplain has two unique roles for the commander: he is a special staff officer and a personal staff officer. The CSM is the only other personal staff member for the commander. As a special staff officer, the Chaplain advises the commander and the staff on religious requirements and needs of the unit and operations. As a personal staff officer, the Chaplain advises the commander on personal religious needs of the command.

Rank and Pay Grade Structure

Knowing the difference between rank and pay grade is very important. Military rank reflects leadership and responsibility. As rank increases, so does responsibility for personnel, equipment, and mission. Pay grades are administrative classifications used to standardize compensation across the military services. Pay grades are divided into three groups: "E" for enlisted, "W" for warrant officer, and "O" for officer. Enlisted pay grades begin at E-1 and finish at E-9; warrant officer pay grades begin at W-1 and finish at W-5; and officer pay grades begin at O-1 and finish at O-10. If your Chaplain has the rank of Captain, his pay grade is O-3; if his rank is Colonel, his pay grade is O-6.

Soldiers are divided into two major categories: officers and enlisted. Officer ranks in the United States Army consist of commissioned officers and warrant officers. The commissioned ranks are the highest in the military and receive a commission from one of four possible sources: United States Military Academy (USMA, West Point), Reserve Officer Training Corps (ROTC), Officer Candidate School (OCS), or by Direct Commission. Chaplains normally fall into the Direct Commission category.

These officers hold presidential commissions and are confirmed at their ranks by the Senate. Within the officer ranks, there are three subcategories: Company Grade Officers (Lieutenants–Captains) in pay grades of O-1 to O-3, Field Grade Officers (Majors–Colonels) in pay grades O-4 to O-6 and General Officers (Brigadier General–General) in pay grades O-7 to O-10.

Warrant officers hold certificates of appointment from their service secretary and are specialists and experts in certain military technologies or capabilities. The lowest-ranking warrant officers serve under a warrant, but they receive commissions from the President upon promotion to Chief Warrant Officer 2. These commissioned warrant officers are direct representatives of the President of the United States. They derive their authority from the same source as commissioned officers but remain specialists, in contrast to commissioned officers, who are generalists.

There are thirteen enlisted ranks in the US Army. Within the enlisted is a subcategory called Non-commissioned Officers (NCOs). NCOs are allowed to issue orders, but they are still considered of lower rank than even the most junior of those in the Officer Corps. In general terms these Army ranks are broken down into three groups—Junior Enlisted (E-1 through E-4), NCOs (E-4 through E-6), and Senior NCOs (E-7 through E-9). All enlisted Soldiers must salute officers, but officers only have to salute those of higher rank.

> Now pay attention because this is important. When you pull into the Commissary parking lot and see the sign that says "FOR GENERAL OFFICERS," it doesn't mean that parking spots marked FOR GENERAL OFFICERS are for officers in general. It means for GENERALS AND THEIR SPOUSES ONLY. No star(s), no parking! You may also see a sign that says CSM, which is the acronym for "Command Sergeant Major." It would be equally unwise to try to snag the CSM's parking spot. (Don't worry—we won't tell that we saw you almost do this.)

Your spouse will have two designations: Chaplain and a military rank. Chaplains of all ranks are introduced as "Chaplain [last name]," but, when addressing a letter or formal invitation, both designations are noted. The address line should be as follows:

CH (CPT) Smith
CH (MAJ) and Mrs. Smith
Mr. and CH (LTC) Smith

US Army Rank and Insignia Chart

Rank (referred to as, in casual conversation)	Abbreviation	Pay Grade	Insignia
Private	PV1	E-1	No insignia
Private	PV2	E-2	1 stripe
Private First Class (Private)	PFC	E-3	1 stripe above 1 arc
Specialist	SPC	E-4	Inverted Chevron w/eagle
Corporal	CPL	E-4	2 stripes
Sergeant	SGT	E-5	3 stripes
Staff Sergeant (Sergeant)	SSG	E-6	4 stripes
Platoon Sergeant (Sergeant)	PSG	E-7	5 stripes
Sergeant First Class (Sergeant)	SFC	E-7	5 stripes
Master Sergeant (Sergeant)	MSG	E-8	6 stripes
First Sergeant (Sergeant)	1SG	E-8	6 stripes w/ diamond
Sergeant Major (Sergeant Major)	SGM	E-9	6 stripes w/star

Rank (referred to as, in casual conversation)	Abbreviation	Pay Grade	Insignia
Command Sergeant Major (Command Sergeant)	CSM	E-9	6 stripes, star within a wreath
Warrant Officer 1 (Mr./Mrs./ Ms.)	WO1	W-1	Silver bar w/ 1 black square
Chief Warrant Officer 2 (Mr./ Mrs./Ms.)	CW2	W-2	Silver bar w/ 2 black squares
Chief Warrant Officer 3 (Mr./ Mrs./Ms.)	CW3	W-3	Silver bar w/ 3 black squares
Chief Warrant Officer 4 (Mr./ Mrs./Ms.)	CW4	W-4	Silver bar w/ 4 black squares
Chief Warrant Officer 5 (Mr./ Mrs./Ms.)	CW5	W-5	Silver bar w/ 4 black squares
Second Lieutenant (Lieutenant)	2LT	O-1	Gold Bar
First Lieutenant (Lieutenant)	1LT	O-2	Silver Bar
Captain	CPT	O-3	Two silver bars

Rank (referred to as, in casual conversation)	**Abbreviation**	**Pay Grade**	**Insignia**
Major	MAJ	O-4	Gold oak leaf
Lieutenant Colonel (Colonel)	LTC	O-5	Silver oak leaf
Colonel	COL	O-6	Silver eagle
Brigadier General (General)	BG	O-7	1 silver star
Major General (General)	MG	O-8	2 silver star
Lieutenant General (General)	LTG	O-9	3 silver star
General	GEN	O-10	4 silver star

Officer Branches

An Officer's branch is the specialty into which he is commissioned or transferred, trained, and developed. Officers are accessed into a single basic branch and will hold that branch designation. They will serve their company grade time developing the leadership and skills associated with their branch and will continue to wear their branch insignia throughout their military service. Your spouse, the Chaplain, is a part of the Chaplain Corps branch of the Army. The Chaplain and Judge Advocate General's Corps are considered Special Branches as well as the Dental and Medical Corps. An example of Combat Army branches are Infantry, Armor and Field Artillery. Combat Support Branch examples are Military Police, Military Intelligence Corps, and the Signal Corps.

Some Trivial but Useful Information

Second Lieutenants, the lowest-ranking officers, are sometimes called "butter bars" because their insignia is one gold bar. This is helpful to remember because gold insignias indicate a lower rank than silver. Colonels are sometimes referred to as a "full bird" because of the insignia—the eagle.

There used to be two levels of Generals, Lieutenant General and General. As the Army grew, so did the need for different levels of Generals. Since Lieutenant Generals were already one level below a General, the new levels of General ranks were added below them. This is why a Major ranks higher than a Lieutenant, but a Major General ranks lower than a Lieutenant General. Confusing, right? However, unless doing a formal introduction, most people refer to a General as a "one star," "two star," and so on, which makes things easier.

Some Trivial and Mostly Useless Information

The five star general rank was created in the midst of World War II to address the fact that several American commanders found themselves in the delicate position of supervising Allied officers of higher rank. Initially, the new rank was to be called Field Marshal, after the British military, but this was nixed due to objections, so instead it was named General of the Army. The four generals who have served as five stars are: George C. Marshall, Douglas MacArthur, Dwight D. Eisenhower, and Omar N. Bradley. When General Bradley died in April of 1981, the five star rank was consigned to history. The rank of "General of the Armies of the United States"—the highest military rank of all time, and the only rank to beat a five star—has been held by George Washington (Revolutionary War) and John J. Pershing (WWI).

The Army, Marines, and Air Force have almost identical ranks (the Air Force was created out of the Army during WWII); the Navy and Coast Guard have identical ranks, but they are different from the Army. A Captain in the Navy is along the same rank as a Colonel in the Army. That's why Captain Kirk and Captain Picard sit in the big chair on Star Trek Enterprise. Chief O'Brien is a Chief Petty Officer (or Warrant Officer in Army-speak), which is why he is alternately referred to as "Chief O'Brien" and "Mr. O'Brien."

Some Very Important Information

A spouse has no official or unofficial rank. None. Zero. Zippo. Nada. If you hear the comment, "She wears her husband's rank," it's not a compliment. "Wearing rank" should be avoided like the plague in a Chaplain's spouse. It is a good practice to refer to your spouse by name rather than mentioning his rank in conversation. When in public and when talking with others, remember to address senior people by their proper title and last names. Manners are always more attractive than pretension.

MILITARY COURTESIES AND TRADITIONS

Protocol

Did you realize it is bad manners to show up at an award ceremony in jeans? Go ahead, ask me how I know that (now). Protocol is the Army's version of "Ask Emily Post." It's a combination of common sense, good manners, and a rich heritage of military history. While there is no question things are becoming more relaxed and casual, there are still times when knowing what's expected will go a long way toward avoiding embarrassing blunders. A number of these situations are addressed below and in the many resources available for military spouses. When in doubt, take your cue from the senior spouse and always remember the protocol top-five must-knows:

1. RSVP
2. Thank-you notes
3. Wear name tags on right side
4. Be punctual
5. Take the first step to introduce yourself at a gathering

Reveille and Retreat

If you are on post outside in the morning for Reveille (flag being raised) or in the evening for Retreat (flag being lowered), stop and stand facing the flag or the sound of the music. This is showing honor to our nation and the flag our Soldiers defend. Soldiers will salute. Family Members (including children) may place their right hands over their hearts. Stand quietly until the music has stopped. If you are in a car, stop, get out, and follow the same procedure. If you have small children in the car, you may remain in the car; however, stop the vehicle until the music stops playing. If you live on post, children should stop their play activities and stand quietly until the music stops. If you are visiting an Air Force or Navy base, you are only required to stop the car and remain seated inside. This is showing honor to our nation and the flag our Soldiers defend.

Flag Etiquette

There is a federal law outlining how to treat our flag. Go to www.usflag.org/flagetiquette.html to read a layman's version of these outlines. One interesting bit concerns Memorial Day. Flags are to be flown at half-staff from dawn to noon to honor the dead; then they are to be dipped or lowered and raised to full height at noon until dusk to honor the living. The flag is to be flown at half-staff in mourning for designated, principal government leaders and upon presidential or gubernatorial order.

Bottom line: If you are going to display a flag, be sure you do it properly. When the flag passes in a procession, or when it is hoisted or lowered, all should face the flag. Soldiers in uniform will salute. All others should place their right hands over their hearts.

What to Wear

There is always much discussion generated about what to wear to the many social functions to which you will undoubtedly be invited. A good rule of thumb to follow is that no matter how friendly the workplace is or how chummy coworkers are, the Army is STILL your spouse's place of work and business. Always maintain a professional image and manner of dress. Inappropriate attire will be noticed. There are technically only three forms of attire (Formal, Informal and Casual). However, you will see many things written on invitations in terms of dress codes. The following is a guide to help you decide WHAT to wear to a function.

Formal

Military Personnel: Army Service Uniform (ASU)/bow tie (men) or neck tab (women); Army white uniform/bow tie (men) or neck tab (women); Army blue mess or white mess with bow tie (men) or neck tab (women).

Civilians: For a ball or dance, white or black tie (men); long or short formal (women). For a formal dinner, tuxedo/bow tie (men); long dress, blouse and skirt, or evening slacks (women).

Informal

Military Personnel: ASU with four-in-hand tie (men)/black neck tab (women); when not in uniform, dark-colored business suit preferred. Civilians: Business suit (men); "dressy" dress or suit (women).

Casual

Military Personnel: May include the Class B uniform or Army Combat Uniform (ACU); check with host/hostess. Civilians: Open-neck shirt (no tie), slacks with sport coat or sweater (men); simple dress, skirt and blouse, or pant suit (women).

Semi-Formal

Although not an official category of dress, the host or hostess who uses this description most likely expects guests to wear a business suit (men) or a cocktail dress (women).

Very Casual

This usually means jeans, shorts, or sundresses. There is no military dress for this category, but jeans with holes, short shorts, or too-sheer sundresses are never appropriate.

Texas Casual, Beach Wear, Etc.

These types of categories are usually "defined" by local custom and policy. It would be best to ask the host or hostess if you are unsure.

Receiving Lines

A protocol officer will be positioned at the beginning of the receiving line. He will ask you to place your glass or food on a tray, remove your chewing gum, or correct any other "no-no's" of receiving line etiquette. Obviously, it's better to do these things before you get that far. At Army functions, the lady precedes the man regardless of which one is the Soldier. This is not the time to catch up with friends, but rather to offer a quick hello, a medium-firm handshake (no fishy-floppies, but common courtesy is a less-than-your-normal firm because of the number of people those in the receiving line must greet), and move along. If the person in the line is well known to you and extends a hug, feel free to reciprocate but, again, there are many people who must get through the line, so keep conversation brief.

Toasting

A list of the toasts and proper responses will usually be provided in the program (so bring your reading glasses). Though they are often a short repeat of the offered toast, some are not. For example, when the toast is offered to the President of the United States, the proper response is, "To the Commander in Chief." A personal/professional non-alcohol policy is not a reason to decline toasting. Many functions will provide a non-alcoholic alternative to wine or champagne. If this is not provided, use your water glass to participate.

Where to Wear a Name Tag

Yes, there's a proper way to wear a name tag. Who knew? And it's not where it's easiest to slap on. It's on your right side so it's most visible when you shake hands.

ARMY GATHERINGS, FUNCTIONS, AND CEREMONIES

Parades

Outdoor review of troops. No formal invitation is required. Wear weather-appropriate clothing. Seating is often provided, but areas may be reserved for high ranking officers, so be sure to ask before you sit down. Stand for "Ruffles & Flourishes" (when a General is present, the band plays it once for each star he/she has) and the General's March. Stand and place your right hand over your heart when the National Anthem is played. When you see the American flag approach, rise when its bearer is six paces from your position and remain standing until it has passed six paces away from you. Stand when the Division song and the Army song are played, and as a courtesy, when a foreign national anthem is played. With all that standing, you might not need to sit down after all.

Change of Command/Responsibility Ceremonies

No formal invitation is needed for attendance. The incoming leader provides refreshments. No gift is required, but if you wish to acknowledge in that way, be sure to bring a gift for both the incoming and outgoing Soldier/spouse.

New Year's Day Receptions

The New Year's Day Reception is a dress up affair and traditionally held on New Year's Day by the commanding officer of a unit. These are normally held at the battalion level or higher. It is one of the few "command performance" occasions, and the military members of the unit should attend unless ill or out of town, even if the spouse cannot attend. A New Year's Day Reception is often a buffet-style meal (appetizers only) and typically runs on a tight schedule. For example, a battalion-oriented reception would be organized by company, and usually held at the Battalion Commander's home. Each company will be assigned a specific time to arrive, as well as a specific time to depart. Be punctual! Dress code will be specified on the invitation. Traditionally, the spouse doesn't attend without the sponsor, but the sponsor may attend without the spouse. However, during times of deployment, an exception may be made by the host.

Dining-In/Dining-Out

Dining-In is an old military tradition that has been passed down from the British. It allows the unit to celebrate its successes and to enjoy its traditions and heritage. It is strictly a military affair and spouses are not included. When spouses are invited, a Dining-In becomes a Dining-Out. This gives the spouses an opportunity to see all the "pomp and circumstance" that goes with the tradition. These are always formal events. The desired uniform will be stated on the invitation, usually Army Service Uniform or the Blue Mess Uniform for officers. Spouses wear evening clothes—long gowns, short or tea-length formals, or formal evening pants. Male spouses should wear appropriate black-tie attire.

Balls

The most formal of all occasions. (Think high school prom without the teenage angst.) Dress code for Soldiers and spouses will be the same as for a Dining-Out. Soldiers wear their dress uniforms. Balls are usually an annual event, although there could be one prior to and at the end of a deployment as an additional way to celebrate. Children are never invited, not even nursing infants.

Teas

Teas are the dressiest daytime event, reserved for very special occasions like welcoming and farewelling commanders' spouses or very senior spouses. Whether or not you know the person being honored, your presence conveys respect and will be appreciated. Respond to your invitation within 24 to 48 hours. Arrive promptly at the time specified on your invitation. These are not drop-ins. Dress up—dress, skirt, or suit is more appropriate than pants. Choose your shoes carefully, as you will be standing during a tea. There will be a receiving line, in which the hostess will introduce you to the guest of honor. There will be a special time set aside when the hostess will celebrate the guest of honor. Be sure to thank your hostess and say goodbye to the guest of honor before you leave.

Hail and Farewells

The Army way of welcoming and saying goodbye all at the same function. No cards or gifts are exchanged unless specific instructions are given on the invitation. If it is held at a restaurant, you will be responsible for the cost of your own meal. Children are not normally included, unless specified on the invitation. When you are being farewelled, your spouse (and possibly you) may be asked to say a few words. It is not necessary to accept this offer, but if you choose to speak, be prepared with short and gracious remarks.

Award Ceremonies

The Army presents many levels of awards in recognition of service, achievement, or valor. The actual ceremonies can vary from an office gathering to a unit formation. The basic elements of this ceremony include the reading of the official orders and the presentation and/or pinning on of the award. Attendees should stand quietly and respectfully while orders are read.

Promotion Ceremonies

Family, friends, and coworkers are invited to honor Soldiers upon their promotions to the next rank. A specific format is usually followed, which includes announcement of the official party, remarks by the host, reading of the promotion orders and award, pinning on of insignia, presentation of award, remarks by the honoree, and a receiving line. The honoree will ask significant persons from his personal or professional life to do the honor of pinning on the new rank. Traditionally, flowers are presented to the spouse. There may be refreshments offered, ranging from cake and punch to more elaborate fare.

Promotion Parties

A time-honored tradition is the promotion party, which is given by an officer or NCO or a group of officers or NCOs with similar dates of rank, shortly after being promoted. It does not have to be a fancy affair but provides a chance to invite friends and their spouses to share their good fortune. Many choose to host a dinner at a local restaurant or at home. As you join in the celebration, be mindful of those around you who may not have been selected on this promotion board. A little sensitivity goes a long way.

Military Weddings

The military uniforms and traditions are what make a military wedding special. The sword or saber arch is one of the most popular military wedding traditions. For the sword or saber arch, six or eight service members line up in pairs on the chapel steps or along the walk. The bride and groom walk under the arch as they leave the chapel. One of the highlights of a military reception is cutting the cake with the groom's sword or saber. The bride holds the sword with the groom's hand over hers. Together they cut the wedding cake. Unlike in civilian life, you may not be automatically invited to every wedding ceremony your spouse performs. When you do attend, you will enjoy the military pageantry.

Military Funerals and Memorial Services

The Army is at its finest when it lays to rest one of its own, and you will not be able to keep from shedding tears. Your spouse will be very well-trained on how a funeral or memorial service is to be conducted, so ask him or her questions about what to expect. In particular, ask what your spouse wants to do at the end of the service when Soldiers pay their final respects. This may be a slow salute, the laying of a unit coin, and/or a whispered word over the memorial helmet, boots, and picture. As a spouse, you should stand quietly beside your Soldier as the salute is offered. If your spouse wishes to lay a coin or say a word, you may walk forward to accompany him or her or wait until he or she is finished. Your attendance at funeral and memorial services is not required, but it's worth the effort to arrange a day off or child care because of what it will mean to your spouse and the rest of the unit to see you there.

Unit Coffees

Unit coffees are usually held monthly and provide a wonderful opportunity to greet new arrivals, to farewell those leaving the unit, to get acquainted with the other spouses in the unit, and to find out what's happening in the unit and on post. Each member of a coffee group may host or co-host a coffee. There will usually be a sign-up sheet. It's always easier to have a co-host, so make friends quickly! Entertain within your budget and comfort level. Snacks with paper plates in your small apartment with some people sitting on the floor are fine and appreciated. Formal china, coffee service, and a large house are not necessary, though they are appreciated, too (except maybe by the people hosting the next coffee!). Large groups often meet at post or community facilities or in meeting rooms at restaurants. Individuals pay for their own meals at restaurant outings, though the host(s) might provide appetizers for the group. Unit welcome committees and care networks (which provide meals during illness or when new babies arrive) may provide information at coffees. Often units will collect "coffee dues," which will cover such things as cards and farewell gifts (yes, this basically means that you are paying for your own farewell gift, but, *hooah*).

When it is your turn to host, coordinate your date and time with your commander's spouse, who will let you know if there are special guests, fiancés to be included, or a baby to welcome. Invitations should arrive at least two weeks in advance with RSVP information. If it is a tradition with your unit to have door prizes (these are often called "opportunities"), have them ready—candles, candy, and scented soaps make appealing gifts. Nametags are helpful with large groups. Plan refreshments within your budget and culinary abilities. Store-bought food is fine and much preferred to an overheated, overworked hostess who can't enjoy her own event. If you have a theme, be sure your invitation includes information on what you would like people to wear or bring. This is your time to shine!

The agenda at unit coffees typically is as follows:

- Thank hostess
- Welcome newcomers and guests
- Farewells
- Family announcements (births, promotions, birthdays, honors . . .)
- Committee reports
- Calendar of events
- Information distribution
- Next coffee date, time, location
- Door-prize, drawing usually called an "opportunity" drawing
- Program, guest speaker

Be a Gracious Guest

Respond to Invitation

An "RSVP" invitation is requesting you reply so that your hostess is able to plan properly. If the invitation indicates "Regrets Only," your hostess is assuming you will attend unless you tell her otherwise. A "no" is as important as a "yes" when planning food and other activities. Always inform your hostess if you have an allergy that requires special preparations, and remember that responding within 48 hours is best. Also, notify the hostess if you cannot attend after RSVPing "yes" due to an unscheduled conflict. Many groups are using electronic invitations, which could get sent to your "spam" folder depending on your computer's settings. You might need to adjust your privacy settings or specifically designate invitations as okay for your inbox.

Who Attends

Only those named on the invitation should attend. No children or houseguests should attend, unless specifically invited. (When you regret because of houseguests, the host or hostess may extend the invitation to include them. The rule is that you really shouldn't ask.)

Coming, Going, and During

Arrive on time, no more than five minutes early or fifteen minutes late. Greet the host, hostess, and/or guests of honor first before socializing with other party guests. Circulate, mingle, and be a pleasant conversationalist. It is traditional to stay at an official function or formal dinner party until the senior person or guest of honor departs. If you must leave early, make your apologies to them first. ALWAYS thank the host and/or hostess as you leave.

Hostess Gift

You may take a hostess gift to a dinner in someone's home. Inexpensive ideas include flowers, wine, candy, hostess soap, note cards, and homemade goodies. Wrap the gift or put it in a gift bag and include a card with your name.

Dinners

At a **buffet,** the hostess will announce when the food is ready. Let the senior person or guests of honor serve themselves first. You may begin eating as soon as you have served and seated yourself. Wait till everyone has been through the line before going back for seconds. At **seated dinners,** guests remain standing behind their chairs until given the signal to sit. The gentleman to the left of each lady will assist her with her chair. Ladies sit immediately. Gentlemen remain standing until the hostess sits. Watch the hostess for your cue to take your napkin, to begin eating, which utensil to use (usually start with the furthest utensil from the plate, with utensils above the plate reserved for dessert).

Alcohol

Alcohol may be served at some functions. If your personal choice or spouse's endorsing agency prohibits you from partaking, a polite and gracious, "No, thank you" is all that's necessary.

Thank You

Everyone appreciates being thanked. The traditional way is a written note, but a phone call or email thank-you is acceptable. The important thing is to express your appreciation to the hostess/host.

Reciprocity

It is appropriate to reciprocate by inviting your host and/or hostess to your home. You needn't repay "dinner for dinner"—customize your entertaining to fit your personal style. Cookouts, coffee, cocktails, or dessert gatherings are all acceptable. There is no time requirement for reciprocating the invitation, but it's always easier before you or they move to a new post. Command performance occasions do not need repayment, such as New Year's Day's Receptions, Hail and

Farewells, and formal or group unit functions. If you have questions about inviting senior people, always check with your senior spouse.

Senior Spouses

Out of respect, never call senior spouses by their first names unless they ask you to do so. Always acknowledge a new senior spouse's presence when he/she joins a group.

When It Is Your Turn to Host

- Relax and be yourself. Enjoy your guests. Make new friends, foster camaraderie.
- There are a variety of invitations to choose from, depending on the mood of the party and the hostess—informal notes, boxed invitations, electronic invitations, or handmade creations. On an invitation use only ONE of the following responses: 1) RSVP or 2) Regrets Only. If using two or more telephone numbers, include the corresponding name or names.
- Indicate the dress code using the "What to Wear" information found earlier in this chapter. It will significantly reduce the time your guests spend pulling outfits out of their closets and tossing them across their beds.
- Plan your menu to fit the occasion and prepare as much as you can in advance. Keep your favorite dinner menus on hand for future use. Consider writing guests' names on your personal menu file so you don't repeat a menu with the same guests. Juice, soft drinks, coffee, tea, and water are appropriate. Be sure to include low/no calorie and decaf options. Alcohol is optional.
- Types of parties

    Cocktail party—drinks and simple hors d'oeuvres

    Cocktail buffet—drinks and heavy hors d'oeuvres

Buffet dinner—full meal, served buffet-style, casual seating

Dinner—guests are seated at tables; meals can be served family style or pre-plated

Organizations

Family Readiness Groups (FRG)

- The Family Readiness Group (FRG) is an organization of Family Members, volunteers, and Soldiers/civilian employees belonging to a unit/organization, who together provide an avenue of mutual support, assistance, and a network of communication among the Family Members, the chain of command, and community resources.
- Chaplain spouses are usually assigned to the HHC/HHB (Headquarters and Headquarters Company/Battery).
- All Soldiers and Family Members are automatically a part of the FRG, although Family Member participation is optional. **Participation is highly encouraged, especially during deployments.**
- FRG leaders are volunteers and are coordinated by a paid Family Readiness Support Assistant (FRSA).
- These are the people who will keep you up to date on all the stuff your spouse is supposed to be telling you but forgets to relay. The FRG provides a major source of support for Families and is also a wonderful opportunity for you to get to know and serve Army Families.

Spouse Organizations

- Historically raised money and supplies from among the citizens for the Soldiers, organized social opportunities (theater, book clubs, quilting groups)

- Most Army posts have separate clubs for officers' spouses and enlisted spouses; although many smaller posts—and even some larger ones—have all-rank spouses clubs.
- Organize and sponsor educational, charitable, cultural, and social activities
- Must conform to Army regulations
- Voluntary board members including president, vice-president, treasurer, and secretary
- Membership with annual dues
- Activities include luncheons, themed/seasonal events, classes (cooking, sewing, etc.), tours and travel, fund raising (bazaars, craft fairs, post thrift shop), scholarships, newsletters

Need to Know Information for New Spouses

Military ID Card

As a new military spouse, you will need a military Identification Card (ID card). Your military ID card is necessary in order to gain access to the valuable services to which your Soldier's service entitles you. This ID card will enable you to use The Exchange (sometimes referred to as the "PX" for Post Exchange), the Commissary, and to receive medical care. ID cards are issued to all Family Members who are ten years or older. To obtain your ID card, you will need the original or certified copy of both your marriage and birth certificates. You will also need your original Social Security card and a government issued photo ID. The service member MUST accompany the Family Member in order to authorize the issuance of the military ID card. Due to its importance, you should always carry your ID card with you and *guard it carefully*. Do not allow children to hold onto their own ID cards until they are old enough to clean their rooms without being asked . . . like that's ever going to happen! If the ID card is lost, the loss must be reported to the Military Police as soon as possible. If your spouse is set to deploy, be sure you check the expiration date on your ID card(s) to update before the deployment if necessary.

Enrollment in DEERS

All Soldiers must ensure that their Family Members are enrolled in Defense Enrollment Eligibility Reporting System (DEERS) to receive medical care. Information is available at www.tricare.mil/DEERS. You **MUST** keep your Family's DEERS information updated and current at all times.

"Sponsor's Social" or "Last Four"

Congratulations! If it took you twenty years to memorize your own Social Security number, you get to start all over now. In the Army culture, your spouse's SS is the one you need to know for many purposes, including medical.

Military Time

Military time is measured on a 24-hour clock versus the 12-hour method of telling time, which many of us are more accustomed to using. Some other parts of the world also measure their time using the 24-hour clock. Military time always contains four numbers and no colons. It may seem a little confusing at first, but once you figure out its system, it will make more sense, come more naturally, and seem very simple. 0800 (referred to as "Oh-eight hundred") is what we normals call 8:00 a.m.; and anything after noon has an extra twelve added to it, so 1:00 p.m. becomes 1300 ("thirteen-hundred").

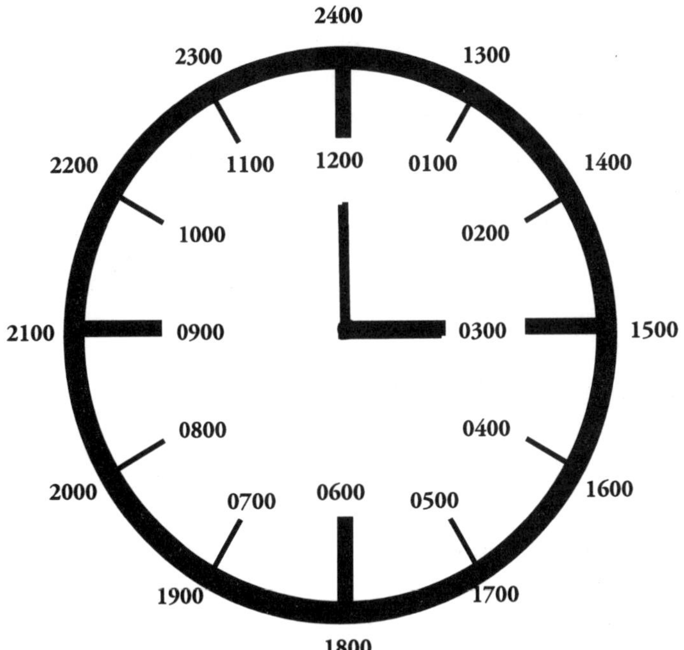
2400
2300
1300
2200
1100
1200
0100
1400
1000
0200
2100
0900
0300
1500
0800
0400
2000
0700
0600
0500
1600
1900
1700
1800

Basic Acronyms

The Army has more acronyms than alphabet soup. Here are a few that might help you make sense of Orders and the LES (Leave and Earnings Statement).

- BAH (Basic Allowance for Housing). When not living in government housing, Soldiers receive BAH according to their pay grade, number of dependents, and geographical location to cover housing costs. To find out how much your BAH will be in any given area, go to: http://military benefits.info/bah-calculator/.
- BAQ (Basic Allowance for Quarters). BAQ is the number of dependents a Soldier claims as needing housing. BAQ has no dollar amount attached to it, though it does help determine the dollar amount of BAH or the size of the house you qualify to have on post.
- BAS (Basic Allowance for Subsistence). Soldiers not receiving meals at a Dining Facility receive BAS to cover the cost of food.
- LES (Leave and Earnings Statement). The LES is a comprehensive statement of a Soldier's leave and earnings showing entitlements, deductions, allotments, leave information, tax withholding information, and Thrift Savings Plan (TSP) information. Your most recent LES can be found 24 hours a day on www.mypay.dfas.mil /mypay.aspx. Your Chaplain will have to register a username and password to be able to view this information. This is also where your W-2 forms will be available for printing at the end of each year. Verify and keep your LES each month. If your pay varies significantly and you don't understand why, or if you have any questions, consult with your disbursing/finance office. When you PCS, there are certain allowances that are granted. These

will be detailed on the LES with a set of acronyms all their own.

- NET, NLT, NMT (No Earlier Than, No Later Than, No More Than). A PCS or TDY order will have a report date. Generally it gives the NLT date and then might either say "early report authorized (NMT 30 days early)" or "NET 05 JAN 15 but NLT 05 FEB 15." Army dates are day/month/year, so the example actually means that you can report no sooner than January 5, 2015, but no later than February 5, 2015. You might also see a NET 0800 & NLT 1300, but since you read all about military time above, you figured that one out already.
- PCS (Permanent Change of Station). The physical move from one duty location to another.
- POV (Personal Operation Vehicle/Privately Owned Vehicle). This refers to your car or truck. And only the Army would create an acronym that takes longer to say than car or truck.
- Permissive TDY (Permissive Temporary Duty). A temporary assignment that does not grant travel pay. Often you get permissive TDY when you are relocating and have to go house- or apartment-hunting or are separating from the military and need to go job-hunting. Permissive TDY may also be granted to the Chaplain for travel business, denominational responsibilities, or special training.
- TDY (Temporary Duty). Duty performed at some location other than the permanently assigned location. A single TDY trip is usually limited to 179 days or less. This covers things like schools or assignments, which are for a shorter duration. It is a usually a "Soldier-only" sponsored move. The Army will reimburse the Soldier for meals and/or lodging as appropriate.

Learn the Army Song

You will be standing and singing this at nearly every Army event you attend. Be proud to know the words.

Introduction
March along, sing our song, with the Army of the free
Count the brave, count the true, who have fought to victory
We're the Army and proud of our name
We're the Army and proudly proclaim
Verse
First to fight for the right,
And to build the Nation's might,
And The Army Goes Rolling Along
Proud of all we have done,
Fighting till the battle's won,
And The Army Goes Rolling Along.
Refrain
Then it's Hi! Hi! Hey!
The Army's on its way.
Count off the cadence loud and strong (TWO! THREE!)
For where e'er we go,
You will always know
That The Army Goes Rolling Along.[1]

You finished reading this chapter—Hooah!

NOTES

1. "'The Army Goes Rolling Along': The Official Song of the United States Army," U.S. Army, www.music.army.mil/music/armysong/.

CHAPTER 3

ALWAYS READY: AN OVERVIEW OF THE ARMY RESERVE AND NATIONAL GUARD

Sandra Gray

Mess Call

Signals mealtime.

With tensions building around the globe, it takes a multi-tiered force of highly trained committed Soldiers to protect our freedoms and uphold democracy. This force consists of Active Duty Soldiers and Soldiers in the Reserve Components. These two groups work in tandem to create the most powerful, well-prepared fighting force in the world" (GoArmy.com). It should be noted that the Total Army consists of three Components: the Active Army, the Army National Guard, and the US Army Reserve.

Since Desert Storm and the continuation of the War on Terror, the Army Family has become a more diversified one with the Reserve Components serving side-by-side with their active duty counterparts both state-side and down range. Though a Reserve Soldier holds a civilian job, he/she is always "on the ready" to serve.

Since 2001, more than one million Soldiers have deployed. Approximately 66 percent of the Army's Active Component, 45 percent of the Army National Guard, and 42 percent of the US Army Reserve wear a combat patch today, which they earned since 9/11.

Most of us are familiar with the active duty side of service, but navigating through the Reserve Component side of the Army may be somewhat foreign territory. It is my hope that this chapter will provide information to us as Chaplain spouses that will help us be more knowledgeable and thus more aware of the unique challenges that face the reserve side of the Army Family. Here we go. . . .

The Reserve Component is divided into two major groups: the US Army Reserves and the Army National Guard. US Army Reserve Soldiers are assigned to one of three major reserve categories (Congressional Research Service):

1. The Ready Reserve—the primary manpower pool of the reserve component

    A. The Selected Reserve—Soldiers are generally required to perform one weekend of training each month (weekend drill) and two weeks of training each year (annual training); can be involuntarily ordered to active duty service or can volunteer

    B. The Individual Ready Reserve (IRR)—Soldiers who have already received military training, either in the Active Component or in the Selected Reserve; can volunteer for training, but not required; can be involuntarily ordered to active duty or can volunteer

    C. The Inactive National Guard (ING)—for practical purposes, the ING is the National Guard equivalent of the IRR

2. The Standby Reserve—contains those individuals who have a temporary disability or hardship and those who hold key defense-related positions in their civilian jobs; reservists are not required to participate in military training; can be involuntarily ordered to active duty or can volunteer

3. The Retired Reserve—either reserve officers or enlisted personnel who are receiving retired pay or those who transfer into the Retired Reserve before they become eligible to receive retired pay (normally occurring at age sixty)

The Army Reserve makes up only 20 percent of the Army's organized units, but it provides about half of the Army's combat support and a quarter of the Army's mobilization base-expansion capability. At 5.3 percent of the Army's budget, the Army Reserve provides a cost-effective solution to the Army's need for specialized capabilities. The Army Reserve's mission, under Title 10 of the US Code, is to provide trained, equipped, and ready Soldiers and cohesive units to meet the global requirements across the full spectrum of operations. The Army Reserve is a key element in the Army multi-component unit force, training with Active and National Guard units to ensure all three components work as a fully integrated team.

Reserve Soldiers spend one weekend a month drilling to keep their skills sharp. For roughly two weeks a year, Reserve Soldiers serve on Active Duty, focusing on challenging field and specialty training. They may even have the opportunity to attend competitive Army training programs such as Airborne and Air Assault schools. With the increased reliance on the Reserve, more units are training in other countries and performing missions. Reserve Soldiers may be called to Active Duty when needed. Today's Army Reserve is over over 200,000 troops strong. Service options for the Army Reserve range from three to six years.

The Army National Guard (ARNG) is the other group that comprises the Reserve Component. The Army National Guard is composed primarily of traditional Guardsmen—civilians who serve their country, state, and community on a part-time basis (usually one weekend each month and two weeks during the summer). Each state, most territories, and the District of Columbia have their own National Guard, as provided for by the Constitution of the United States.

While the Guard originally focused on protecting local communities, it eventually grew into a force that complements the Active Duty Army when help is needed anywhere in the world. The National Guard has a unique dual mission that consists of both Federal and State roles. Its versatility enables the Guard to respond to domestic emergencies, overseas combat missions, counterdrug efforts, reconstruction missions and more.

For state missions, the governor, through the state Adjutant General, commands Guard forces. The governor can call the National Guard into action during local or statewide emergencies, such as storms, fires, earthquakes, or civil disturbances.

In addition, the President of the United States can activate the National Guard for participation in federal missions. Examples of federal activations include Guard units deployed to Kosovo and the Sinai for stabilization operations, and units deployed to the Middle East and other locations in the war on terrorism. When federalized, Guard units are commanded by the Combatant Commander of the theatre in which they are operating.

Deployment

Deploying as a Chaplain in the Reserve Components can take several forms. Chaplains often go to war with their own units, but they also go to war with other units (called cross-leveling) across the US or with a Chaplain detachment. A Chaplain detachment typically goes to war as a two-person team (56A & 56M) or a five-member team. Chaplain detachments augment deployed active duty divisions and provide direct religious support to the command group. They are utilized as the Division Chaplain sees fit. Reserve Component Chaplains often go to war with units in another state, thus leaving their Families in a community that does not have a support network in place. When spouses of deployed Reserve Component Chaplains are left alone, there is usually not a military base or many military Families around them. They must be more proactive to find the resources they need by utilizing social networks and Reserve Component support programs. Sometimes, when Reserve Component Chaplains return from combat there is no one from their unit at the airport to receive them except their Families.

When National Guard Chaplains deploy, they usually go to war with their units. The National Guard is made up of Soldiers almost entirely from the state—and many times the very community—from which the unit originates. It is easier to get know unit members and stay in contact with them. Many National Guardsmen work together in different units in their state throughout their career. The National Guard contains all types of units to include combat units unlike the US Army Reserve that only contains combat support units and combat service support units. Sometimes National Guard Chaplains deploy with other units, but not as often as US Army Reserve Chaplains.

There are many programs to support you throughout the deployment cycle, from mobilization through the service member's reintegration. Guard and Reserve Families may not have much time to prepare for deployment, so it's important to know the support and information resources in advance. Knowing as much as you can about the military, the deployment process, your benefits, and the support available to you will help you manage the home front with strength and confidence.

Your command leadership will distribute information to you as efficiently as possible, but be realistic about the availability and frequency of communications. Command may use several different methods to keep you and your Family informed, including a unit website or answering machine, email, toll-free phone number, or automated multimedia communication systems.

The Department of Defense (DoD) and each branch of the Military Services provide online information for military Families, including those in the Guard and Reserve. These websites will inform you about services, points of contact, links to additional sources of support, and opportunities to interact with other military Families. If you are a National Guard Family, register on the Joint Services Support site at www.jointservicessupport.org/ for information on resources in your state, online forums, e-learning opportunities, and local event calendars. This site also provides information and referrals on quality-of-life issues. If you are a military Reserve Family, you can obtain information from the Joint Service Support site that will help connect you to local support resources.

Military commands typically host "yellow ribbon" events to help Families prepare for and stay strong during and after a deployment. Through the Yellow Ribbon Reintegration Program (YRRP), the National Guard and Reserve prepare service members and Families for deployment, sustain them during deployment, and provide information and support to help with reintegration with Families, communities, and employers upon their return and release from active duty. At pre-deployment events, you and the service member will learn about enrolling in the Defense Enrollment Eligibility Reporting System (DEERS), military pay, financial readiness, Family-care plans, TRICARE, and other benefits. You'll also learn about Family support through the military in such areas as education, counseling, child care, and religious support.

Events during deployment provide information and outreach to Family Members to assist with the impact of separation and allow them to connect with other Families. After service members return home, Yellow Ribbon activities help Families reconnect and readjust with information on communication challenges, relationship stress, combat stress issues, Department of Veterans Affairs (VA) benefits, employment, and more. You'll get information in briefings and group discussions and can ask questions. You'll also meet unit leaders, Family support professionals, and volunteers who will be important resources during the deployment. Yellow Ribbon events are posted online at www.yellowribbon.mil and www.jointservicessup port.org/YRRP. Knowing about and using the resources available to you is essential to Family readiness. During a deployment, you may have financial or legal questions, need support for your children, be concerned about your emotional well-being, or just want to connect with other military Families. Getting support early, before concerns become problems, will help you stay strong.

Military OneSource is a free twenty-four-hour service available to all Active Duty, Guard, and Reserve members (regardless of activation status) and their Families. Consultants provide information and make referrals on a wide range of issues, to include helping military Families navigate each stage in the deployment cycle. Free face-to-face, online, or phone counseling sessions are available. Go to www .militaryonesource.mil to learn more.

Family Assistance Centers (FACs) are located in every state to serve geographically dispersed military Families. FACs provide information, outreach, and referrals to services in your community and serve all Active and Reserve service members and Families, not just the National Guard. To find the nearest FAC, use the Resource Finder at the Joint Services Support website www.jointservicessup port.org/. Immediate Family Members of Active Duty, Guard, or Reserve members are entitled to use services at military installations. Fleet and Family Support Centers, Marine Corps Community Services, Airman and Family Readiness Centers, and Army Community Service Centers offer a wide range of professional support services as well as information and referral to community resources.

If you live near a military installation, a visit to the Family Support Programs will give you an idea of the services available. The Service branch of the installation isn't important; installation Family program professionals are accustomed to serving all activated personnel and their Families without regard to Service branch. Go to www.militaryinstallations.dod.mil/ to find contact information.

Guard and Reserve commands have organized Family support systems of staff and volunteers. Family Assistance Coordinators, Family Readiness Assistants, Family Readiness Officers, or other designated Family support specialists are your links to unit information and support.

Getting to know key staff and volunteers before your Chaplain deploys can make it easier to ask for help later. Call the unit to connect with these resources, and stay in touch during the deployment. If you move or get a new phone number, notify the unit points of contact so you won't miss out on important information and activities.

Families of Reserve Component members deployed are often surprised to discover how many people in their community have some connection to a deployed service member. Ask neighbors, coworkers, school personnel, or leaders in your religious organization if they know someone with a spouse, child, or significant other on active duty, and get in touch.

Mutual support is also available online. Searching the websites referenced here will help you find online military Family discussion and support groups for both adults and youth. And look for support outside the military community as well. Above all, don't try to go it alone. Having a support system at home helps Families avoid burdening their service members with worries that might distract them from the mission.

Helping others can be an effective and positive technique when dealing with deployment. Unit Family readiness groups and other programs rely on the voluntary efforts of Family Members to achieve their mission. Your group will have an important role for you to play in welcoming new members, planning social activities to bring Families together, or providing support for others in need. These groups need volunteers before, during, and after the deployment, but especially during down times when it's more of a challenge to keep Families interested and involved.

As you focus on taking care of home and Family during your loved one's deployment, don't forget to take care of yourself as well. Try to have realistic expectations of yourself, and keep in mind that Family separations and deployments offer a unique opportunity to nurture your own physical, emotional, and spiritual well-being.

Medical Benefits

Depending on the Chaplain's duty status, Family Members may be eligible for TRICARE. TRICARE is the Department of Defense health care program that provides medical and dental care services for eligible uniformed Services members and other eligible DoD beneficiaries. Eligibility for TRICARE is determined by the uniformed Services and reported to the Defense Enrollment Eligibility Reporting System (DEERS). All eligible beneficiaries must have their eligibility status recorded in DEERS.

TRICARE beneficiaries can be divided into two main categories: sponsors and Family Members. Sponsors are usually active duty service members, National Guard/Reserve members, or retired service members. "Sponsor" refers to the person who is serving or who has served on active duty or in the National Guard or Reserves. The phrase "National Guard and Reserve" refers to members of the Army National Guard, Army Reserve, Navy Reserve, Marine Corps Reserve, Air National Guard, Air Force Reserve, and US Coast Guard Reserve.

Members of the Individual Ready Reserve (IRR) may purchase the TRICARE Dental Program, but usually do not qualify for any other TRICARE benefits when not on active duty orders or immediately following a period of activation. Service member and Family health and dental options are different depending on the sponsor's current military status.

Service members on military duty for thirty days or less may qualify to purchase TRICARE Reserve Select, a premium-based, voluntary health plan that provides comprehensive health coverage for the sponsor and Family. Traditional, drilling National Guard and Reserve members are eligible for the TRICARE Reserve Select health plan. The service member may also qualify for Line of Duty Care for any injury or illness sustained in the line of duty, including traveling to and from the place of duty.

For dental care, the sponsor and Family can enroll in the TRICARE Dental Program. You will enroll separately and pay separate monthly premiums.

When activated for more than thirty consecutive days (called or ordered to active duty for more than thirty consecutive days under federal orders), the service member becomes eligible for the same health and dental benefits as active duty service members. The service member will enroll in one of the following Prime options upon arrival at the final duty station: TRICARE Prime, TRICARE Prime Remote, TRICARE Prime Overseas, TRICARE Prime Remote Overseas.

If the service member is enrolled in the TRICARE Dental Program when called to active duty, the coverage is automatically terminated. The service member is now covered by active duty dental benefits and receives dental care at military dental treatment facilities and through the TRICARE Active Duty Dental Program.

The service member's Family becomes eligible for the same TRICARE benefits as active duty Family Members when the service member is on active duty for more than thirty consecutive days. The Family can use any of the following plans depending on where they live when the service member is activated: TRICARE Prime, TRICARE Prime Remote, TRICARE Standard and Extra, TRICARE Prime Overseas, TRICARE Prime Remote Overseas, TRICARE Standard Overseas, US Family Health Plan, TRICARE Young Adult (for dependent adult children up to age twenty-six).

If the service member's Family is enrolled in the TRICARE Dental Program, their coverage continues uninterrupted and their premiums are reduced to the "active duty Family Member" rates. If not already enrolled, they can enroll in the TRICARE Dental Program at any time.

If the service member is issued delayed-effective-date active duty orders for more than thirty consecutive days in support of a contingency operation, Guard and Reserve members may qualify up to 180 days early for active duty TRICARE benefits. This "pre-activation benefit" begins on the date the orders are issued, but not earlier than 180 days before reporting to active duty.

During the pre-activation period, service members are covered as "active duty service members" and receive active duty medical and dental benefits. Eligible Family Members are covered as "active duty Family Members" and can enroll in one of TRICARE's Prime options or use TRICARE Standard and Extra.

The Service personnel office will tell members if they are eligible for pre-activation benefits when they receive their delayed-effective-date active duty orders. If the service member does not meet these "early eligibility" requirements, your coverage (and your Family's coverage) will begin on the first day of the service member's orders.

When the service member leaves active duty, or deactivates, the Family's health plan options may be different if the service member was called to active duty in support of a contingency operation. If activated in support of a contingency operation:

- Sponsor is immediately covered by the Transitional Assistance Management Program (TAMP) for 180 days. TAMP coverage begins on the first day after leaving active duty service. Family Members are also covered during the TAMP period.

- After TAMP ends, service members may qualify to purchase TRICARE Reserve Select for personal and Family coverage.

- If service members don't qualify for TRICARE Reserve Select, another option is to purchase the Continued Health Care Benefit Program.

- Service members continue to be covered under active duty dental benefits during TAMP. After TAMP ends, TRICARE Dental Program coverage will automatically resume (if previously enrolled) and monthly premiums resume until the 12-month minimum enrollment period is reached.

If the service member's Family is enrolled in the TRICARE Dental Program, their coverage continues uninterrupted; however, their premium payments will revert back to their original rates.

If the service member was not activated in support of a contingency operation, the Family does not qualify for TAMP and active duty benefits (including dental) end immediately.

When a service member retires, he or she may qualify to purchase TRICARE Retired Reserve for personal and Family coverage. At age sixty (and when you begin receiving retired pay), you become eligible for the same benefits as all other retired service members. For dental care, the member may purchase the TRICARE Retiree Dental Program for personal and Family coverage.

Additionally, adult children who "age out" at twenty-one (or twenty-three if enrolled in college full time) may qualify to purchase TRICARE Young Adult.

Identification Cards for Military Family Members

Normally, Reserve Component Family Members and other dependents receive a DD Form 1173-1, the DoD Guard and Reserve Family Member ID card. These ID cards do not authorize eligibility for medical benefits. They will assist Family Members in accessing these privileges when accompanied by a copy of the service member's orders to active duty. ID cards do authorize access to commissary, exchange, and certain Morale, Welfare and Recreation (MWR) privileges. The DoD Guard and Reserve Family Member ID card serves as proof that the individual has been pre-enrolled in DEERS. This is an important first step in obtaining Family Member and dependent medical treatment when the service member is called to active duty for more than thirty consecutive days.

When the Reserve Component service member is called to active duty for more than thirty consecutive days, part of the processing for entry on active duty should be the completion of DD Form 1172 (Application for Department of Defense Identification Card-DEERS Enrollment) for each eligible Family Member. This application, along with the DD Form 1173-1, will allow Family Members and dependents to receive the DD Form 1173, Uniformed Service Identification and Privilege Card. This card will authorize appropriate medical benefits and privileges for the period of active duty specified on the member's orders.

Shopping on Post

The Defense Commissary Agency operates a worldwide chain of commissaries providing groceries to military personnel, retirees, and their Families in a safe and secure shopping environment. Shoppers save an average of more than 30 percent on their purchases compared to commercial prices—savings amounting to thousands of dollars annually. Authorized commissary patrons include active duty, Guard and Reserve members, military retirees, Medal of Honor recipients, 100 percent disabled veterans, and their authorized Family Members. Since November 2003, members of the Guard and Reserve—including the Ready Reserve, Selected Reserve, Individual Ready Reserve, Inactive National Guard, Guard and Reserve retirees and their authorized Family Members—have enjoyed unlimited access to commissaries in the United States, Guam, and Puerto Rico. A military ID is required at all commissaries.

Military Installation Exchanges provide quality merchandise and services to customers at competitively low prices. Authorized personnel include uniformed or retired uniformed personnel and their Families, either on active duty or serving in any category of the Reserve Component. A military ID card is required for all exchange services.

Family, Morale, Welfare, and Recreation (FMWR)

FMWR activities include arts and crafts facilities, bowling centers, golf courses, libraries, outdoor recreation, recreation centers, youth services activities and recreation membership clubs. Occasionally, local FMWR facilities may offer significant discounts on popular local and national Family attractions. In most instances, Guard and Reserve members and their dependents are eligible to use all facilities on the same basis as active duty personnel. Local installation and facility commanders do have the authority to establish priorities for FMWR activities that are in high demand and unable to accommodate all who desire to participate.

Child Care

The DoD Military Child Development System (CDS) is a benefit available to active duty members, retirees, Guard and Reserve members, and DoD civilian personnel. Availability of the facilities and programs varies depending on the location of the installation, resources, and the needs of the local community. The availability of child care is also affected by the status of the service member and the priority of the Family on the waiting list. In some instances, for example, Reserve and Guard personnel must be activated in order to use military child care facilities and programs.

Space-A

Space Available (Space-A) travel is a great program for our active duty, Guard, Reserve, retired, and eligible Family Members. Please understand, Air Mobility Command's (AMC) primary mission is to support our war fighters. Once duty and safety requirements are met, available seats will be offered to passengers awaiting transportation. Therefore, you must be prepared to possibly wait a few days or arrange alternate transportation. Remember, Space-A travel is a privilege, and AMC cannot guarantee movement to your desired location or on any particular schedule.

When not on active duty, authorized National Guard members and Reservists as well as authorized Reserve Component members entitled to retired pay at age sixty (gray area retirees) may fly within the Continental United States (CONUS) and directly within/between the CONUS and Alaska, Hawaii, Puerto Rico, the US Virgin Islands, Guam, and American Samoa. Dependents are not authorized to travel Space-A with these members. Reserve or Guard members placed on active duty for more than thirty consecutive days may travel Space-A to any location authorized for Space-A travel upon presentation of a military ID card, orders placing the member on active duty, and a valid leave authorization or evidence of pass status as required by the Service concerned. Dependents are authorized to travel when accompanied by members on active duty in excess of thirty days. For Space-A travel eligibility, once the retirement age of sixty is reached and the member is receiving retirement pay, no distinction is made between members retired from the Reserves/Guard and members retired from active duty. Dependents of these retirees are authorized to travel Space-A when accompanied by the sponsor.

Legal Assistance

The Service members Civil Relief Act (SCRA) provides protection to anyone entering or called to and on active duty in the Armed Forces. Members of the National Guard and Reserve are covered by SCRA when in active federal service and while serving on active duty. The SCRA provides important safeguards to members on active duty status in the area of financial management including rental agreements, security deposits, evictions, installment contracts, interest rate limits on pre-service consumer debt and mortgage loans, civil judicial proceedings and income tax payments. One of the most widely known benefits under the SCRA is the ability to reduce preservice consumer debt and mortgage interest rates to 6 percent if military service materially affects your ability to make payments. If you believe being called to active military service will impact your ability to meet financial obligations, please contact the nearest legal assistance office to determine if the SCRA offers you protection.

The Military Services have legal assistance offices available to assist service members with legal issues while the member is on active duty. Typical legal services involve consultation and assistance on wills, powers of attorney, child support questions, Family matters, contractual disputes, and more. Although legal assistance officers cannot represent Family Members in court, they can negotiate on your behalf. Generally, the Military Services offer limited legal assistance to Guard and Reserve members during inactive duty training periods to prepare legal documents needed (wills and powers of attorney) in the event of an involuntary call to active duty. Each Military Service has specific regulations regarding the extent of legal assistance they provide. The nearest military legal assistance office can be found through the Armed Forces Legal Assistance (AFLA) Legal Services Locator found by visiting www.jagcnet.army.mil/legal.

Department of Veterans Affairs

Like the active duty counterparts, Guard and Reserve service members can take advantage of benefits and services offered by the Department of Veterans Affairs. Certain benefits—such as medical care—may require active duty service, but many Guard and Reserve members who have never been called to active duty will still qualify for the VA's most popular benefits.

Those called to active duty since Sept. 11, 2001, may be eligible for the Post-9/11 GI Bill. These programs, administered by the VA, also help Guard and Reserve members pay for undergraduate and graduate programs, apprenticeships, and other programs. More information on these benefits is available on the VA's GI Bill website.

If you're a member of the National Guard or Reserves, you're eligible for a VA loan guaranty after you have completed six years of service in the Selected Reserve. However, if you are called to active duty, you must serve only ninety days before you are eligible. For more information, visit the VA's Home Loan Guaranty website, or call the Loan Eligibility Center at 888-244-6711.

A percentage of the loan—between .5 and 2.40 percent—is charged as a funding fee. Guard and Reserve members pay the higher fee, but the amount is reduced if you are making a down payment of at least five percent. The funding fee can be included in the loan.

Life Insurance

National Guard and Reserve members can purchase up to $400,000 of life insurance through the VA's low-cost Service members' Group Life Insurance program. To qualify, you must be assigned to a unit in which you are required to perform active duty or active duty for training and will be scheduled to perform at least twelve periods of inactive duty creditable for retirement purposes. The insurance coverage is in effect 365 days of the year, not just when you are drilling or training.

Life insurance coverage is available in increments of $50,000. Currently, the VA charges 7 cents per month per $1,000 of coverage, regardless of the service member's age. For a $400,000 policy, your cost would be $28 per month. You can purchase up to $100,000 of additional life insurance coverage for your spouse and up to $10,000 of coverage for each dependent child through the VA's Family SGLI program.

After you leave the Guard or Reserve, you may choose to convert your SGLI to Veterans' Group Life Insurance. Visit the VA's Life Insurance website at www.benefits.va.gov/insurance/.

Retirement

National Guard and Reserve service members who complete a minimum of twenty "qualifying" years of service (creditable retirement years) become eligible for retired pay at age sixty.

A qualifying year, under this system, is a year in which the service member earns at least fifty retirement points during their retirement year. Inactive point credit is earned for inactive duty training,

Reserve membership, equivalent instruction, and correspondence courses.

Note: A law passed in early 2008 allows Reserve and Guard members with twenty or more years to begin drawing retirement benefits before age sixty if they deploy for war or national emergency. For every ninety consecutive days spent mobilized, members of the Guard and Reserve will see their start date for annuities reduced by three months. But this law only applies for deployment time served after January 28, 2008.

By law, members may receive credit for up to sixty inactive points for retirement years that ended before September 23, 1996, up to seventy-five inactive points for retirement years ending on or after September 23, 1996, and before October 30, 2000, and up to ninety points in the retirement year that includes October 30, 2000, and in any subsequent year of service. Points from these sources may be added to points earned from active duty and active duty for training for a maximum total of 365 or 366 points per retirement year. Points are credited on the following basis:

- One point for each day of active service (active duty or active duty for training).
- Fifteen points for each year of membership in a Reserve Component (Guard and Reserve).
- One point for each unit training assembly.
- One point for each day in which a member is in a funeral honors duty status.
- Satisfactory completion of accredited correspondence courses at one point for each three credit hours earned.

Visit the Army Reserve Retirement Pay Calculator at www.hrc.army.mil/Calculators/RetirementCalc.aspx to get an estimate of your monthly retirement pay at age sixty.

The Secretary of the military department concerned notifies, in writing, members of the Reserve Forces who have completed the eligibility requirements for retirement and receipt of retired pay at age sixty. Notice is sent to the member within one year of reaching eligibility. Reserve Component members generally have three options upon receiving notice of eligibility:

1. Remain in the Ready Reserve and continue to perform inactive duty training, annual training, and active duty training depending on their training and pay category, or remain on the active status list of the Standby Reserve and continue to perform unpaid training for the purpose of accumulating retirement points.

2. Transfer to the Retired Reserve. A member in this category may participate in inactive duty training provided:

   a. Such training is at no expense to the Government.

   b. Members are not entitled to pay or retirement points.

   c. No official record of such participation is maintained.

   d. Members request discharge from the Reserve Components.

Note: Regardless of the option chosen, the member is entitled to receive retired pay at age sixty, but must apply for it.

Reserve Component Retirement Pay Systems

Upon reaching age sixty, a Guard or Reserve retiree may begin receiving retired pay. There are currently two Reserve retirement systems that parallel the systems for active duty: the Final Basic Pay System and the High-Three System. To determine which retirement system a Reserve Component member is under, look at the same criteria that determines the retirement system for the active force—the Date of Initial Entry to Military Service (DIEMS). That is the date an individual first became a member of a uniformed service. Note: The date an individual first became a member of a uniformed service is the sole determining factor in determining which retirement system is used when computing retired pay.

Formulas for Computing Retired Pay

- If you first entered a uniformed service before **September 8, 1980**:
  Compute your retired pay based on length of service by multiplying the basic monthly pay for your retired grade at the time of retirement by the years of creditable active federal service at the rate of 2.5 percent for each whole year of service. This is called the **Final Pay** retirement system. That means you get 50 percent for twenty years of service up to a maximum of 75 percent.

- If you first entered a uniformed service* between **September 8, 1980, and July 31, 1986**:
  Compute your retired pay using the same formula as the Final Pay system above, except you use the average basic pay for your three highest paid years (thirty-six months) rather than final basic pay. This is called the High 36. Under the **High 36** system you get 50 percent for twenty years of service up to a maximum of 75 percent.

- Your years of service are used to determine the value of each point. Your retirement points are multiplied by the approximate value of a point to produce the estimate monthly retired pay value. For example an E-9 with twenty years in 2009 would receive a valuation of approximately 0.360 per point whereas the same retiree would get 0.432 for thirty years of service.

An important factor: A member who retires under either system receives longevity credit for those years while a member of the Retired Reserve awaiting pay at age sixty. However, this does not apply to a former member who is entitled to retired pay under either the Final Basic Pay System or the High-three System. A former member is defined as an individual who elected discharge rather than transfer to the Retired Reserve any time after receiving notification of eligibility to receive Reserve retired pay at age sixty. In the case of a former member, regardless of the system under which the individual will receive Reserve retired pay, longevity credit ceases on the date the former member was discharged.

Whether your loved one is supporting a military operation overseas, performing duty in a local or regional location, or performing training at the local armory or reserve center, you may face challenges during these periods similar to active military service. The geographic dispersion of many Guard and Reserve Families is unique and at times can make it more difficult to obtain information. It also may be more difficult to access various support services that are normally available at active duty installations. We hope that the information provided here has given you a good starting point for acquiring needed knowledge, and will inspire you to conduct further research. Remember that we all are joined together in one Army—Active Duty, Reserve, and Guard. Together we are a part of the Army Family.

Websites

www.nationalguard.com/
http://www.nationalguard.mil/
http://ra.defense.gov/mobilization/
http://ra.defense.gov/
www.usar.army.mil/
https://www.facebook.com/usarmyreserve
www.nationalguard.mil/resources
www.usar.army.mil/ourstory
www.arfp.org/

Chapter 4

Your New Hometown

Tonia Gutting

Sick Call

Signals all troops needing medical attention
to report to the dispensary.

Like an overstuffed chair at Starbucks, a fudge shop in a mountain resort town, or the Slurpee machine at 7-Eleven, amenities on Army posts quickly become familiar. It takes villages to run the Army, and most posts are complete communities within themselves. Don't hide out on post without experiencing the locale, but do enjoy the advantages found right in your new neighborhood. Soon the cadence of running Soldiers, the lullaby of Taps, even the boom of cannons will feel like home.

Have your ID card ready to take advantage of everything from getting through the post's front gate to buying a new dress at the PX. Here is what you can expect on most Army posts:

HOME AND WORK

Housing—Neighborhoods are usually grouped by rank, and vary broadly from post to post, except for the dull-white paint used on the interior walls. Barracks are where single Soldiers live.

Chapels—Buildings where worship services are held.

Chaplains' Offices—There is no set standard concerning where Chaplains' offices are located. This is based on availability and needs. Most of the Combat or Combat Support Unit Chaplains' offices are found in their unit areas. Garrison Chaplains and their staff are usually located in sections near or where their headquarters staff is housed. The Officers in Charge (OICs) and Non-commissioned Officers in Charge (NCOICs) of chapels have offices in their designated chapels.

Workplace Buildings—You will find everything from storage sheds to commanders' offices clustered according to units and functions. Buildings are often referred to by numbers and are marked accordingly.

Training Grounds—Large land areas where Soldiers drill. Some parts may be available for recreation such as hiking, hunting, and fishing. Beware of signs indicating areas where live ammunition is used.

Places to Spend Money

Commissary—Provides high-quality groceries at low prices. It is a great way to stretch the Family dollar. Baggers work for tips, so be prepared unless you use the self-checkout lane. Paydays and the days before holidays are always very crowded.

PX (The Post Exchange)—The PX is similar to a department store and sells clothing, medicines, furniture, pet supplies, auto parts, and fishing gear. The PX typically is housed in a mini-mall with shops such as:

- Beauty salon and barber shop
- Food court
- Military clothing sales: Soldiers' uniforms and supplies
- Alterations and dry cleaning
- Optometry shop
- Flower shop
- Concessions or vendors who display and sell their wares, such as a sunglass kiosk or a cellular phone store

DFAC—The dining facility is a cafeteria where Soldiers eat; Families may use this also. Especially on holidays, notably Christmas and Thanksgiving, the DFACs lay out quite a spread at unbeatable prices.

Other dining options—May include chain restaurants.

Thrift Store—Always a good place to buy and sell. These are typically operated by volunteers; profits are used to benefit the post community.

Lemon Lot—The Lemon Lot is a designated area where people can park used vehicles they wish to sell. Especially when overseas, Army Families often buy and sell "hoopties" from the Lemon Lot. They can be excellent second cars.

Lodging—Whether the rooms are called *Army lodging, temporary lodging, guest housing, or transient lodging,* the terms all mean the same thing—they are the Army's equivalent of hotels. You will become familiar with this as you most often will spend the first few days and the last few days of each assignment in Army lodging. Additionally, you may be able to take advantage of these accommodations during leisure travel time, but always call ahead to be sure there is space available. Post campgrounds may be available at some locations.

Shoppette/Express/Gas Station—For late-night diaper and milk runs or quick snacks, these convenience stores can save the day.

Places to Have Fun

Playgrounds and Parks—From old-fashioned grills to baseball diamonds, parks vary in size, features, and location.

Bowling Centers—Fun gathering places for league bowling, birthday parties, and unit or chapel functions, bowling centers usually offer some type of food service such as hamburgers or pizza.

Movie Theaters—Typically, prices are lower than off-post theaters but selection and showings are limited.

Running Tracks/Ball Fields

Swimming Pools

Fitness Centers/Gyms—Depending on the size of the post, most centers provide athletic and training facilities including exercise and weight rooms, saunas, and various sports-related courts. Family members may use the centers, with some age restrictions. Check out the programs offered by your fitness center.

Libraries

Ranges—Archery, rifle, and clay pigeon shooting.

CYSS (Child Youth and School Services)—CYSS provides comprehensive child and youth programs. Recreational team sports, arts and crafts classes, dance and gymnastics classes are available. Contact CYSS Central Registration Office to enroll.

Services

Military Police—Known as MPs, they are first responders for any emergency. They are also responsible for neighborhood patrol and traffic control. The MP station is your first destination if a Family Member loses an ID card.

Fire Department

Medical Facilities—Most posts have some type of medical care available for Family Members. Providers may be both civilian and military. Not all Army posts have hospital/ER/Urgent Care. ***Always be sure to familiarize yourself with your emergency medical options as soon as you arrive at a new duty station.***

Dental—In the United States, on-post care is generally reserved for Soldiers; Family Members will use off-post providers. Some overseas assignments will accommodate Family Members.

OSJA/JAG—The Army's legal team can assist with many legal issues, including rental problems, creating wills, obtaining powers of attorney, and notary services. JAG opens tax offices each year to file tax returns at no cost for Soldiers and Family Members.

The Child Development Center—Army Child Development Centers (CDCs) are on-post childcare centers that offer full-day, part-day, and hourly care for children, generally from six weeks old through five years old. Registration through the CYSS Central Registration Office is required prior to enrollment.

Education Center—The Education Center provides counseling services, testing services, and the Army Learning Center and education programs.

Veterinary Clinic—Most Army posts have a veterinary clinic. These clinics require that your pet be registered and they also provide standard pet services for a fee. Expect that your pet will be required to have an identification chip.

Stables—Trail rides, clinics, and rental spaces for Family Members' horses may be available.

Auto Craft Shop—Provides a place where you can perform self-help services on your vehicles. Professionals are available to help or advise.

Post Office—Just like the ones in the civilian world, but very convenient when they are located on your post.

Outdoor Recreation—This office specializes in creating fun, local experiences. Look here to rent everything from bicycles to RVs. They have equipment for every sport you can imagine, as well as opportunities to participate in excursions and trips.

Information, Tickets, and Reservations (ITR) or Leisure and Travel Services (LTS)—This is the place to find travel information and, often, discounted tickets to regional and national attractions.

Army Community Services (ACS)—Start here for most any need, from a fax service to relocation, to English as a Second Language, to Family Members with special needs, to emergency loans and employment opportunities. ACS also offers nonmedical counseling through the Military Family Life Consultant program. If ACS can't help, they know who can. ***When you arrive at a new post, be sure to attend their post/area orientation for newcomers!***

ACS Lending Closet—Basic household items can be checked out for temporary use; especially helpful when arriving and departing a duty station.

Self-Help Store—Found mainly overseas, self-help stores provide home maintenance items such as rakes, lightbulbs, curtain hooks, paint, and recycling bags.

USO—Often found in airports, and sometimes on posts, the USO is a haven for the weary. They offer food, rest, and recreation for Military ID card holders.

American Red Cross—Provides rapid communications between Soldiers and Families in the event of serious personal and Family problems such as a need for financial assistance, for emergency leave, and for disaster assistance. Be sure to give the Red Cross telephone number to your parents or others back home who might need to reach you or your Soldier in an emergency.

You will find that each duty station has its own character and design, but Army posts and the services they offer will begin to feel and look even more familiar and comfortable to you as the years go by.

Put your feet up—you are home.

CHAPTER 5

RELIGIOUS ACTIVITIES ON POST

Aby Dolinger and Kelly Croom

Church Call

Signals religious services are about to begin. The call may also be used to announce the formation of a funeral escort.

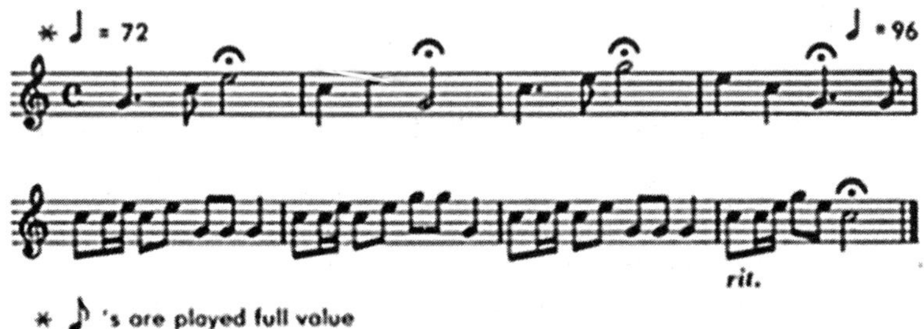

Whether this is your first military installation or you've spent the better half of your life on various installations around the world, each Army post offers a variety of religious programs and opportunities for service. They all have varying characteristics, needs, and operational tempo.

What Religious Facilities Can Be Found on an Army Post?

Typically, there will be one or more buildings designated as chapels or worship centers. The same building might be used for various religions or denominations. Rooms or areas within the worship center may be designated for specific faith groups only. On rare occasions, a chapel may be utilized by only one specific faith group.

The Chaplain and the Chaplain Assistant may have an office in the chapel, or their offices may be housed with their Army unit. The Garrison Chaplain usually assigns a Chaplain Officer in Charge (OIC) in charge of services and personnel for each chapel and a Non-commissioned Officer in Charge (NCOIC) in charge of facility needs.

Some Army posts have a Family Life Center, which may be manned by Chaplains who have been through special counseling training. Children and youth programs may meet at the chapel or in another community building on post. Some installations host religious activities in a chapel "coffee house" facility.

What Religious Services and Support Can Be Found on an Army Post?

Chapel services for every religious need are provided on post, according to regulations and availability of resources. Additionally, most Army installations offer auxiliary programs, such as men's and women's studies. Chapel congregations often sponsor fellowship meals and picnics. Many have youth groups; some are led by professional youth ministers and others by Army Chaplains or chapel volunteers. The Garrison Chaplain may sponsor fellowship or training events, such as large concerts, Bible study training, or marriage enrichment events. Special programs for holidays and events, like Chaplain-sponsored community lunches with devotional messages, are additional opportunities for fellowship.

Religious care is available to all Army Families. Soldiers and Family Members with a counseling need are encouraged to seek out their Unit Chaplain or a professional Family counselor on post. Army hospitals are staffed with Hospital Chaplains who minister directly to patients and staff as well as to Family Members. Many hospitals have a chapel or prayer room. Sometimes needs are met through referrals to off-post services.

The Unit Chaplain and Chaplain Assistant often plan ecumenical prayer breakfasts or luncheons, which may be held in the troop dining facility or in another post community center. A meal is served, and attendees enjoy special music and a devotional speaker. In addition, a post-wide prayer breakfast or luncheon may be planned in conjunction with the National Day of Prayer.

Chaplains also sponsor retreats and workshops for single Soldiers, couples, or Families. These may be held on or off-post; they could be a few hours to a few days in duration. Contracted childcare providers are usually available to care for the attendees' children.

Who Is Responsible for On-Post Religious Activities?

The Garrison Commander is responsible for the religious programs on an installation, and the Garrison Chaplain plans and executes those programs for the Commander. Garrison Chaplains (who may also be known as Installation Chaplains) coordinate all available resources—to include Chaplains and Chaplain Assistants assigned to combat or combat support units—to execute the programs. Things work best when everyone understands his or her duties and responsibilities to support the Garrison Religious Program, as synchronized support to the Senior Commander's mission. The Garrison Chaplain assesses the needs and interests of the Army community and combines facilities, resources, and personnel to meet those needs.

Chaplains are expected, under the direction and supervision of the Garrison Command Chaplain, to support the post religious programs. The Garrison Chaplain will let your spouse know in which areas his or her services are required. Besides the normal worship service support, there are key programs that need both Chaplains and Chaplain Assistants to make them work: religious education, youth ministry, duty rosters, and sponsorship of auxiliaries (i.e., Protestant Women of the Chapel (PWOC), Catholic Women of the Chapel (CWOC), and Protestant Men of the Chapel (PMOC).

A key staff member is the Director of Religious Education (DRE). A paid civilian professional, the DRE compiles a comprehensive religious education schedule for the post and requests resources needed to support the religious education programs. The DRE also recruits and trains volunteers for these programs. Other staff members may be paid contractors, such as musicians or childcare workers.

Chapel-related program offerings can be extensive, and volunteers are essential to their success. Because of the many unit and community commitments, chapel volunteers are usually in high demand.

As Chaplain spouses, it can be our privilege to help provide quality and meaningful religious support and programs on our installations. Chaplain spouses are free to match their talents, time, interests, and training to specific activities when volunteering. Volunteering your time and talents benefits your spouse, your unit, and your installation's ministry. Be aware that, depending on the position, some chapel volunteers must pass a background check and receive training.

Volunteers are encouraged to log their volunteer hours in the Volunteer Management Information System (VMIS), an online computer program sponsored by the Garrison Commander. This is a concrete way for the Garrison Commander to evaluate and address community needs and determine funding requirements for religious programs. A record of many volunteer hours invested in religious programs helps to justify the programs' existence.

How Are Religious Activities Funded?

There are major differences between civilian congregation funding and military chapel funding. For example, there are two "pots" of money used to fund chapel programs (bear in mind that both of these pots belong to the Army): Appropriated Funds (AF), which are taxpayer dollars appropriated by Congress; and Non-Appropriated Funds (NAF), from chapel tithes and offerings. Regulations govern how funds can be used. AF monies are spent on "mission essential" programs; both monies can be spent on "mission enhancement" activities. The Chaplain Funds Manager/Resource Manager, a Garrison Chaplain's staff member, manages the procedures for requesting, approving, and spending these monies. Unlike a civilian congregation's spending procedures, one may not spend first and be reimbursed later, even when presenting a vendor receipt. Chaplains are trained on local procedures, and volunteers work with their activity's Chaplain sponsor when requesting funds.

If you are interested in starting a new religious program on your post, first contact your Unit Chaplain or leader of the chapel. You may then be encouraged to vet your idea with the Director of Religious Education or Garrison Chaplain. It is possible to receive support from the Chaplain's office, such as securing a meeting space, funding for materials, fellowship supplies, and Watch Care (an Army term for childcare) expenses. You may discover by speaking to the Chaplain that a similar ministry already exists.

Although the Army chapel may look similar to a civilian worship center from the outside, you will find a richness of diversity, ideas, and experiences inside that combine to embrace the similar and minimize the differences.

Chapter 6

We're Moving Where?

Sarah Ball

First Sergeant's Call

Signals that the First Sergeant is about to form the company.

Jerry Seinfeld once said, "To live is to keep moving." As Army spouses, we can certainly echo that statement! Moving is a regular part of our grand Army adventures. The experiences we have as we move can include stress and uncertainty, but they can also lead to new opportunities and friendships.

This is a collection of some of the wisdom and experience of Chaplain spouses who have gone before you, and we hope that it will lead to successful and enjoyable moving experiences for you!

Let the Fun Begin

There are many reasons for a move in the Army. The Army may need your spouse to fill a position somewhere or attend a school for further training. Often, a move allows your spouse to gain job experience or education that will further his career and better equip him or her as a Chaplain. You'll have the opportunity to talk together and fill out a preference form (dream sheet) listing assignment locations you'd prefer. Keep this updated, but remember that the needs of the Army will always prevail, so don't be disappointed when you are assigned to a location you might not have chosen.

Sometimes, you and your spouse will have plenty of time to prepare for a new assignment. Other times, new jobs will become available unexpectedly or the Army will have a sudden need your spouse can fill. In a perfect world, we'd all have months to plan for our moves and everything would go exactly as scripted. In reality, the most successful movers are the ones who live by the motto, "*Semper Gumby*—Always Flexible."

If you have a Family Member with an ongoing medical condition that requires regular medical treatment, contact your installation's Exceptional Family Member Program (EFMP) for information about screening and mandatory enrollment requirements. All Family Members *must be* screened in order to be approved for overseas or remote location assignments. This helps ensure that your Chaplain will be assigned to locations where your Family Members will have adequate care.

Typically, your move process begins when your spouse receives word that he or she has a new assignment coming. Your spouse will be instructed to attend a Levy Briefing, at which necessary forms relevant to the upcoming PCS orders will be updated. At this time he or she will note which Family Members are to be included in the move and make requests for Professional Gear allowances for both of you, if applicable. More information on what constitutes Professional Gear can be found at www.SDDC.army.mil.

The notification does not become official until a Request for Orders (RFO) is received. Next, your Soldier will receive official Permanent Change of Station (PCS) orders, which allow you to begin arrangements for your move.

Keep in mind, orders can and do change even after you have an RFO or PCS orders in hand. In the fluid world of Army life, be aware that locations may change and your assignments may be shorter or longer than you'd like. You probably won't be the Family who gets new orders to Kansas after your household goods have already left for Germany. But it does happen!

If your spouse's orders are for an accompanied move, he or she is allowed to move his or her dependents (that's you) to the new duty station. If the orders are for an unaccompanied tour, then your spouse is not able to take Family Members along.

If your spouse's new duty station is overseas (including Hawaii and Alaska), it will be considered OCONUS (Outside the Continental United States). Moves within the continental US are called CONUS (Continental United States).

Your timeline for moving will depend on the report date listed on your spouse's orders. This is the date by which he or she must sign in at the new location. Many Families take some leave time between signing out of their old duty station and signing in at the new location. They use this time for traveling, vacation, or visiting Family.

Your spouse will attend a briefing at his or her current duty station to receive some initial information on the moving process. After that briefing, he or she can access the Defense Personal Property System online to set up your move. At this time the DPS website (www.move.mil) will allow you to manage the move of your household goods. On the site, you can request specific dates for a moving company to pack and transport your items. You can also select a PPM (Personally Procured Move—often called a DITY) if you'd rather move your household goods yourself.

To DITY or Not to DITY (Do-It-Yourself)

The moving process requires lots of decisions, but one of the biggest ones you'll make is how you'd like your household goods moved. You have several options: a full move by a commercial carrier, a move by a commercial carrier plus a partial DITY, or a full DITY. Here's how it breaks down, with a few pros and cons to consider.

Full move by commercial carrier: A Transportation Service Provider (TSP) will be contracted by the Army to move all of your household goods (minus a handful of restricted items). You will request specific dates for them to pack and load your goods, but you will have to work out the final schedule with the TSP according to their availability. The TSP will be responsible for packing your goods, loading them on a commercial moving truck, driving the truck to your new destination, and unloading and unpacking the items. (Many people choose not to have the movers unpack for them.)

Using a TSP for your entire move requires the least physical labor and offers the greatest convenience. If items are broken in transit, the TSP reimburses you at full replacement value for your goods. However, the experience of watching packers and loaders handle your items can be stressful, since they may not pack and manage items in the same way that you would.

Move by a commercial carrier plus a partial DITY: In this option, you send the majority of your household goods with a TSP, following the same process described above. However, you pack a portion of your household goods and move them yourself. Household goods you might consider moving yourself include clothing, dishes or food items to use during transition, liquids, medications, and items that a TSP will not move. You can also choose to transport valuable items this way if you feel they will be more secure with you. You will need to weigh the vehicles you use while empty and again while fully loaded to find the weight of the household goods you are moving. There are no restrictions as to the type of POV or equipment used to perform personally procured transportation of HHG. Government vehicles cannot be used.

Even a few hundred pounds of personal items can translate into a decent reimbursement, which can help with some of the other financial stresses of moving. If your TSP shipment reaches or exceeds your weight limit, you can always choose not to submit your partial DITY paperwork after the move. You won't be paid for what you self-transport, but you also won't be charged for that excess weight!

Full DITY: In this type of move, you assume responsibility for moving all of your household goods yourself. The government pays you for the weight that you move, up to 95 percent of the amount they would have paid a TSP to move your household goods. If you choose to do this type of move, the DPS website where you manage your move will help you estimate your potential reimbursement.

DITY moves can be done in a couple of ways. You can rent a truck, trailer, or other equipment and do all packing, loading, driving, and unloading yourself. Another DITY option is called "you load/they drive." In this type of DITY, you pack and load your goods into a commercial trailer or vehicle. The commercial company drives your goods to your new destination, and you unload and unpack your goods.

Doing a full DITY allows you to organize, pack, and handle your goods yourself. If you are moving a long distance (reimbursement rates depend on distance moved), you can potentially earn some money for your hard work. Be sure to calculate your costs carefully in advance, factoring in transportation rentals and gas, moving supplies for packing, and possible tax consequences. Also, be aware that your own insurance and pocketbook will need to cover any items damaged in transit. If you decide to DITY, there are multiple websites and online videos that will help walk you through the options and the process.

Who Pays for This?

The government covers many moving expenses through an assortment of allowances and reimbursements. Ask for specifics at your spouse's first transportation briefing and do some research online for the most up-to-date numbers. Militaryavenue.com covers some of the major allowances and entitlements.

Dislocation Allowance (DLA) is money intended to help with the costs of relocating and miscellaneous travel costs. There are some kinds of moves that do not receive DLA: moving to your first duty station, moving locally, and a few other situations. The amount of DLA depends on your spouse's rank and dependent status.

Monetary Allowance in Lieu of Transportation (MALT) is a mileage reimbursement paid when a Soldier and/or the Soldier's Family drive to their new duty station, based on the Official Military Table of Distances.

Per Diem Allowance helps reimburse your cost of meals and lodging while traveling. The amount is calculated using the distance you travel and the number and ages of dependents in your Family.

All three of the allowances listed above can apply to CONUS or OCONUS assignments (see explanations below). You can request up to 80 percent of these three allowances in advance before your move to help pay for costs along the way. You will receive the remainder when your move is complete and you file your moving paperwork.

In addition to these allowances, the government also assists with some costs of temporary lodging while you are in transition. If you are moving within the continental US, you can receive **Temporary**

Lodging Expense (TLE), a reimbursement for up to ten days of hotel expenses. For overseas moves, **Temporary Lodging Allowance (TLA)** helps defer your lodging costs while you wait for housing.

Here is something the Army does not pay for—**Overweight Household Goods.** The Joint Federal Travel Regulations (JFTR) prescribes the maximum Permanent Change of Station (PCS) and Non-Temporary Storage (NTS) weight allowances that you can ship and/or store at government expense based on the member's rank and dependency status. The JFTR also prescribes Temporary Duty (TDY) weight allowance based on the member's rank. Weight allowances do not include Professional Books, Papers and Equipment (PBP&E/Pro-Gear) or required medical equipment.

Exceeding your authorized weight allowance on a move can cost you a lot of money. Charges for excess weight can range from several hundred to several thousand dollars.

Notification of overweight charges can occur many months after your move is completed. This can be a really unpleasant surprise, so try to estimate the weight of your household goods as carefully as possible.

The weight tables and entitlement resources can be found at: www.move.mil/documents/DOD/Weight_Allowance_Table_JFTR_Vol1.pdf

Across the Distant Ocean

If the Army has presented you with the opportunity to see foreign lands and exotic places (an OCONUS assignment), then you have some additional questions to ask. Once your spouse receives orders, put together a list of essential questions to ask at the transportation briefing. Each overseas location has its own unique living situations and guidelines for moving. Once you research the specifics of your OCONUS destination, you can begin to plan your Family's move (and all the traveling you will do while living overseas!).

Here are a few topics to ask about as you talk with your transportation office:

- What will our weight limit be for household goods? Typically, overseas moves allow an expedited shipment of a few essentials (your unaccompanied or "hold" baggage), followed by the remainder of your household goods in a later shipment.

- What items are not allowed on this move? This information may depend on the customs rules of the country you are entering.

- What arrangements are available for storing items we will not be taking overseas?

- Can we ship our vehicle? In general, the military will ship one vehicle to your OCONUS assignment. Military Families often find it beneficial to buy a vehicle in their new country that is suitable to local driving conditions.

- What are the guidelines for my pets? Most of the time, Families may transport two pets with them overseas. This is usually limited to cats or dogs, and additional vaccinations may be needed. Bear in mind that there are certain times of year when pets cannot be transported due to high temperatures. All costs and arrangements for moving your pets are your responsibility.

- What passports and visas are required, and how do we go about getting them? Be sure to allow plenty of time to complete this process before your move.

Once you've got the major parts of your move sketched out, it's time to research your new home. Prior to your move, your Chaplain will be assigned a sponsor at your new duty station and this Soldier will be able to answer questions for you. Ask around in your circle of friends as well. Many military spouses have friends scattered at duty stations all over the world, and their friends may already be in your new area. Most military Families are happy to answer questions—they've usually benefited from others doing the same for them. Ask them about housing, schools, commissary availability, chapel programs, youth services, and all the other things that are important to your Family life.

. . . Or Just a Few States Away

Whether you are moving to Germany or Georgia, many of the same questions will come to mind. Where will we live? How good are the schools there? What kind of recreation is available? What resources and programs does the post have to offer? Doing some advance reconnaissance on your new area can help you make wise choices and build excitement for your move.

If your schedule and budget allow, you may consider an advance trip to your next duty station to check out schools and housing. During a short visit, consider driving around the post and its surrounding areas with maps in hand. Which areas do you like best? Visit schools and talk to their staff; assess the feel of each educational environment. Focus on researching the aspects of life and education that are priorities for your Family—sports, special education services, specific clubs, academic rigor, gifted and talented programs, or whatever is most important to your Family. Websites such as www.greatschools.org and others can give you a lot of background information to narrow your search for schools.

An advance visit to your new area may also help you find your next home. You may have several options: live on post (in "housing" or "quarters"), live off post in a rental, or live off post and buy a home. Every Family has different priorities in choosing a home, so spend time talking with your spouse about the things that are important to your Family. Good communication of your thoughts and priorities will make the decision process smoother. Be aware of your monthly Basic Allowance for Housing (BAH) as you examine your options.

In the past, the housing on military installations was managed by government housing offices. Over the last few years, many locations have switched to "privatized housing"—that is, a private company has contracted with the government to manage the military housing. The process of privatization has brought many positive changes to military housing. Many military installations have newly built or renovated homes to offer. Military housing communities have also added community centers and recreational bonuses like skate parks, splash parks, and new playgrounds.

Contact the housing office at your new duty station to discuss housing options. They will be able to tell you about the kinds of housing available to your Family, as well as potential wait times. Some of this information may be available through the main website for your new duty station or on other websites like www.housing.Army.mil.

If you decide to look at options off post, you can learn a lot about potential homes online. There is an array of websites that will help you learn more about home and rental prices in various neighborhoods. By watching these sites over a period of time, you can also get a sense of how quickly home sales or rentals are moving. In a slower-moving market, you may be able to line up a rental during your advance visit, since landlords are more eager to find reliable tenants. In a hot market, you may have to be more aggressive in your hunt and even start paying rent early (which the Army does not cover) to hold your rental home.

The Department of Defense sponsors the Automated Housing Referral Network (www.ahrn.com) to help connect military Families with available housing. Privately run websites like www.militarybyowner.com focus on home sale and rental listings near military installations. Sometimes a local realtor will be willing to show you rentals, hoping to earn your business if you decide instead to purchase a home. Property management companies often have multiple listings for rent in your target area. Call ahead and make appointments with specific property managers before traveling out to visit. You don't want to plan your visit on a holiday weekend and then discover that the property managers are all unavailable. Any lease you sign should include a military clause, which lets you out of your lease in case of new orders. Your local JAG office can help with checking the specific language for you.

Ready, Set, Go!

Once you have your PCS orders in hand and moving dates scheduled, you can begin prepping for moving day. Military.com has great checklists to help you prepare in the weeks leading up to moving day. Here are a few highlights:

> "A place for everything and everything in its place. The more organized you are before a move (things sorted and put away), the easier it will be after the move. The quicker you are able to unpack, the shorter and less stressful the transition will be." —Becci

Three Months before Your Move

- Notify your landlord of your upcoming move, but don't lock in an exact departure date just yet.
- Make an inventory of your household items, focusing on high-value items. Use video or pictures; keep this file with you when you travel. Don't send this with your household goods!
- Notify clubs, organizations, Family, and friends.
- Gather records from medical, dental, and optical offices as needed.
- Go through closets and drawers; donate unneeded items to charity or have a garage sale. This process will also help keep your household goods under the weight limit!
- If you are planning a DITY with rented equipment, research your choices and make a reservation.

Two Months before Your Move

- Begin using up canned food items, liquid soaps and lotions, and other consumables.

- If anyone in your Family has other employment, notify the employer of your upcoming move. Give an end date for your work schedule and request a letter of referral. Update résumés for use in your new area.
- If you will need childcare in your new area, begin looking for childcare providers.
- Check enrollment dates and requirements for schools at your next duty station. If possible, complete school and sports physicals before moving, so you have up-to-date physicals for your new registrations.
- Make travel reservations for your trip and any vacationing you plan to do along the way.
- Complete any needed auto maintenance.
- Check with your vet to see that all pets' immunizations are up-to-date. Get copies of pet medical records.

One Month before Your Move

- Call your TSP's local office and talk to them about finalizing dates. Verify your packing and loading dates. Schedule a walk-through with one of their staff members. They will look at your household items for things that require special packing (A piano? Three flat screen TVs? Ninety cartons of books?). They can also let you know what specific items their company will not transport. If you believe you may be close to your weight allowance, this is the time to request an appointment for your Soldier to meet the movers on moving day to weigh the truck before your items are loaded, so an accurate measurement is assured and you have a copy of the documentation.
- Reserve lodging at your current location and your next duty station for the time you will be moving. Most military installations have lodging options (many of these are now

run by private hotel chains). If you prefer to stay in hotel accommodations off post, check with the military lodging to see if you need a Statement of Nonavailability. In the past, military Families were encouraged to use on-post lodging unless it was unavailable, but this has gradually changed in the last few years.

- If you do not have an address yet in your new area, obtain a post office box or other address to use for temporary mail forwarding.
- Arrange to pick up school records or ask about the procedures for having them transferred to your children's new schools.
- If you do not have a cell phone for each vehicle your Family will be driving, consider purchasing an inexpensive prepaid phone or a set of walkie-talkies to communicate during your travels.
- Retrieve dry cleaning and items you have loaned out. Return library materials and other things you have borrowed.
- Notify utility companies of your move and schedule end dates for services. Cancel local subscriptions and delivery services.

Three Weeks before Your Move

- Contact your credit card companies and notify them of your upcoming move. Ask them to enter your travel dates in their systems. Some credit card companies have very vigilant fraud detection systems that will shut your cards down after you purchase gas in two different states—not a great convenience when you are on the move!
- Renew and pick up prescriptions. Obtain paper copies of your prescriptions in case refills are needed on the road. Pack medications carefully in leak-proof containers.

- Separate professional books and gear into separate piles and label them clearly for the packers.
- Begin washing and cleaning curtains and rugs. Be sure to allow ample time for rugs to dry before they are rolled and wrapped for shipping.
- Make arrangements for pet and childcare on your packing and loading days.

One Week before Your Move

- Remove wall accessories like curtain hardware, shelves, and racks. Bag and label small hardware.
- Buy a large assortment of Ziploc-type bags. They are useful for bagging small parts, silverware, small toy assortments, and much more. You may wish to bag the contents of entire drawers or shelves—the movers will pack the bags intact, so you can easily unpack them at the other end.
- Pull out items from attics, crawl spaces, under stairwells, or any other storage area that does not allow full standing room.
- Disconnect and drain hoses. Gather backyard toys, planters, and yard items into one area for packing.
- Drain oil and gas from your lawn mower and other lawn equipment. Disconnect spark plugs.
- Dispose of flammable items, including matches, lighters, aerosol cans, acids, chemicals, ammunition, paint, and thinners. Many moving companies will not move propane tanks, so consider gifting your grill tank to a neighbor.
- Disconnect cables, wires, speakers, and other electronic equipment. Inventory serial numbers on high-value items.

Consider setting your hard drive or back-up drive aside to travel in your personal vehicles.

- Set aside the cleaning materials you will use after your house is empty.

The Final Days before Your Move

- Designate one area of your home for items that will travel with you (See "Travel Well"). Placing these in a separate room will prevent confusion for the packers—an extra bedroom, a walk-in closet, even a bathroom. Label the door clearly with a "DO NOT PACK" sign for the benefit of your packers.
- Be aware of items that are often overlooked and could be packed by mistake—the oven broiler pan, if it stays with your house, house keys and garage door openers, manuals that belong to your current house, books and supplies that belong to employers or schools.
- If you are moving OCONUS, separate linens, dishes, and other items for your unaccompanied baggage shipment.
- Do a final sweep of your kitchen, bathroom, and medicine cabinets. All liquid or flammable items must now be disposed of or packed for your vehicles.
- Secure your valuables to travel with you. Remember to include jewelry, watches, cash, and checkbooks.
- Return your cable TV box or other rented equipment. Get a receipt to keep with your files in case of later issues as you close the account.
- If you are sending your personal computer with the movers rather than hand carrying it with you, it is a good idea to copy your hard drive and keep the copy with you.

- Clean your refrigerator and freezer, allowing them time to dry with the door propped. Fill socks with baking soda or charcoal briquettes and place them inside to avoid musty smells.

- Remove pictures and mirrors from wall; take lightbulbs out of lamps.

- Disconnect your washer and dryer; drain all hoses thoroughly.

Your Moving Day(s)

- When your scheduled packing date arrives, be prepared to get up early and have everything in order.

- Do a final sweep of the house—no dirty dishes, dirty laundry, or trash left in trash cans. The packers will wrap everything "as is"! Many Chaplains' spouses have reported being greeted at the other end of a move by a securely wrapped but very smelly bag of trash.

- Deliver your children and pets to their sitters early, so that you are in place for the truck to arrive.

- Remove purses, wallets, and other valuables from sight and secure them in a locked area (your vehicle may be a good option).

- If at all possible, have another adult available in your home to help supervise packers and loaders.

- As your movers disassemble furniture, ask them to bag and label each set of hardware.

> "Often, many things do not go according to plan, especially during moves. Allow yourself to have wiggle room, even with a plan B or C, and let go trying to manage or control everything."
> —Brenda

- Have snacks and drinks available for yourself and the movers (if you desire). Some Families like to provide lunch for their moving crew. This is not required, but some moving crews seem to expect it.

- Communicate kindly but firmly if you would like the packers or movers to do something differently. They do not know which items are most valuable to you, so you may request extra paper as they pack your mother's china, a separate wardrobe box for your husband's valuable guitars, or individual boxes for your fragile items or special collections.

- If you wish to stay overnight in your home until the final loading day, ask the packers to leave your beds intact until the last day. They can disassemble your beds just before the truck is loaded.

- Consider requesting a box for "First Night Linens." Your packers can label an empty box for you to fill with sheets and towels that you will need during your first night in your new home. Their label will help you find the box quickly on your first day of unpacking.

- Once the packers have filled many boxes, one of their crew will begin to inventory items. The person conducting inventory sticks colored numbers onto each box and writes an inventory list. Remember that Professional Gear needs to be labeled on the inventory; it can then be subtracted out from the weight of your household goods.

- At the end of the packing process, a driver will come to begin loading your goods on his truck. He will also conduct inventory—his list contains your furniture and items that are not in boxes. He will look closely for preexisting scratches and damage on your items and note them on his list. Ask for his inventory sheets as he completes each page. You need time to review his remarks and check the damage codes he has noted. Be sure his notations of damage are accurate.

- Check your house thoroughly for forgotten items—look behind doors, in high cabinets, and in the stove broiler drawer. Once your movers leave, they will not return for forgotten items.
- Watch the loading process carefully and ensure that every separate item has an inventory tag. You will not be reimbursed for lost or damaged items if they were not inventoried.
- Tipping is not expected or required, but some military Families like to tip their moving crews. If you wish to tip, you may want to distribute the money to your crew—the driver may or may not share tips with the rest of the crew.

Travel Well

The makers of Lincoln luxury cars once tried to persuade Americans that they could not travel well without a Lincoln. In truth, any well-packed vehicle can be the difference between crisis mode and low-stress travel. As your space allows, load up on these essentials:

- Important papers—fill an accordion file folder or binder with your Family's essential documents:

  IDs, passports, Social Security cards, marriage and birth certificates

  Auto and property titles, insurance documents

  Multiple copies of PCS orders, Powers of Attorney (POA), and leave forms

  Medical and dental records, immunizations, prescription and medication information

Emergency contact information, phone and address book

School transcripts, childcare information, sports physicals

Pet records and immunizations

Passwords, including financial and online accounts

Moving paperwork—keep copies of HHG inventories and receipts for moving expenses, lodging, and gas in one place. You will need these soon!

- Extra car keys
- Cell phones and chargers
- Carsick Kit—if you travel with children, pets, or anyone prone to motion sickness, this can be a lifesaver! (It also makes a great going-away present for friends who are on the move.)

Use a plastic container with a snap-on lid—a gallon ice cream bucket or a quart-size drink container, for example

Gallon-size Ziploc-type bags for . . . any potential circumstance

Antibacterial wipes and hand lotion

Small containers of Febreze-type deodorizer and stain remover

Breath fresheners

Bottled water

> "My 'Battle Book' is a must-have! It is the first thing I would grab in an emergency—birth certificates, serial numbers for electronics, military unit rosters, frequent flyer miles; you name it—it's in there!"
> —Kelly

For the kids—consider giving each child a backpack or container to pack with his own favorite items. This provides some security during lots of changes; it also limits how much space they can fill in your vehicle! Some ideas are:

- Toys for traveling and hotel rooms
- A special bedtime storybook or two
- Security blankets or special stuffed animals
- Last-minute gifts and photos from friends and classmates
- For small children, consider packing each day's outfit, including underwear and socks, in separate Ziploc-type bags. This is a great timesaver and helps keep luggage organized.

Other kid-related essentials—depending on the age of your children and the amount of travel time you anticipate, consider these options:

- Portable DVD player and assorted DVDs, electronic games, and a battery recharger to keep these items running for hours. A healthy budget for batteries may be the best money you ever spend for a long distance trip.
- A bag of surprises to be revealed whenever a little pick-me-up is needed. Include small toys, "new" books from the thrift store, special snacks, or travel games for the car.
- Medical Kit—keep a small container or travel bag with your usual medications, plus a few extras in case of unexpected illness.

  Thermometer

  Band-Aids and antibiotic lotion

  Anti-itch cream and antihistamines for allergies

Cold, flu, and headache remedies; cough drops and throat lozenges

Antacids and your favorite digestive remedies

Multi-vitamins or other supplements

Experienced pet owners suggest:

- Make sure all pet vaccinations are up-to-date, especially if you will be boarding pets on either end of your trip. If you are driving, taking pet beds or sleeping mats will make your pets more comfortable.
- If you are flying, be sure your pet's kennel fits the airline regulations.
- If your pet is unaccustomed to being in a kennel, begin using the kennel a month or so before your move to build familiarity.
- Obtain a Certificate of Veterinary Inspection (health certificate) from a federally accredited veterinarian within ten days of flying; know the temperature limits for your pet to fly. Don't wait until the last minute!
- Attach a zippered pencil bag to the side of your kennel and include a leash, copies of health certification, your contact information, and a small Ziploc-type bag of pet food.
- Find out about possible quarantines on overseas moves. How long and in what conditions are pets quarantined? Some overseas living situations may not allow pets. Check out PCSPets.com and DogsOnDeployment.org.
- Restaurants with outdoor seating areas may allow you to have your pet on a leash so he or she isn't stuck in the car.

Keep a portable food and water dish with you and a bag packed with all your pet needs for the trip.

- AAA's travel books are great because they list which hotels allow pets.
- Find out if government lodging is pet-friendly. If not, consider staying off post where pets are allowed.

When the Truck Pulls Away

After long hours of loading boxes and wrapping furniture, your moving crew finally closes the truck doors. Your spouse signs a stack of moving paperwork, and the truck rolls away. Now what?

Typically, this is the point when you grab your broom and get busy. If you are currently living in military housing, you should have a checklist from the housing manager of items to clean. Cleaning standards have eased in the new age of privatized housing, so "broom standards" are much easier for you to accomplish. Sweep and mop, wipe out cabinets, clean bathrooms, and work your way down the list.

Depending on your circumstances, you may consider hiring a cleaner to do your final clean-out. Some managers will require carpet shampooing, particularly if you have pets, and this can also be done by a professional company if you prefer. Be sure to keep receipts either way as proof that you have completed the carpet cleaning. Ask your manager about wall touch-ups—do they prefer for you to spackle holes yourself or leave them for the professionals?

The following will be helpful to have on hand at both ends of your move:

- Tool kit—a few basic tools will get you smoothly out of your old house and into your new home:

    Spackle, paintbrush, and paint for last minute wall touch-ups

Screwdriver, wrench, or specialty tools for disassembling and reassembling furniture. Your movers will do some of this, but if they show up without the right tools, you don't want them to get too creative!

Tape measure—plan your furniture layout in your new space.

Hammer and nails, assorted hardware for hanging pictures and curtains

- Cleaning Supplies—fill a crate or plastic tote with supplies for cleaning your old space and touching up your new one. If anyone in your Family is sensitive to chemical smells, consider using a tote with a snap-on lid to contain odors while traveling.

  Dusting cloths and spray—your bookshelves, desks, and dressers are never easier to clean than when they are completely empty.

  Your favorite products for cleaning windows, bathrooms, and floors

  Magic eraser sponges for doors and walls

  Dish soap and laundry detergent—you'll be surprised at how often you pull these out while traveling!

  Vacuum cleaner—consider borrowing a friend's vacuum if you don't have room in your vehicle for this.

  Carpet cleaner—if you don't own an appliance that can shampoo carpets, borrow or rent one to save yourself charges for dirty carpet.

At this point in the moving process, it is completely okay to feel exhausted and a little emotional. Take breaks whenever possible, and choose easy meal options. Visit a favorite restaurant one more time. Soak in the bath tub or hot tub at your hotel.

When it comes time to say good-bye to friends, choose the route that brings you closure. Some military spouses want to see everyone one last time, give dozens of hugs, and give last-minute thank-you notes, cards, and gifts. On the other hand, some Families want to quietly slip away, avoiding the emotional pain of saying good-bye. In the military community, many good-bye moments are really just "See you later!" departures, because friends often appear again at future duty stations.

As you load your vehicles and drive out (don't forget to stop at a weigh station if you are doing a DITY or partial DITY!), help your Family focus on the positive things that lie ahead. Will you be stopping at Grandma's house for a visit? Will your next duty station have opportunities for hiking? Visiting the beach? Building huge snow forts? Build some excitement for your Family's next stage of life.

When the Truck Arrives

Wouldn't it be wonderful if you arrived at your new home in an HGTV moment? On the home and garden shows, people always walk into tastefully decorated homes full of color with flowers blooming in the yard. They "ooh" and "aah" and everything is perfect. We wish!

Your arrival at your new home may come quickly or slowly. If you were able to line up a rental home in advance, you may be moving in quickly. Military housing might be ready and waiting, or it may require some waiting by you. Some military Families spend extended time in hotels, working through the home-buying process or looking for a suitable rental.

Most installations have an Army Community Service (ACS) Lending Closet. If your transition time stretches longer than a few days, you may want to set up temporary housekeeping with some of their free loaner items. The Lending Closet typically has things like inflatable mattresses, folding tables and chairs, high chairs, dishes, pots and pans.

If you have a place lined up and waiting for you, you may be able to do a "direct delivery" move. This means that you drive quickly to your new home in order to beat the moving truck to your destination. The moving truck comes directly to your new home and delivers your goods without any transfers on or off the truck. The big advantage of this delivery is that you avoid a lot of potential damage by supervising your possessions every time they are moved—both on and off the truck. There is also a smaller chance of your household goods becoming mixed up with another shipment or lost, since they stay on the truck during the entire process.

A direct delivery move typically cannot be arranged until the last minute, since it depends on the timeline of the driver. You won't meet your driver until loading day, at which point you can ask him how quickly he plans to complete the trip. You also need to talk to the TSP that sent the driver, to ensure that your tentative arrangement with the driver fits their schedule. (Note: Many military Families refer to a direct delivery move as "door to door," but the transportation system uses "door to door" to mean something different.)

If a direct delivery move is not workable, your household goods will typically be offloaded into storage at a warehouse until you are ready to receive delivery. Once you notify your TSP of your new address, the TSP will organize a crew to deliver your items.

While You Wait for the Truck

- Walk through your home, photographing and documenting damage and imperfections to avoid being charged for these upon exiting. Report these immediately to your landlord or property manager.

- Arrange for utility services, phone, cable, and trash disposal. Ask your new neighbors what companies they recommend.

- Find out what your options are for recycling packing materials. No matter how many boxes the movers haul away at the end of the day, you will have paper and cardboard to dispose of later.
- Decide on placement of your large furniture items. Your moving crew will place your furniture one time—any rearranging will be your job!
- Label each room with a taped sign on the door so your movers get boxes to the right rooms.
- If you have several days to wait for your delivery, consider painting rooms that you will want painted. Check with your housing manager about rules regarding paint first. If you have favorite color schemes for certain rooms, keep paint samples and fabric swatches in your accordion folder of important papers.

During Unloading

- If you will want any boxes or areas of the house unpacked, let your delivery crew know when they first arrive. You are entitled to unpacking, but many crews are not accustomed to this request. Don't wait till late in the day to clarify your expectations.
- Check off inventory numbers as items come into the house. Direct movers to the locations where you'd like items placed.
- If items are visibly damaged when they arrive, note the item number for later damage claims.
- You are entitled to reassembly of all furniture that the movers disassembled at your original home.
- The movers should remove all packing materials when they leave.

- Some people like to order pizza or other lunch items for their unloaders; this is entirely up to you. Unloaders always appreciate drinks to be provided. As mentioned earlier, tipping is an option.

Settling In

Once your truck is fully unloaded and all the driver's paperwork has been signed, you can begin to unpack and settle in. The boxes may seem overwhelming at first, so be strategic in your unpacking. What do you need first? Which rooms of the house are most important to your Family routines?

Many Families focus on the kitchen first, just to have normal home-cooked meals again. If you have children who are old enough to unpack some items, they may enjoy unpacking and arranging their own bedrooms. Be careful to shake out all your packing paper and boxes carefully—small items are very easy to miss!

As you work through your boxes, keep a running list of any items that you find in damaged condition from the move. Note the inventory number on the box or piece of furniture. Take pictures of the damage; do not throw away any broken items yet. Your moving company may have the option to claim broken items for salvage if they reimburse you for the items.

Go through all your boxes and containers, even the ones that you don't currently need. You may be surprised at where you find odds and ends stashed by the movers! (Hardware for the futon couch in the grill? Why not?!) You also need to verify that the contents of your seasonal decor tubs and storage totes are unbroken before you complete your damage claim.

If you find items that are broken or damaged, you may complete a claim through the move.mil website. Loss or damage must be reported through the website within seventy-five days of completing your move. Once your damage report is filed, you have up to nine months from your move date to finish filing your claim. The TSP has the option to repair your items to their original condition or pay you for the repairs. If your items cannot be repaired to their original condition, you will receive full replacement value for them.

The claims process can take time and negotiation to complete. If you have specific information on your furniture or possessions, it will help validate your claim and obtain a correct settlement amount. The damage claim form will ask you for information about when you purchased the item and its purchase price. If you can find an exact or comparable item currently for sale (the Internet is your friend for this!), it will help you make your case with the TSP.

Once the TSP makes you an offer to settle your claim, you can accept their payment and the claim is closed. If you reject their offer, you can provide more information and try to negotiate further. If you are unable to reach an agreeable settlement with your TSP, you can use the move.mil website to transfer your claim to the Military Claims Office (MCO). When you transfer your claim to the MCO, the MCO will reimburse you only for depreciated value of your items. The MCO will then try to obtain the full replacement value of your items from the TSP. If they succeed, you will receive the remainder of the full value.

After you've reduced your mountain of boxes to a pile of flattened cardboard, your house will begin to feel more like your home. Find out whether your empty boxes will be picked up or whether you will have to dispose of them yourself. Now it's time to venture out into your new community—find your favorite stores, try some restaurants, and take care of the nuts and bolts that connect you to your new duty station. Here are a few things to remember:

- Determine whether you will need a new driver's license or car registration. In many states it won't be necessary, but the MP station on post should know. Check the Department of Motor Vehicles website to see what special rules or discounts apply to military in your new state.
- Register your children for school.
- Set up mail forwarding to your new address, and begin notifying people of your new address.

- Call your bank, credit card companies, and insurance companies to give them your new information. Your insurance company may need to review your policies or write new ones for your new state.

- Visit the Child and Youth Services office on your new post to register your kids with their system and get information on childcare options, recreational classes, and sports.

- Contact TRICARE to transfer your medical care to your new duty station.

- Verify that the DEERS system has your new address and correct information added for *every* Family Member.

- If any of your Family Members will need referrals to specialists for ongoing treatment (such as physical therapy, ophthalmology, dermatology), set up an appointment with your new primary care manager to make those referrals for you.

- Consider subscribing to a website that reviews local services. The reviews are screened and can guide you to quality businesses and service providers in your area.

- Take an hour now and then to do something fun in your new area. Go for a short hike, try out the community swimming pool, or visit a craft or antique store.

> "Set your home up as fast as possible and focus on building relationships quickly. Find a support system at each installation and watch for God to give you his best new plan at each one. Moving is a chance to 'start fresh' and 'reinvent yourself.' It's a great way to wipe out your calendar and begin again, selectively planning your time."
> —Kelly

Building Community

In the middle of a move, you may feel like your life is one long to-do list. Moving all your worldly possessions and your precious Family across many miles is a hefty task. Once the dust has settled a bit, and you've found your sheets, towels, and essentials, set your list down and meet some people. If you have landed in a friendly community during warm weather, you may have neighbors showing up at your door before the moving truck leaves. If your home is more isolated or the weather is cold, you may need to initiate some "hellos" across the snowy driveways in the morning.

> "I am naturally very shy. I have to work to overcome my shyness each move I make to put myself out there to make friends quickly. It is always worth it, but something I have to work at."
> —Sherry

Beyond your neighborhood, you will find circles of potential new friends in your unit's Family Readiness Group, your post chapel and programs, and Chaplain spouse coffee groups. If your post offers a "Welcome to __________" class, take it! The first meeting or two may require some courage on your part, but stepping into new groups quickly will help you feel settled and connected. In times of challenge, your new friends will be your supporters and encouragers.

Helpful Websites

www.greatschools.org—Contains school data and reviews for public and private schools nationwide.

www.kidshealth.org—Search "moving" and find articles written both for you and your child to read about moving with children.

http://www.transcom.mil/dtr/part-iv/dtr_part_iv_app_k_1.pdf

www.militarybyowner.com—Lists homes for sale or rent near military installations.

www.military.com—Type "moving" or "relocation" in their search box and you will find articles, blogs, and checklists from experienced movers.

https://www.housing.army.mil/—The Army's gateway to finding information regarding Family and unaccompanied housing, both on post and in the local community worldwide.

www.militaryonesource.mil—This site contains many resources, including lots of articles on moving.

www.move.mil—The Department of Defense's official website for managing your household goods shipment.

www.petswelcome.com—Locate pet-friendly hotels.

CHAPTER 7

YOU'RE NOT IN KANSAS ANYMORE: LIVING OVERSEAS

Natalie Rauch

OFFICER'S CALL

Signals all officers to assemble at a designated place.

"GO!" Consider orders for an Outside Continental United States (OCONUS) assignment as a great adventure!

"GO!" Jump in when you arrive and experience the amazing opportunity you have to see another part of the world!

"GO!" Fully embrace the chance to make friends and learn about another culture!

The prospect of living outside the Continental US is a challenge and an opportunity like no other. You'll consider the pros and cons of accompanied versus unaccompanied tours and decide what's best for your Family at that time.

The orders say, "_______________ (OCONUS)." And then it starts. As soon as the orders arrive, the opinions and advice rush in like water over a waterfall. "Oh, you'll love it there." "It's such a pretty part of the country." "We were stationed there too, and it was an amazing assignment." There is a temptation to say: "It's just a dot on the map to me." Embrace the military experience as fully as you can. You will not regret it . . . especially when it comes to living overseas.

When you receive orders for an OCONUS assignment, get as much information as you can in order to schedule everything at the proper time and in the proper order. Be sure to attend any briefings available. There are so many decisions to make. What do we bring with us? What furniture/appliances should be put in storage? When do we leave? There are websites that will advise you. Talk to friends. Check for a Facebook page for the new installation.

All information below is a general guide. Anything your installation or transportation office tells you will take precedence.

Appliances: Most foreign countries use 220 volt electricity, which is quite different than the US 110V. In some cases the Army may issue you necessary appliances with compatible voltage such as ovens, refrigerators, washers, and dryers. It may be mandatory to store your large American appliances while serving OCONUS. In this case, the storage cost is paid by the military. You will need transformers or adapters for your 110V lamps and small appliances. Look at the Post Thrift Store/Shop to find a great deal on used transformers and small appliances with appropriate voltage. Some military housing is wired for both American and local voltage, so you may wish to bring your small appliances like irons and toasters, in case you might be able to use them.

Bank accounts: Expect to open a bank account on post to handle some of your local transactions such as phone and Internet services, and utilities. This is also a convenient place to exchange currency.

Car:

- Insurance and liens: Contact your auto insurance provider to determine the steps you need to take to be fully covered in your new location. If you still owe money on your vehicle, you must secure from the lien holder a shipment authorization letter on official letterhead.

- Car warranty: The factory warranty on your car might not be honored in another country. This is especially likely for an extended warranty.

- On the road: Driving can be quite different and more challenging in another country. You will see smaller vehicles in many countries because gas is much more expensive and roads aren't as wide. You will need to study and pass a driver's exam to obtain a military driver's license. You must possess a stateside driver's license to begin that process. Request or download the study materials for this test even before you arrive in country. Call as soon as you sign in to the new installation to get a seat at the next available testing. The new driver's license will probably be a requirement before you can rent a car overseas. In order to be safe (and in order to pass the test), you will need to have a good knowledge of the traffic signs, which are very different from American signs. Realize that people may drive much more aggressively and at high speeds. There are also many more motorcycles, scooters, and bicycles on the road, who have the same rights of way as those driving automobiles. In some countries you will have sidewalks with designated lanes for pedestrians and bicyclists. Be very careful.

- Roadside assistance: Plans similar to AAA are sometimes available from companies in the country where you are residing. They can be well worth the investment.
- Shipping your vehicle: Normally the Army authorizes shipping one vehicle to your new assignment. If you choose to ship a second vehicle, it will be at your own expense. Your car must be in good condition to pass the inspection at the Vehicle Processing Center (VPC). You might consider keeping your oversized car at home. Parking spaces, not to mention roads, are much smaller overseas than in America. What works for many serving overseas is to purchase a used car once you reach your new OCONUS assignment, and then resell it when you PCS. Many times you come out even, and sometimes even make some money on the deal. One huge advantage to purchasing a car made in your host country is that repair parts are a lot cheaper and the inconvenience of waiting for them to be shipped from the US is avoided.

Cell phones: Check your current cell phone contract to find out about overseas usage. Military orders may not be sufficient to release you from a contract. You may find that your American phone service can be adapted or that you must purchase a new phone overseas. Options may include both smartphones with contract plans and basic pay-as-you-go phones. The latter are often available inexpensively at the Shoppette/Express on post. Remember that Skype is a great way to be in touch with Family back in the US.

COLA: Cost of Living Allowance is paid to your Soldier to offset the added expense of living overseas. The rate varies according to location. The overseas COLA calculator can be found online at www.defensetravel.dod.mil/site/colaCalc.cfm.

Dependent Student Travel: Dependent students may be eligible for one funded round-trip per year while the service member is assigned overseas. The student must be enrolled in an academic program in a college, university, or postsecondary vocational education school. The student must also meet all qualifications, and be included on the Soldier's orders.

Department of Defense Education Activity (DoDEA)/ Department of Defense Dependents Schools (DoDDS): Most OCONUS assignments offer DoDDS schools for dependent children. It is worth the time to do Internet and phone research to determine which programs and sports are offered, and exactly what paperwork you will need. Be aware also that course offerings may vary among DoDDS schools. Because school start and end dates vary widely, securing a copy of the school calendar is essential when you are planning your PCS.

DVDs and electronics: DVDs purchased outside of the US may not play on a US DVD player. Often, you can purchase TVs and other electronics with dual voltage capabilities. The PX is an excellent place to find these. Some may need to be switched manually to the alternate voltage; others will change automatically.

Exceptional Family Member Program (EFMP) screenings: Please schedule EFMP screening appointments as soon as you receive orders. These screenings for all Family Members are a requirement for Command Sponsorship.

Guest house: Depending on your installation, Family housing may or may not be available when you arrive. Guest housing is available at most locations and provides short-term accommodations for military Families in transition between duty stations. Overseas guest lodging is usually wired to the voltage for that country, so check out your post's thrift store if you need a hair dryer or other personal care appliances.

Health Care: Healthcare is available for routine, urgent, and specialty care at all overseas assignments. When necessary care is not available at on-post health facilities, your Primary Care Manager (PCM) will make a referral to obtain health care on the local economy. This care is fully covered by your Army health insurance. You may request a translator if you feel you might need one prior to a host nation medical appointment. Foreign medical facilities do have different customs, and modesty standards may differ. It is best to be mentally prepared for this cultural difference. When arriving at an overseas assignment, you must immediately update and transfer coverage for all dependents in **Defense Enrollment Eligibility Reporting System** (DEERS).

Homeschooling: Talk to your school liaison to find out about groups and resources available in your new community. Use the Internet as a resource to learn about legalities and how to begin. As a military Family on orders, you are allowed to homeschool even if the country in which you reside does not allow homeschooling (Germany, for example). Military Families fall under the Status of Forces Agreement (SOFA). Please contact the DODDs school system to see if there is any paperwork to complete.

Newcomers' classes: Take advantage of any "welcome" classes your installation's ACS offers. These will instruct you on local customs and teach you some common phrases that are used in your new country. Sometimes these classes are offered to children as well as adults. Learn as much of the new language as you can. Locals are overjoyed to meet someone who is trying to learn their language.

> "Attending the Newcomers' Classes is invaluable! Sign up as soon as you arrive at your new location. It is a great way to meet and make new friends early on. Some posts even offer classes for kids!"
> —Karen

Family Morale, Welfare, and Recreation Programs: FMWR sponsors recreational services and trips for Soldiers and Families. You can find arts and crafts, library programs, fitness, and special events sponsored by your FMWR. They also put on outdoor recreational trips, adventure tours, shopping trips, festivals, and numerous events for single Soldiers.

Mail: As your Chaplain completes in-processing, your Family may be issued an Army Post Office (APO) or Military Post Office (MPO) box at a Community Mail Room (CMR) on post. You will be able to send and receive mail to and from the US paying regular domestic postage rates, which are far less expensive than international rates. When shopping online, check to be sure that your retailer delivers to APO boxes. You may discover that some items are restricted from shipping.

Overseas housing: Depending on the availability of on-post housing, you may have permission to look off-post for housing. If housing is available, the Installation Commander can mandate that you live in government housing. Advantages of living on-post: Children always have friends to play with, and it helps make their transition easier by making them feel they are living in a "little America" with the PX and Commissary, bowling alley, movie theaters, and other American amenities. Advantages to living off-post: You and your Family have the opportunity to immerse yourselves in the culture of your host nation. You will find yourself interacting with the locals and speaking the language more frequently. If you have school-age children, make sure the home you choose is on the route of the American school bus.

Passports: You will need two passports when PCSing overseas. One is a no-fee passport issued by the government for traveling on orders to and from the country you are stationed in and the second is a Tourist Passport to use when you travel at all other times.

- Government No-Fee Passport—Each Family Member, regardless of age, is required to have a no-fee passport with a Status of Forces Agreement Stamp. A SOFA stamp gives legal rights that exempt the holder from the host country's immigration laws regarding alien registration. You must have this when traveling on orders to and from the country in which you are stationed. Your spouse will accompany you and your Family Members to the office on post where you will apply for these. It should be one of the first tasks you attend to when you receive orders, as it may take many weeks to be processed.

- Tourist Passport—To travel on your own as a tourist, you will need to have a Tourist Passport. All US Post Offices have services to facilitate obtaining US Tourist Passports. When applying for a passport you must bring the following: original or certified copy of a birth certificate, passport application, two recent passport photos, proof of identity (a valid driver's license or other photo ID), and an application fee. The normal time necessary to obtain a passport is eight to twelve weeks. You must apply in person if this is your first passport or if you are under sixteen. Please research passport requirements in advance!

- VISA—A few countries, such as Italy, may require you to apply for a VISA to live there. You will be notified if this applies to you.

Pets: Each country has its unique set of requirements regarding bringing pets into the country. Some areas are very strict, and it is important to do your research as early as possible because relocating pets can be a lengthy and involved process. The timetable for obtaining examination statements and certifications can be very tight. Contact the Animal and Plant Health Inspection Service (APHIS) Veterinary Area Office of the state from which your pet will be transported.

Flying with pets can be complicated, so be sure to check on flight availability and restrictions as you plan your travel.

Rationing: From gasoline in Europe to groceries in Korea, you will find that although you can purchase many of your favorite American items on post, in some countries the quantities are restricted. You will be alerted to these things at your ACS Newcomers' Orientation.

Shopping and Dining: Some of the most fun things about living overseas are shopping in local markets and sampling different cuisines. American credit cards are not always accepted in other countries; if they are, you may be charged hefty fees. Therefore it is a good idea to become accustomed to carrying cash in the form of local currency. Some countries may allow you to shop tax free—for example, Germany has a "sales tax" of 19 percent called Value Added Tax. US personnel stationed in Europe qualify for relief from this tax. Please check with your VAT office on post before you make a major purchase to get the details. There is a fee for a tax relief form so the forms are not normally used for minor day-to-day purchases. Enjoy exploring all the unique shopping opportunities in every country you visit. Soon you will find that the souvenirs you collect allow your home to tell the beautiful story of your Army travels.

Ask your new neighbors for restaurant recommendations, but don't be afraid to strike out on your own and discover some local flavor. Try to become quickly acquainted with local customs and courtesies for dining. For example, tips may be included in your bill, though some servers have come to expect tips from Americans anyway. Dining may be at a more relaxed pace than you are used to, you may find dogs under your table, and if you are seated at a large table, you may find strangers joining you. Be open to these quirky experiences—they often turn out to be lots of fun!

Voting: If you are overseas during an election year, please allow plenty of time to register to vote and to get your absentee ballot. Each community will have a point of contact to answer questions and assist you.

Though it may seem overwhelming at times to live on foreign soil, the Army does its best to provide its Families a great deal of support. We represent the Army and our country, and we should make the effort to be good ambassadors and considerate neighbors.

Definitions

Accompanied assignment: Orders include Family Members.

Unaccompanied assignment: Orders do not include Family Members.

Concurrent travel: The Family has permission to travel at the same time as the sponsor to the overseas location.

Nonconcurrent travel: The Family's travel is delayed. After the sponsor arrives and finds housing, travel orders are then cut for Family Members.

Command sponsored assignment: Family authorized to PCS to new duty station.

Non-command sponsored: If the Family Members want to join the sponsor without command sponsorship, please understand what restrictions you will have once you arrive. (See next chapter.)

Helpful Websites

www.veteransunited.com/spouse/how-do-military-families-adjust-to-living-overseas/
www.militaryonesource.mil/
www.move.mil
www.military.com

Moving with Pets

www.aphis.usda.gov

Shipping Your POV

www.military.com/off-duty/autos/shipping-car-overseas-checklist.html
www.military.com/money/pcs-dity-move/shipping-a-car-overseas.html

Passports

www.travel.state.gov/passport/passport_1738.html

Voting

www.fvap.gov/

CHAPTER 8

WHEN THEY ARE AWAY: DEPLOYMENTS AND SEPARATIONS

Sarah Crosswhite and Emma Kelley

Mail Call

Signals personnel to assemble for the distribution of mail.

Army spouses have always been the cornerstones of support for their Soldiers and their community. They are the continuity for our homes, hearth and Family. When the Soldiers deploy, the spouses take on the additional role of mother or father; they handle all of the household chores, pay the bills and take care of each other. Without their support, we—as Soldiers—could not be successful. Our spouses enable us to deploy on missions with the knowledge and confidence that they are there for us.

—Welcome to the Army Family: A First Guide for Army Spouses and Family Members

As one would expect, a military Family will inevitably encounter periods of time in which the Soldier is apart from his or her Family. Sometimes you will feel as if it is all you can do to endure this time; sometimes it will be an opportunity to stretch and thrive. No one else has your exact life experiences, preferences, and expectations. No one else is married to your spouse and no one else is living your marriage. It is up to you and your Family to decide how you will function best during times of separation.

There are many different kinds of separations, including the following:

Temporary Duty (TDY). This is duty performed at some location other than the permanent assigned location. A single TDY trip is usually limited to 179 days or less. Some examples include staff assistance visits, denominational meetings, and Chaplain Corps or unit training.

Field Training Exercises (FTX). These are designed to simulate and prepare Soldiers for a combat environment. Each battalion will have its own unique training cycle. These will vary depending on the type of battalion. Expect a combat arms unit to have a considerable amount of time in the field. Some units that are not combat-focused will have less time in the field. The FTX can range from a few days to a few weeks. Most Chaplains really enjoy these exercises because it gives them great opportunities to know and minister to the Soldiers in their units.

Unaccompanied Tour of Duty. Unaccompanied Tours of Duty are those in which only the Soldier is authorized to go. Family Members are not Command Sponsored, meaning that if the Family chooses to go along, they will not be eligible to receive military benefits or privileges. Therefore most Families opt to remain behind. The Family's options may vary but there should be enough time to make necessary decisions before your Chaplain departs.

Voluntary Geographic Separations. Sometimes, the Family's needs dictate that the Soldier may move to a new duty station either ahead of or without his or her Family. For example, if a prospective move coincides with a child's senior year of high school, or if an aging parent needs care, the Family might decide to remain in their current location while the Chaplain moves to the next assignment. As with unaccompanied tours and deployments, advance planning and strategizing will serve you well. See the next section on deployment for helpful ideas that can be used in many circumstances of separation. Unlike a deployment situation, both Unaccompanied Tours and Voluntary Geographic Separations usually leave the Family without a unit support structure even though they will have overall Army support.

Dual Military Couple on Separate Assignments. Today's Army often finds two-career couples having to make difficult choices, as their assignments sometimes mandate serving in two different locations. Although the Army makes an effort to accommodate dual military couples, the needs of the Army prevail.

Deployment. Probably the longest and most stressful separation a military Family will endure is the deployment of the Chaplain on a mission without Family Members. Deployments may take the form of training, combat operations, or disaster and humanitarian relief. The length of a deployment depends on the unit's mission and can range from a three- to six-week training mission to a year or longer mission in support of combat operations. This can be an individual or unit deployment. Deployments can happen with little or no notice.

Deployments are a fact of military life. There is much written on coping with deployments and reunions. Read as much as you can get your hands on. Talk with as many people as you can who have been through at least one deployment. Talk with other spouses and talk with other Soldiers. Keep in mind that you can learn as much about what *not* to do as you can about what to do. Explore the web to find helpful resources to prepare you for this season.

The Phases of Deployment

Although it may not be noticeable when each distinct phase begins and ends, service members and their Families progress through a deployment cycle.

Pre-Deployment Phase

What's going on with the service member?

Your Chaplain will be alerted for possible deployment and will receive orders to mobilize. Upon receiving a mobilization alert, preparation for deployment begins, including required briefings, additional training, medical and dental evaluations, and possibly counseling to ensure that service members are ready and able to be deployed. The pre-deployment phase ends when service members or their units physically leave the home installation for the theater of operations.

What's going on at home?

This is the time for decisions and details. Major issues that need to be addressed include decisions about where the Family will reside while the Soldier is away. Some spouses opt to remain in place, taking advantage of all the resources and support offered by the Army and unit communities. Others may choose to live near Family. In either case, decisions about children's schools and Family dynamics will need to be considered. Another important area to consider is finances. Deciding together in advance how to operate the Family budget will eliminate surprises for either party. A deployment may yield extra pay, so discussion may be ongoing about whether to save, invest, or spend this money. Decide as a Family how discipline and Family rules will be handled. Discuss ways to stay connected with one another. As a Family, commit to praying consistently during this time and throughout the deployment cycle.

Make a plan and have it in place to provide practical support for your Family in the event of accident or emergency at home. Apart from the Family Care Plan required of some Soldiers, it is a good idea for the parent staying behind to have a plan in writing. List who will care for your children should you become ill or involved in an accident, and how to reach that person. Post this in a place that can easily be found—on your refrigerator, for example.

It's always a good idea to be organized, but never more so than when you are facing a deployment. Take the time to work thoroughly with your spouse through the following list. Once done, this file can easily be updated for years to come, and you'll have peace of mind knowing the information is at your fingertips.

- Powers of Attorney for each spouse as applicable
- Birth/marriage/adoption Certificates
- SSNs for all Family Members
- Automobile titles, loan paperwork
- Immunization records for Family Members and pets
- Required documents for Family Members' military ID Card renewal (if these will expire during a deployment)

- Wills for both spouses
- Insurance policies
- Passports, Visas
- Multiple copies of current PCS orders
- Current LES
- Certificates of naturalization, citizenship, death
- Inventory of household goods
- Documents related to military service
- Real estate documents
- Copies of recent tax returns
- List of credit cards and bank accounts
- Safe deposit box information
- Court orders relating to divorce, child support, or child custody, if any
- Safe deposit box key and location information

Also essential to have on hand are: an extra set of keys to your home, car, and mailbox; emergency numbers for medical providers; contact information for the Rear Detachment Commander; the mailing address of your deployed spouse; car and home repair provider contact information; warranty information; school records; current addresses and telephone numbers of all members of immediate Families for both spouses; contact information for the Red Cross, ACS, and JAG.

Be sure you are able to access necessary funds in order to handle your finances when your spouse is deployed. If you do not have a joint checking account, this would be a good time to get one. Prepare your home, vehicles, and appliances to run smoothly and safely.

A wonderful idea that requires a little advance planning is to video your Soldier reading books or telling stories for your children to enjoy while mom or dad is away. Recorded goodnight prayers and devotions may be especially meaningful.

Deployment Phase

What's going on with the Soldier?

The deployment phase of the cycle begins with the physical movement of individuals and units from their home installation to the designated theater of operations. This phase of the deployment cycle may be a very stressful time for service members and their Families as they face the realities of a deployment and what that means for them. The remainder of the deployment phase primarily involves the performance of military duties in support of the mission either in the theater of operations (overseas) or within the United States. Near the end of the deployment phase, the unit will begin preparations for its return to the home installation, culminating with the unit's return home, which is called redeployment.

What's going on at home?

The whirl of preparation is over. The Chaplain and his or her unit have plowed through paperwork, gathered their gear, and kissed the kids. You've all made it through the tear-filled farewell ceremonies, and now you are on your own.

Fortunately, you do not have to try to be a lone ranger. If you have chosen to remain close by, you will be able to participate in and take advantage of a multitude of opportunities for support that will smooth the way ahead.

Get to know your Rear Detachment. The Rear Detachment (RD) staff consists of unit military members who remain at the home installation during a deployment. They are responsible for the remaining personnel and equipment, and for providing assistance to Families of deployed Soldiers. Upon deployment, the Rear Detachment Commander (RDC) officially assumes the duties of the Unit Commander and maintains regular contact with the deployed Unit Commander at the mission site. This person is often the first source of information for Family Members during unit separation and serves as the link connecting the FRG, Families, Soldiers (both deployed and non-deployed), and community resources. Always keep the RD informed of any address or telephone number changes if you go out of town. You will want them to know how to contact you in case of an emergency.

Unit FRGs. FRGs foster a sense of belonging to the unit and community and provide a vehicle for Families to develop friendships while they gain information about the unit and community. In addition, they provide information referral and share support during deployments. Through successful FRG efforts, many spouses have developed a more positive attitude and a better understanding of the Army mission. This is great a place for you to receive support and also offer it to others.

Red Cross Emergency Communication Service. Red Cross Messages serve many purposes, from notifying a service member of an illness or death in the Family to announcing the birth of a service member's child or grandchild. Red Cross-verified information assists commanding officers in making decisions regarding emergency leave in a timely manner. No matter where a service member or Family is stationed, all can rest assured that the Red Cross will deliver their notifications in time of crisis. In the United States, including Alaska, Hawaii, and Puerto Rico, you may reach the Red Cross 24 hours a day at 1-877-272-7337. If you are living overseas, contact your local Red Cross Office. The Red Cross must always verify that the information they are relaying is correct. They will do so by contacting the appropriate authority (i.e., the hospital or funeral home), who in turn will need permission from the responsible party in order to release this private information. Giving necessary permission before you call the Red Cross will speed the process.

You will want to have the following information readily available to give to the Red Cross at the time of the call:

- Soldier's legal full name
- Rank
- Branch of service (Army, Navy, Air Force, Marines, Coast Guard)
- Social Security number and date of birth
- Military unit address
- Information about the deployed unit and home base unit (for deployed service members only)
- Full name of ill, injured, or deceased person
- Hospital or funeral home providing care
- Name of the doctor treating the person
- Contact information of a Family Member who can provide additional information
- Detailed information about the crisis and recommendation of Family or doctor as to whether Soldier is to be notified only or asked to come home
- Leave address that the Soldier should go to if the Soldier will be coming back
- How many days of leave the Soldier will need to resolve the problem

It's also good for all concerned to know that the commander has the ultimate decision whether to allow a Soldier to go on emergency leave, dependent on mission requirements.

Red Cross messages can include:

- Verification of critical illness or death of an immediate Family Member, to include grandparents of military or their spouse. (There are case-by-case exceptions on occasion.)
- Birth announcements. Prebirth announcements in the case of serious medical problems for mother and/or baby.
- Health and welfare, depression/suicide issues, or interruptions of normal communications.
- Breakdown of childcare plans. Verification from doctor or from other sources that caused breakdown in childcare.

Be sure to inform the Rear Detachment about your Red Cross emergency situation so that they are able to provide additional support, because messages from the Red Cross are not automatically given to the Rear Detachment.

Care Team. While most spouses will face the normal challenges associated with deployments, some will end up facing what might be the hardest challenge of their lives—the loss or severe injury of their Soldiers. A Care Team is a group of volunteer Family Members who are trained to provide immediate, short-term care and support to Families of deceased and seriously injured Soldiers. The volunteers usually come from the same battalion or brigade as the affected Soldier and Family. After an initial assessment of needs and at the request of the affected Family, the Care Team can offer any or all of the following support services to the Family: home care assistance, childcare support, meal support, transportation, call support, or assistance to visiting Family.

Army Community Services (ACS). Here you will find a wealth of resources and information, including Army Family Team Building (AFTB), which is an educational program designed to orient you to

> "During a deployment, having military friends nearby is vital. These gals will listen when you need to vent, probably will know who you need to call when you have a real problem, will feed your children if you just can't muster up the motivation, and will provide many hours of desperately needed adult company."
> —Becci

Army life. Not only will you build your knowledge of the Army, you will have the chance to meet and make new friends. If ACS doesn't have the information you are looking for, they know where to find it. Great stuff!

Chapel Community. Don't forget, your chapel community can be a rock during this time. We are often accustomed to *serving* in a chapel environment, but this is a good time to allow others to reach out to you. Don't hesitate to accept a meal if it's offered to you; don't hesitate to be a student instead of leading a group. Enjoy the fellowship of people who are like-minded.

Managing Separation. Now that you've seen all of the forms of support that are available to you, it is up to you to decide how to put those pieces together. No two strategies will look just alike; it's worth the effort to find what works best for your Family. Here are some general suggestions that we hope will help.

Self-Care

- Time passes much faster with a friend. It would be ideal to have a "battle buddy" whose spouse is also deployed, but the most important thing is to nurture a close friendship with someone you trust.

- Plan something to look forward to. It will really lift your spirits. Repeat as necessary!

- Get enough rest. You may be busier than you've ever been, and you may not feel like sleeping when your spouse is not beside you, but do make rest a priority.

- Eat well and eat right. Preserving Family meal time is worth the effort, but there is nothing wrong with treating yourselves to a shortcut now and then.

- Routines are helpful, especially for children. The predictability and comfort of establishing routines bring calm and order to a Family.

- Be a smart scheduler. No Family can do everything; choose the obligations and activities that are most important, and pace yourselves.

- Know at least three of your neighbors. You may need their help during an emergency. They can also be a wonderful source of day-to-day support.

- Get out of the house. Whether for a daily walk, a day trip for some new scenery, or an actual vacation, enjoy the refreshment of a change of pace. Take a friend. Don't wait for the phone to ring—take the lead.

- Make time for yourself. Check with your local CYSS for deployment benefits that may include a certain amount of hours of free childcare a month. Also find out if children are eligible for discounts for Schools of Knowledge, Inspiration, Exploration & Skills (SKIES) sports.

- Journal, write, or blog. If this is something that soothes you or helps you process daily life, by all means do it. Indulge your creative self with whatever you like the best—whether it is crafting, art, or music.

- Loneliness, stress, doubts, and fears are all normal and to be expected. If you need extra emotional support, seek it out. Don't forget that there are always other Chaplain spouses around.

Children

Because they can't fully understand the absence, children are often hardest hit emotionally by deployments. Children's ages help determine how able they are to cope with separations. Infants and toddlers are simply unable to process the concept. Toddlers' sense of time's passage is poor, and they may continue to ask for the absent parent even if you try to explain the length of time the parent will be gone. Preschoolers may be fearful of abandonment and feel guilty ("Did Dad leave because I was bad?"). School-age children may hide their emotions and show grief in various subtle ways. Middle-schoolers may assert their independence, and teens may rebel against the overwhelming idea of having to shoulder adult responsibilities. Group activities, sports, scouts, and volunteerism are great ideas for kids of all ages during this time. As with any time of life, our children tend to mirror both the best and worst in us. Choosing to maintain a hopeful and positive attitude as often as you can is good medicine for all.

Staying Connected

As a Couple

- Study a devotional together or choose a book you both want to read and discuss.
- Pray together.
- Email and write letters.
- Create a blog or Facebook page just for your Family.
- Send photos of special occasions and Family life. Encourage your Soldier to also send lots of photos of his or her new home and friends. Ask for "selfies"—not just scenery.
- Find an online or printable game to play. Competition can be fun, even from a distance!

As a Family

- Have fun with your kids preparing packages of surprises and goodies to mail to your Soldier.
- Take full advantage of today's wonderful technologies. Skype, video conferencing, and phone calls, when they are available, are excellent substitutes for in-person conversation.
- Encourage kids to draw pictures, write letters, and compose emails.
- Play your prerecorded videos and send your Soldier recordings of you and the children as well.
- Keep your Soldier in the school loop by providing a copy of the school calendar, sports schedule, important dates, and teacher contact information.
- Young children may enjoy having a Deployment Doll to cuddle. Check with your FRG or ACS for information on how to acquire one.
- Create a personalized photo book.
- Some may find it helpful to make a countdown calendar to have a tangible reminder of the number of days until your Family is reunited. There are lots of ideas available online.

Though all of the above are great suggestions, your personal Family style may be to do none of the above, and that is okay too. Some find that downplaying the absence and answering children's questions as they arise reduces anxiety.

Operations Security. OPSEC and personal security are important to remember during deployment. For the sake of your Soldier's safety, never publicly discuss the unit's travel dates or location. For the sake of your personal safety, don't make your spouse's absence a matter of public knowledge; especially watch what you post and say online and how you respond when someone calls on the telephone and asks for your spouse. Also, realize that suddenly changing the way you conduct your home and yourself may advertise your Soldier's absence. Using good judgment is a must. Information about OPSEC is given out at FRG meetings, and units will pass along the information.

Official Information. Keep your eye on the ball. Don't allow media reports to upset you. Be careful not to glue yourself to the TV or constantly search the Internet for bad news. Trust that your Soldier is safe. When gossip and rumors are flying throughout the unit community, let it stop with you. Feeding a frenzy of fear is never a way to help anyone. Always rely on the official word from the Command.

Your entire Family will find its own rhythm as the days go by. Though you're apart, try not to view this as a "lost time." All of you will discover new strengths, unexpected joys, and periods of growth. It may feel daunting to observe how often another deployed Family is able to communicate, or (especially for females) to watch another spouse manage to look fabulous, work full time, tend to her Family, and consistently send elaborate care packages to her Soldier. Please resist the urge to compare. You will find the best way for your Family to thrive—have confidence in that!

HOMECOMING

YAY!! Ladies, get your nails done and get out your best outfit. Gentlemen, it's time for that shave and haircut. Let your children unleash their creativity and make some awesome welcome home signs and banners. It is time for the Chaplain and the unit to come home. Update any change in phone numbers or email with the Rear Detachment and FRG. These will be your sources for current information on when and where you will be able to meet your Solider. Keep in mind that flight times can change and be at unusual times of day. Some units choose to have a small ceremony when the unit returns before they are released to their Families. Discuss and decide with your Soldier who will be present at the homecoming ceremony—spouse and children, only spouse, extended Family?

As you prepare for this joyful reunion, realize that both you and your spouse have changed during this time apart, so prepare your heart for the fact that it will take a while for everyone to be comfortable together again. In your pre-homecoming discussions, talk about your immediate plans once the Soldier arrives. Will you go on block leave? Will you have Family Members staying with you? Make some plans for how those initial days or weeks will be spent. Will the kids stay home from school a few days? Will your spouse prefer to keep busy or to relax? Will you celebrate with a big home-cooked meal or a special dinner out? Keep your communication honest and truthful. Commit to being patient and understanding with each other as you both realize that deployment changes everyone, and there will be adjustments ahead.

Reintegration Phase

What's going on with the Soldier?

During this phase, service members return to their home installation. Your Soldier will attend additional briefings, training, medical evaluations, and counseling to assist in reintegrating into normal life. These briefings and evaluations provide service members with critical information should they experience any emotional or physical issues later on as a result of the deployment.

There may be unit functions, battalion or brigade memorials, change of command ceremonies, lunches, or balls to attend. These will vary depending on the unit and type of deployment. It is helpful to attend these to get a feel for the camaraderie among the Soldiers and to learn more about their deployment.

Many units will schedule what is called "block leave," which is a substantial chunk of time off. Ideally you will already have discussed prior to homecoming what your Family plans to do with this time. There may be training holidays, half days, or liberal leave days as well. Some Families choose to stay at home and spend time together, some choose to travel to see Family Members, and some go on a road trip or a vacation. Enjoy!

What's going on at home?

There is much to celebrate. It is easy to strain your energy, your time, and your budget trying to make up for time not spent together during the deployment. You certainly deserve a treat, but work together to manage your resources wisely. By now you have discovered that the readjustment process takes a lot of work and intentionality. You can expect a brief "honeymoon period," where every difficulty is eclipsed by the fact that you are all safe and together again. Sooner or later, however, reality will return and you will begin the gradual process of knitting a houseful of changed people into the smooth fabric of a Family once again. Please don't forget that it is absolutely normal that *each* Family Member has changed, sometimes radically, during the deployment. Your Family will not and cannot operate the way it did before; and it may take some hard work to incorporate boundaries, responsibilities, and positions in the household. As you might have guessed, the two keys to success in this endeavor are communication and patience. Male Chaplains' spouses: Your husband may love the more independent and capable new you, or he may need to be reassured he is very much needed. There are two things husbands fear most about their wives: one is that they won't be able to survive without them, and the other is that they will! Assure your husband, "I have learned to live without you, but I haven't learned to like it." Female Chaplains' spouses: Prepare for lots of emotions as your Soldier reassumes her role as wife and mother.

Some Soldiers may return home ready to take charge immediately. Others return with some hesitation to re-enter the Family system. It is not easy to pick up where they left off. They may appear indecisive and feel like an outsider. Obviously neither of these extremes is helpful or healthy. This is the time when you sit down together with love, understanding, and patience to work out your new normal. It will be a gradual process and sometimes not without bumps in the road, but you will get there. Be a good listener. Your Soldier may not share every deployment experience right away; he or she might not share anything at all. It may take time to restore a comfortable intimate relationship, it may take time to restore a comfortable parenting rhythm, and it may take time before the Soldier is able to fully relax. Celebrate together the personal growth each has achieved during the separation.

Children are a part of the military Family and they have also sacrificed. They need to be given time to adjust after a deployment or separation. They will also be trying to adjust to new roles and Family leadership. They will need Family time and individual time with the Soldier who has been gone. The children have grown, developed, and acquired skills since the Soldier has seen them last. Mom or Dad may have missed a lot, but the joy of catching up will be sweet.

PTSD

Post Traumatic Stress Disorder (PTSD) is a psychological or physical reaction that develops after a distressing event that is not normal for a human to experience. Wars, natural disasters, and abuse are some events that can bring about PTSD. Not every Soldier who returns from combat will end up with PTSD. There are many factors that contribute, such as the amount of time a Soldier served under combat conditions, as well as the number of traumatic experiences that the Soldier was involved in. PTSD is when the traumatic, life-threatening event becomes imprinted in the image and emotions of the Soldier's mind.

Returning troops may appear withdrawn, edgy, nervous, depressed, aggressive, anxious, hypersensitive, unable to sleep or enjoy life.

Symptoms of PTSD:

- Nightmares, flashbacks, or recurring memories
- Feeling detached from other people
- Avoidance, poor concentration

- Trouble sleeping, night sweats
- Anger and rage, irritability, easily startled, being constantly on guard
- Exaggerated or abnormal startle responses, intense alertness all the time
- Feeling of helplessness
- Overwhelming waves of emotions
- Feelings of terror

If Soldiers have symptoms and feel they need help, they can take the DoD Mental Health Self-Assessment at www.militarymentalhealth.org/ or they can get help from Behavioral Health at www.behavioralhealth.Army.mil. Often the friendship or mentorship of another Chaplain who has experienced deployment can be of great assistance. Remember that seeking help is a sign of strength that helps protect your loved ones, your career, and your mental and physical health. If you believe your spouse needs help, encourage him or her to get it.

Spouses should continue learning the Army system. Recognize the need to maintain the skills you have learned. They will serve you well for future deployments and separations. Staying involved in religious activities, hobbies, and sports will help your Family continue to grow closer together.

Emotional Cycle of Deployment

Many Chaplain Families will experience more than one deployment. Each one will be unique, but all will follow the same general emotional cycle.

Stage 1: Anticipation of Departure. In this stage, spouses may alternately feel denial and anticipation of loss. As reality sinks in, tempers may flare as couples attempt to take care of all the items on a Family pre-deployment checklist, while striving to make time for "memorable moments." Stage 1 may begin again before a couple or Family has even had time to renegotiate a shared vision of who they are after the changes from the last deployment.

Stage 2: Detachment and Withdrawal. This occurs the last few days before leaving. In this stage, service members become more and more psychologically prepared for deployment, focusing on the mission and their unit. Bonding with their fellow service members is essential to unit cohesion, but this may create emotional distance within the marriage. Sadness and anger occur as couples attempt to protect themselves from the hurt of separation. At this stage, marital problems may escalate more often and more frequently. When a husband or wife must repeatedly create emotional distance, they may gradually shut down their emotions. It may seem easier to just feel numb rather than sad, but the lack of emotional connection to your spouse can lead to difficulties in a marriage.

Stage 3: Emotional Disorganization. This occurs the first six weeks after departure. With back-to-back deployments, one might think that this stage of adjusting to new responsibilities and being alone would get easier. Although a military spouse may be familiar with the routine, he or she may also be experiencing burnout and fatigue from the last deployment and feel overwhelmed at starting this stage again.

Stage 4: Recovery and Stabilization. Here spouses realize they are fundamentally resilient and able to cope with the deployment. They develop increased confidence and a positive outlook. With back-to-back deployments, however, spouses may find it hard to muster the emotional strength required, but many resources are available to provide needed support.

Stage 5: Anticipation of Return. This occurs around six weeks before the Soldier returns home. This is generally a happy and hectic time spent preparing for the return of the service member. Spouses, children, and parents of the service member need to talk about realistic plans and expectations for the return and reunion.

Stage 6: Return Adjustment and Renegotiation. This occurs up to six weeks after reunion. Couples and Families must reset their expectations and renegotiate their roles during this stage. The key to successful adjustment and renegotiation is open communication. Families also need to be prepared to deal with the effects of combat stress on the returning service member. Such stress and trauma can be difficult to deal with. Troops with combat stress are often irritable, guarded, and want to be alone. Some may use alcohol or drugs in a failed attempt to numb the emotional pain they are experiencing. Attempts at renegotiation may result in increasing marital arguments.

Stage 7: Reintegration and Stabilization. This stage can take up to six months as the couple and Family stabilize their relationships anew. As noted with stage 6, the presence of combat stress can severely disrupt the stabilization process. Reintegration and stabilization can hit more roadblocks when a Family must make a Permanent Change of Station (PCS) move immediately upon the return of the service member. Back-to-back deployments create stress as Families stabilize only to begin stage 1 once again.

Learning about the feelings that you may experience, as well as utilizing the resources that are available to you, can help you maintain a strong military Family team.

CHAPTER 9

LIVING THE LIFE OF AN ARMY SPOUSE

Carol Woodbery and Ann Watson

Fire Call

Signals that there is a fire on the post or in the vicinity. The call is also used for fire drill.

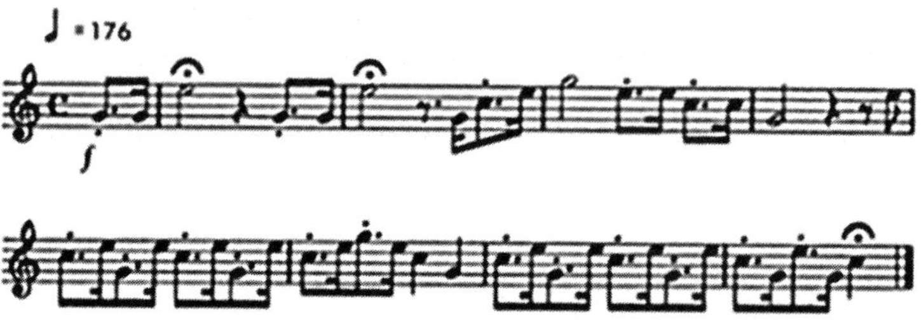

You are a patriot—the sort of citizen that all of us should be, but so few of us are. You live with sacrifice, because you believe in the rights and ideals that your husband defends. Although you wear no uniform, you are a part of that defense—a vital link in the chain of freedom. Although you wear no medals and will reap no glory on the field of battle, you are a hero in the truest sense of the word. You are a military spouse.

—Gene Thomas quoting Navy Chief Petty Officer Jeff Edwards

ATTITUDE

There is much to be learned during your journey as an Army spouse; a willingness to learn will take you far. View it as an adventure. This is the life you have been given—live it! It will not be as easy or as comfortable as living in the same town for twenty years, but it will be *rich*! Embrace this life with enthusiasm; it will knit your Family closer than you ever dreamed, and enrich your community as well.

Parents' attitudes often set the standard for their children. Developing a Family mission statement or slogan is one way to "rally the troops"; examples might be "All for one, and one for all!" and "Sharp minds; soft hearts!" Your location will change, schools will change, friends will change, your Chaplain's jobs and positions will change, but your Family team will be your one constant.

There are many things in the military that a spouse cannot control; in fact, sometimes that list seems to be endless. Deployments, promotions, or constant moving can be viewed as obstacles or opportunities.

The past cannot be changed, difficult people will still be difficult, and mistakes will still be made. Not every move will be great, not every job will be easy, or even enjoyable. But seek contentment by choosing to laugh rather than scream. Most Army spouses find a sense of humor to be extremely helpful when meeting challenges.

At each duty station, decisions are made: where to be involved; how much time, if any, to invest outside the Family; where to live; how to educate children, and so on. Due to the habitual and sometimes formidable life changes associated with the military lifestyle, flexibility is key. Sometimes changes happen quickly. Rapid and frequent deployments, and even living arrangements, can change in a matter of days or hours.

Be willing to learn the logistics of your spouse's workday: where the office is and what is required of you if you are allowed to visit there. Get to know his or her coworkers and assistants; learn to recognize unit patches and acronyms, and talk with your Soldier about career goals, not only for this job but also for those ahead.

Practicing positive social interaction results in a happier outlook and lots of opportunities to enlarge your circle of friends and build community. Choosing to be happy each day adds up to a lifetime of contentment. Military life is not the easiest of lifestyles and, overall, attitude really is everything.

Adjectives to live by:

BROAD-MINDED, CALM, SUPPORTIVE, ENTHUSIASTIC, OPTIMISTIC, SELF-CONFIDENT

OPPORTUNITIES

Our lives are defined by opportunities, even the ones we miss.
—F. Scott Fitzgerald, *The Curious Case of Benjamin Button*

An Army spouse has opportunities to travel and have experiences that others may find unbelievable. Military assignments place

Families in unfamiliar cultures, sometimes surrounded by people who speak, believe, live, eat, shop, or interact in ways that are quite foreign. The Army spouse has the privilege of being a goodwill ambassador by expressing interest and appreciation of cultural differences and similarities.

Military installations provide cultural opportunities, but Army spouses may seek other ways to experience the area where they live. Much can be learned by shopping at local grocery stores, by attending musical concerts or religious services, by befriending nonmilitary neighbors, and by exploring parks and other outdoor activities. The Army spouse can utilize military resources to further education, to seek employment, to grow spiritually, to become physically fit, to develop marketable skills, or to pursue a hobby.

Opportunity can be described as "a favorable junction of circumstances." Every PCS move can be another "favorable junction." In that vein, a military spouse has the unique opportunity to make deep and lasting friendships at every change of station, both in this country and in other countries. What an incredible chance to immerse yourself in a culture that most people could only experience as tourists. Many children of military parents have seen wonders of the world that some of their civilian counterparts will never see. Moving can be difficult, but the rewards make the effort worthwhile.

Adjectives to live by:

ADVENTURESOME, WILLING, PROACTIVE, IMAGINATIVE, HUMOROUS, CREATIVE

VOLUNTEERING

Although military spouses usually have employment opportunities, many choose to volunteer their time. Volunteering is a win-win situation—not only benefiting those you serve, but also giving you a chance to build a résumé and meet new people. Volunteering also enriches lives and builds character. Don't be afraid of stepping up in an unfamiliar area. You may discover hidden talents you never imagined!

There are so many great organizations and activities—so how will you choose? Army Community Service (ACS) is a good place to start, but you may find your own niche volunteering in your children's schools or extra-curricular activities, various chapel programs, unit Family Readiness Groups, the Red Cross, or installation-wide spouse groups. Your own interests may lead to off-post volunteering as well, perhaps in a garden club, an after-school arts program, or youth sports league.

> "Being involved in the FRG has helped me stay busy, but also helped me to be involved with the spouses of other deployed Soldiers. They have become good friends." —Jennifer

As you become more involved in your unit, more opportunities will be presented. **Discuss with your spouse the areas of service, if any, that are most important to you both. Don't feel obligated to everyone, but do your best in any position you take on.**

Keeping a record of volunteer hours is useful for installation administrators and ACS, as well as for your own encouragement and potential future employment. Logging volunteer hours can help later in a résumé. It serves as a record for teens who need such information for college applications and scholarships. Although altruistic volunteers are not overly concerned with rewards or recognition, the Army Community Service usually hosts a yearly award ceremony when volunteers are honored for support of the installation. Some installations offer discounts or coupons for their top volunteers. Most units should have a volunteer coordinator; see yours to be sure your hours are recorded.

Adjectives to live by:

GENEROUS, ENERGETIC, COMPASSIONATE, SELFLESS

EMPLOYMENT

Employment opportunities do exist for military spouses "within the gate," including jobs with the Post Exchange (AAFES), the commissary (DeCA), and schools on military installations (DoDEA Schools). Federal government job listings are available at usajobs.gov. ACS is a great place to begin your employment search; they offer classes as well as assistance with résumés and job searches. One program you will want to become familiar with, if you are interested in federal employment, is the Military Spouse Preference Program (MSPP). For off-post employment, check Military Spouse Employment Partnership (MSEP). Be flexible—this may be your opportunity to work in fields you never dreamed of.

> "Don't try and do it all. Know your limits and abide by them. Take time for God, your Family, and yourself."
> —Dixie

Maintaining a current résumé is a huge time saver. Keep the following updated in one place—it will enable you to apply for jobs without undue stress: addresses of former places of employment, supervisors' names and phone numbers, chronological list of positions held with dates of employment, a list of your former residence addresses and dates of residence. Have a file containing letters of reference.

> "I use my volunteer experience teaching quilting at the Post Craft Shop on my résumé when I apply to teach at a local quilt shop or lecture to quilt guilds."
> —Abigail

Adjectives to live by:

PERSEVERING, RESOURCEFUL, FLEXIBLE, ORGANIZED, COMPETENT

Seasons of Life

Whether you are a military spouse or not, the passage of time and the seasons of life can be quite similar. You get married and start a new life together, possibly start a Family, the children grow up, then leave home, parents grow older, and grandchildren arrive. You may start a job, begin, complete, or postpone your education, or add a new degree along the way. Other seasons such as experiencing a serious health issue, losing loved ones, caring for aging parents or a special needs child may come your way. The course of a military career often spans decades, and Families will find themselves in many of these different stages. There will be times when you'll be able to pitch in as a super-volunteer. There will be times when feeding your children and tackling the laundry will be more than you can face. Give yourself a break and know that both extremes are temporary. Realize that most of us are doing the best we can. Compassion, communication, and choosing not to make assumptions are key.

Something that may be unique to the military lifestyle is that you may encounter more frequent seasons of adjustment and loneliness. Arriving at new places can be challenging. Making new friends every couple of years can seem exhausting. But having the chance to reinvent yourself once in a while can be a great thing. You'll soon learn that the difficult seasons cycle quickly around, and plenty of good seasons are ahead. Each season has a special beauty and usefulness of its own.

Sometimes time seems to progress impossibly slowly, especially during deployments, when children are young, or communication with loved ones is limited. These times are as valuable to the big picture as the happiest of times, so look for ways to treasure and enjoy them. You can't get a minute back, and as you stretch to make the moments count, you may enjoy great self-discovery and spiritual growth.

Later in life, time may seem to fly. There may be less to do at home, but there are plenty of opportunities to share the wisdom you've earned. The season of retirement will bring yet another set of changes and adjustments. Start planning for later years early. It will come sooner than you think. No matter our stage of life, our accumulated experience can serve to encourage and benefit those alongside us and behind us on the path.

Adjectives to live by:

CONSIDERATE, COURTEOUS, DIPLOMATIC, DISCREET, INTUITIVE

SUPPORT NETWORKS

The transient nature of our lives doesn't automatically lend itself to a sense of belonging; therefore we need to be intentional about building support structures to ensure our well-being. The Army community offers us numerous support networks, but it is up to us to seek out those that enhance our well-being and provide the foundation we need to thrive.

Adherence to a faith tradition is one layer of a good support system. Fellow faith group members and leaders can be important resources for comfort and strength. The Chaplain Family and the Army Family offer a foundation on which to rest, as they will be a constant wherever you go. Those who understand our unique lifestyle are so valuable.

The Army will teach your spouse about situational awareness. For you, staying informed of news on a global, national, and local scale will allow you to function more knowledgeably and comfortably in times of constant change. Learning more about the Army and the Chaplain Corps can give you confidence; decision making is easier when you have resources and information. Do your research not only online and in printed publications, like your post newspaper and the *Army Times*, but also by networking with people who have been where you are. *And always, always share what you learn!*

Maintaining friendships of all kinds makes life rich and interesting. It is helpful to know that friendships exist at many depths and breadths. There are individuals with whom the military spouse has deep and meaningful, but brief, connections. "Battle buddies" stand side by side through a period of mutual hardship. There are Family friends from previous assignments with whom only holiday greetings are exchanged. Then there are the delightful friendships that are renewed as duty stations intersect, often more than once. What a treasure to pick up right where we left off! Social media sites allow friends of all kinds to stay in touch—but do venture beyond social media. A wonderful aspect of Army life is that you'll have lots of opportunities to meet and become close to people with whom you'd never have crossed paths otherwise. Don't hesitate to reach out, just because your time at a given location is short; everyone's in that situation. A unique and fabulous result of this is that we make friends "fast and faithful"! You'll be amazed at how willing Army spouses are to help out with each other's children, offer transportation, bring meals, and unpack boxes. We all need each other, and the journey is so much happier with friends!

Adjectives to live by:

OPEN, DEPENDABLE, KIND, HELPFUL

All in the Family

One of life's richest blessings is the privilege of having friends who are like Family, and the other side of that coin is having Family Members who are counted as friends. We've discussed the fact that change is one of the only constants in the military world—but the best constant of all is the nuclear Family. Your spouse and children are the only ones who will take every step of the journey with you. You'll endure the stresses together, and you'll enjoy experiences your civilian friends can only dream of. The resulting closeness is priceless.

Not surprisingly, you'll find that many fellow Soldiers and spouses come from generations of military Families—and that your own children may pursue the military as a career. It seems that our children enjoy being part of the big, big world, and that they feel most at home on Army posts!

Your extended Family won't always be nearby to celebrate holidays and special occasions, not to mention everyday life. The Family back home is sacrificing by not seeing your Family as often as they'd like, and they may feel disconnected or afraid of the risks inherent in Soldiering—risks we have learned to live with. Your Family may feel excluded when they aren't able to attend milestone events, and need to know they are valued and missed. It is important to appreciate the struggle and to accept these situations, but it is especially sweet when you are able to celebrate together. Do make the effort to keep in close touch with Family using Skype, email, and even old-fashioned letters. Helping relatives understand our way of life and including them as much as possible will strengthen the ties that keep our Families entwined.

Adjectives to live by:

WARM-HEARTED, SENSITIVE, PATIENT, LOVING, COMMUNICATIVE

Look beside each Soldier and you will find the people who fight with them. The spouses, the sons, the daughters, the Families, we serve too. Their victories are our victories, their defeats are our defeats. We keep trying, we keep loving, we keep believing. I am proud of the role we play in maintaining peace in our country and in the world. I am proud to stand beside a man whose integrity shines like a diamond in the dust. And I am proud to call myself an Army wife.

—Army Wives

Chapter 10

No Better Life: Embracing the Chaplain's Spouse Journey

Rosemarie Sniffin

Adjutant's Call

Signals that the adjutant is about to form the guard, battalion, or brigade. The bugler plays the bugle part of the call.

I am a part of all that I have met;
Yet all experience is an arch wherethro'
Gleams that untravell'd world, whose margin fades
For ever and for ever when I move.
How dull it is to pause, to make an end,
To rust unburnish'd, not to shine in use!
As tho' to breathe were life. Life piled on life
Were all too little . . .
For my purpose holds
To sail beyond the sunset, and the baths
Of all the western stars . . .
That which we are, we are,
One equal temper of heroic hearts,
Made weak by time and fate, but strong in will
To strive, to seek, to find, and not to yield.

—Alfred Lord Tennyson, "Ulysses"

Literary historians would agree that when Tennyson wrote these stirring, heroic words, he was not thinking (exclusively) of the Chaplain spouse. But this poetic image—of unexplored lands of opportunity and adventure; travel and toil in new and uncertain places—does fit the life cycle of a Chaplain spouse. We are not the captain of the ship; we cannot determine where the vessel (and our Family) will land and when we will depart. Our Army time offers rich and rewarding opportunities for friends, work, travel, and ministry that we would *never* have if not for the Chaplain Corps. In the midst of this great adventure will come hardships and disappointments—just as in any life. But the journey by our Chaplain's side offers us the rare, rich chance to reflect and say, "as tho' to breathe were life! Life piled on life were all too little!"

Like the aged Ulysses, the experienced Chaplain spouse can gratefully recall not just the challenges of multiple moves, but the beauty of unique stops along the way: hikes through the Alps and visits to King Ludwig's Bavarian castles; growing hibiscus and bulging hydrangeas in South Carolina; Kansas farm visits and antique shopping; wandering the spice markets of Korea. And it is not just the travel that enriches; it is the Army people we meet. In early assignments we are tightly connected to a smaller unit, the battalion. In later positions our spouse is more likely to supervise young leaders and be an integral part of larger units—a brigade, division, or corps; the Pentagon or the Chaplain School. Whatever the assignment, we meet and work alongside Families who carry the honor and the responsibility of protecting our great nation.

> "I don't look at the Army as some nebulous, oppressive entity that works to take my husband from me. I see the time that he spends away as his work, but also as my gift to the people who he is helping."
> —Sara

Our journey guarantees a level of dynamic change that can be very exciting—and never dull. While other pastoral roles minister to one denomination and multiple generations of Families, the Chaplain Family will worship, work, and live with various denominations and other faiths. And while we age . . . the Soldiers stay young!

The Army mission, to defend and protect our nation, requires multiple moves to best train all leaders in many different roles and positions. And as our Chaplain cycles through the positions and posts, we have the option to engage differently in each new assignment. But in *every* position, in every state, and on any continent, we have the privilege of helping military Families. *How* we reach out—

whether volunteering at the chapel, working on post, pursuing a degree, or joining a home school co-op—will not only enrich our own lives, but the lives of others.

Military ministry is different from ministry in the civilian world. Some faith traditions customarily expect that when they hire a clergy person who is married, they are getting two "employees" for the price of one. In other faith traditions, the clergy and spouse view themselves as a ministry team. However in the Army's view, boundaries are very clear. The Army has commissioned the Chaplain only. There is no officially defined role that you are required to assume as a Chaplain spouse. Therefore you have the privilege of choosing your level of involvement in the Army Community.

Be aware that regardless what niche you choose to carve out for yourself, you will have intangible influence because you are married to the Chaplain. If we treat those in authority with respect and honor, our Chaplain's position will be strengthened as one who respects and honors superiors. If we treat all Army folks graciously and kindly, our Chaplain's potential to minister increases. The golden rule somehow seems more intense as a Chaplain spouse!

On the flipside, if we are seen as elusive and self-contained, grumbling over multiple moves and too much time alone, or bored, the job of our spouse can be more difficult. Our Chaplain is defined by his or her faith as well as the Army rank. Our faith, while not a patch displayed on a uniform, is always perceived. Our faith can be the awkward elephant in the room or a glorious glow we embrace. What a wonderful opportunity—and tremendous responsibility—to live out our beliefs in the Army world. If we join the journey as joyfully as possible, we add to the results. If we withhold our gifts, energy, and kindness, we are (fairly or not) judged a little more harshly—and the influence we and our Chaplains might have is diminished.

Nurture the living. Care for the wounded. Honor the fallen. These ten words define in simple language the role of the Chaplain. As our Chaplain's closest ally, we can either embrace this call or set it aside. We can observe, or we can come alongside and help

Army Families. For some, the most scenic and rewarding journey emerges when we seek out ways to nurture, care for, and honor Army Families.

Your own personality, experience, energy level, and career decisions will determine *how or if* you "come alongside," and different posts, opportunities, and changing Family obligations allow us to redefine our role in each new location. At one point the Family Readiness Group may need leadership that you can give. Post chapels' needs are varied and endless—anything from children's church leader, worship team, PWOC, Sunday school teacher, and making meals for the sick to organizing social gatherings.

Unit functions offer tremendous opportunities to nurture. Sometimes just attending Family Readiness Group (FRG) meetings or fund raising events encourages others with our presence. Other times more involved, intense volunteer work may fit: an FRG or Boy/Girl Scout Leader, soccer coach, unit event organizer for a formal or welcome home celebration.

There will be times when we are able to simultaneously nurture Army Families and also gain a variety of professional experience. Some spouses have held positions of community influence that neatly fit their career goals: teaching on post, working at the Legal Assistance Office, pursuing educational dreams; while at the next PCS (ironically termed *Permanent* Change of Station) they are free to change careers or focus more on Family. These "position" labels do not tell the whole story, however. Whatever job we take, from attorney to homeschool parent, we are still known as "the Chaplain's spouse."

Our spouses have sworn an oath to uphold the Constitution and serve our country—to defend it from enemies foreign and domestic. Some of us may say, "But my Chaplain joined the Army, and I didn't." It's a very rare and noble thing to promise your life to an ideal. Our spouses have not only promised to give their lives for their country, they have promised to minister and serve those making the same vow. A richer life would be difficult to find. Our journey, walking beside our Chaplains, can be so amazing. We can enjoy meeting

Americans of every geographic area, learning about other faiths and cultures, encouraging those who suffer and grieve because of the high price of freedom.

Respecting All Faiths

In the poem "Ulysses," the old king looks back and relishes the *journey* he's taken and now defines himself as "part of all that I have met." Our journey will not only offer us the chance to grow in our own beliefs but also to taste and see other cultures and beliefs. This does not mean we absorb all faiths and diminish our own. It does mean we are made fuller and richer from associations and friendships—from time with those with whom we otherwise may never have shared a meal or a meeting.

> "I've always tried to convey the belief that there is strength in our diversity. We can all grow in learning about each other's traditions and beliefs if we respect each other's differences." —Jeanne

Our faith rightly defines us. Our beliefs lead us and increasingly mold us to what God has made us to be. In the Chaplain Corps we have the privilege to lead others in our faith *and* to appreciate different religions. In the civilian world limited opportunities exist where various worship groups meet and socialize. Rarely, if ever, will you find a Muslim, Catholic, and Baptist at the same event! Conversely, this happens all the time in the Army. If we embrace this core American value of religious freedom, we can both stand for what we believe in and support the Chaplain Corps mission. We can be justly proud of not just some vague "American notion," but actually live out a founding principle of our country. Living the Army life is actually a great civics experiment. In our unique position as Chaplain spouses, we have great influence on the mood and atmosphere of events.

Special Relationships

That which we are we are. . . . One equal temper of heroic hearts.
—Alfred Lord Tennyson, "Ulysses"

Two unique relationships present themselves to a Chaplain spouse, relationships to be protected and cherished. One is obvious: our marriage to the Chaplain. The other one is less so but still very important: our relationship with the commander's spouse.

Nurturing our marriages is important during this journey. The sheer emotional demands on *any* military Family are great. Especially the time spent apart—TDY (Temporary Duties Away), deployments to war zones, training, and schooling—can make our marriage, at times, a lonely one. There can be a tendency to feel isolated or left out, but it is always a choice. Abraham Lincoln, a man of noted periods of depression, once famously said, "Most folks are about as happy as they make up their minds up to be." President Lincoln was not married to a deployed Chaplain—*still,* he has a good point! We must realize that the marriage vows to love, honor, and cherish are going to be tested on this journey. Time apart, intense or negative work environments, being passed over for promotions, challenges with our children, and distance from close friends and relatives make for incredible growing opportunities in our marriages. We are in this together. We are an Army Family serving Army Families, "one equal temper of heroic hearts

> "Keeping a marriage strong during a military career requires a lot of forgiveness and flexibility. Keeping a Chaplain's marriage strong requires that and a whole lot more. I believe you must be called and committed to this ministry as a couple to stay strong as a couple."
> —Kitty

> "I am the safe sounding board. No competition. Just a listening ear that can be trusted to keep a confidence."
> —Connie

. . . made weak by time and fate, but strong in will to strive, to seek, to find, and not to yield." Protect your marriage. Set time aside, if at all possible and in some creative ways, to share and lift one another up. For as wonderful as the Chaplain journey is, it will end someday. Our marriages continue. In the midst of this adventure, look upon marriage as a precious gift that binds us even more greatly than the call to the Chaplain Corps.

Developing a relationship with the commander's spouse is an area of opportunity sometimes overlooked for the Chaplain's spouse. The Chaplain is unique in that he or she is a personal and special staff officer working directly for the commander. So while accountable to the top military leader in the unit, he or she is also (and more importantly) the spiritual and emotional support within the unit for this leader. The commander's spouse may also need support. Commanders have tremendous pressures and responsibilities for the very lives of all Soldiers under their authority. Their spouses feel that pressure too. We can be a great help to these spouses. Some will accept our help and wonderful friendships can develop. Others may feel uncomfortable with

> "Our battalion commander's wife had supported her husband through more deployments than she could remember. We were in the thick of the latest one. When she answered the phone, I asked, 'How you doin'?' Her response was very telling of the stress and pressure of being a leadership spouse, holding everyone else together. Returning endless text messages, phone calls, and emails. Bearing the heavy burden of her husband's responsibility to his Soldiers along with caring for all the Family Members at home. She said, 'Is that all? You don't need anything? You are calling just to see how I am doing? No one has done that in quite some time.' My heart was pierced through, and thus was born my passion for serving leadership spouses."
> —Malinda

us (perhaps because of faith differences or earlier difficulties with folks in religious authority) and draw apart. If the commander's spouse prefers to keep us at a distance, we can and should always make it our practice to be empathetic and caring so that he or she can endure the pressures and serve our Soldiers and their Families well too. Whatever the situation, take the risk to reach out, to care. We can meet for lunch, help with fund raisers, participate in the FRG, and remember the commander's Family in our prayers. At whatever level we interact, one component is key: confidentiality. Any sensitive or personal conversation, shared concern, or struggle *cannot* be repeated, but must be kept in a sacred trust. Our unique role as Chaplains' spouses may help us genuinely empathize and offer us greater understanding of the isolation and role of the commander's spouse.

No Better Life

No honest spouse will tell you the journey is easy. No honest spouse will paint a picture of perfect sunsets, easy transitions, and smooth sailing. But many an experienced spouse, like the aged Ulysses, will tell you the ride is worth it. In the end we are "heroic hearts," made stronger by the moves, the adventures, and the challenges of this Army life.

Nurture the living. Care for the wounded. Honor the fallen. It is entirely plausible that our spouses will answer all those callings in a single day, definitely in their life cycle as Chaplains. It's not an easy task, at times not a pretty one, but the journey rewards us all in the end. The opportunity to be a part of our Army as helpmate and spiritual influence while Soldiers and their Families face life's most intense demands is a gift to be embraced. The Chaplain Corps gives us a beautiful life journey—all personalities, faiths, talents, and strengths are needed to bolster today's military Families. No better life awaits those seeking to know their God, honor their country, and support their spouses in the US Army Chaplain Corps.

Chaplain Spouse Years

CAPTAIN YEARS

Battalion Chaplain

It has been said numerous times, that these are the best years in the Army. Learn and enjoy!

Key Players

Battalion Commander (CO)— Lieutenant Colonel (LTC)
Battalion Executive Officer (XO)—Major (MAJ)

Your Chaplain will be assigned usually to the Headquarters Company (HQ) with a Captain as the Company Commander.

This is your time to

- get to know the spouse of the Company Commander, the Battalion Commander, the CSM as well as other Battalion Chaplains' spouses in the Brigade
- get to know your battalion spouses and their Families plus the single Soldiers
- ask questions, don't be afraid
- listen, observe, learn from others, especially the brigade Chaplain's spouse and your commander's spouse
- discover and find your niche
- adapt and get to know the Army culture

You will probably realize

- your peers in the battalion may be younger than you
- individuals in the unit may have differing expectations of you
- because your Chaplain is a Captain (or soon will be), you may be expected to know more than you actually do
- the unit is very close-knit

Remember

- you do not wear any rank

- you may be one of the newest-to-the-Army members of the unit
- you will make some mistakes as everyone does, which is okay, but those in the unit seek authenticity and care from you
- to be yourself

Be sure to

- get a unit roster
- engage people in a caring and supportive way
- stay informed
- learn all about what your spouse does as a Chaplain
- respect confidentiality

Social

- activities mostly revolve around your battalion
- a few brigade functions
- your FRG will play an important role
- Brigade UMT get-togethers
- a few higher command unit events
- community events

MAJOR YEARS

Brigade

This will be the first time your Chaplain serves in a supervisory role.

Key Players

Brigade Commander (CO)—Colonel (COL)
Brigade Executive Officer—LTC

Other possible Chaplain assignments include Division Deputy, Family Life Chaplain, Ethics Instructor, Recruiting, Chaplain School Instructor, and so on.

This is your time to

- mentor your battalion Chaplain spouses; get to know them, pass along information, reach out to them, make them feel welcome, check on them
- do your best to connect and support your Brigade Commander's spouse

You will probably realize

- a brigade is not as social as a battalion
- you may not feel as much a part of the unit as when you were with a battalion
- you may want to seek other places to serve and be involved
- you are growing in your knowledge and experience as an Army spouse

Remember

- to get to know the UMTs in your brigade; socialize, and have fun together
- don't be intimidated by rank
- others will seek out your experiences and knowledge
- you will have more opportunities for leadership
- *no* is not a bad word
- be yourself

Be sure to

- establish priorities according to your needs as well as your Family's needs
- take one day at a time
- continue learning about the Army world

Social

- most activities revolve around your brigade
- Brigade UMT get-togethers

- some higher command unit events
- community events

LIEUTENANT COLONEL YEARS

These are positions of greater responsibility. No matter the position of your Chaplain, supporting and caring for the Army Family is the top priority.

Possible Positions: Division Chaplain, Garrison Chaplain (on a small post), Chaplain for a large brigade, staff positions in higher commands

This is a time

- to be approachable
- to mentor other Chaplain spouses
- to possibly be in more of a leadership role and supportive role with other Chaplain spouses

You will probably realize

- others are looking more carefully at how you handle yourself
- others will consider you as a role model
- others will expect you to be well informed and knowledgeable of the Army
- every position for your spouse brings new challenges and a new set of group dynamics

Remember

- there is no path for your Chaplain that guarantees success—the best formula for your spouse is to work with others as a team, do his or her best, and serve with passion and care
- no matter the position of your Chaplain, he or she is serving

- sometimes the grass is not greener on the other side
- graciousness and humility go a long way—no matter the rank or position
- be yourself

Be sure to

- take care of yourself and your Family
- enjoy the journey
- stop and remember all you have accomplished

Social

- activities revolve around your unit
- higher command events
- community events

COLONEL YEARS

Possible Positions: Corps Chaplain, Installation Chaplain, Hospital Chaplain; Chaplain of Army Commands, Army Service Commands, Direct Reporting Units; USACHCS Commandant and USACHCS staff positions, Chief of Chaplains' staff positions

This is a time

- to know and use your strengths
- to treat everyone the same—always treat others with respect and care
- during which you may take on more responsibilities

You will probably realize

- you will be in more of an advisory role
- you are much more visible

- you will do a bit more entertaining
- you still have to find your place to fit in

Remember

- to take advantage of workshops, training, seminars
- be an encourager and motivator
- to be excited about serving the Army Family
- to be yourself

Be sure to

- make the most of each day, as the years pass by very quickly
- acknowledge your season of life
- begin thinking about and preparing for Army retirement

Socially

- UMT and Unit functions will be at a higher level
- may be in spotlight more—such as be seated at head tables and participating in receiving lines
- community events

Good Things to Know

When your Chaplain is on the promotion list, it is a joyous occasion. At the same time, you will inevitably share in the disappointment of those who were passed over for promotion. Always be mindful of those who are not on the list and be caring and supportive toward them. If your Chaplain is not on the promotion list, it is not the end of the world. Remember, there will be another promotion board the following year. Encourage your spouse to remember the reason he or she entered the Army—to serve Soldiers, with honor and care.

Chaplain Assistants' Spouses—Your personal relationship with the Chaplain Assistant's spouse is unique. It will vary for each individual. Many welcome a relationship with the Chaplain's spouse; others prefer more distance or no relationship at all. Some enjoy being involved with the UMTs while others don't. But passing along information, expressing sincere care and concern are almost always welcome.

UMT/Chaplain Staff/Chaplain Spouses' Social Suggestions:

- birthday cakes in office
- cards for anniversary, birthday, new babies, condolences
- office lunches, breakfasts
- send in cookies/goodies
- potlucks, dinners in your home
- baby basket at a gathering, baby cups, baby shower as appropriate
- hail and farewells
- cookouts, picnics, couples night out

Chaplains' Spouses' Coffees/Groups

Do connect to the Chaplains' spouses' group at each duty station. Almost all Army posts have a Chaplains' spouses' group. The group will not automatically receive your contact information, so when you arrive at a duty station, ask your Chaplain to pass the information along to his supervisor. It can be difficult at some locations for the spouse group to be aware of incoming spouses; so alert your friends, reach out to another Chaplain's spouse if you don't hear from the group within a few weeks, and always let the group know when you become aware of a new arrival.

The Chaplains' spouses' group is made up of all Chaplain spouses on the installation and is usually led by the spouse of the Senior Chaplain on post or several "senior" spouses on post. The main purpose of these groups is to promote friendship, share information, and support one another as Chaplain spouses. An added bonus is that they provide a wonderful opportunity for spouses to learn from each other.

Installations come in all sizes and varieties. The Chaplains' spouses' groups will reflect this. On some installations, the group might be composed of Unit Ministry Team (UMT) spouses, which includes both Chaplain spouses and Chaplain Assistant spouses. Other posts will have groups just for Chaplain spouses. At large installations, the group might be divided into two or more groups. For example, Fort Bragg and Fort Hood are large posts so the group is often broken into smaller groups for a better opportunity for fellowship. On most other posts, all Chaplain spouses will meet as one group.

Typically the Chaplain spouses will meet once a month; at some posts, they meet every other month. The group, for example, could meet for a monthly Saturday breakfast, meet the first Thursday evening of the month, or at the discretion of the host. Occasionally the host will have a low-key program, a group mixer, or game, but most of all, everyone loves to chat and catch up with one another. Attendance is not required, but do take advantage of participating when you can. Here, most of us discover new friends who we treasure for years to come. It is so encouraging as well as relaxing to be with other Chaplain spouses—we share a common bond. It is a great feeling to be among a group where all feel safe and connected while having lots of fun. We are all in this together!

It is unknown when this tradition began, but the benefits are remarkable. Many of us will accompany our Chaplain many miles from our Families and friends. Yet, within weeks of arriving, we will have a wonderful opportunity to make connections and begin lasting friendships.

A Note to Those Leading a Spouse Group

If you are ever in the position to lead a Chaplains' spouses' group, keep in mind to always be supportive, inclusive of all, and gracious. You set the atmosphere for the group and many take their cues from you. The key ingredients to remember are cooperation, nurture, and service. This is a time for you to serve your fellow Chaplain spouses with love and care. Also keep in mind that we are a very diverse group, representing many faiths and traditions. We never want to exclude or appear to exclude anyone, or make anyone feel they don't belong.

Make your gathering a social time of getting to know one another, sharing information, and just having fun. The atmosphere created should be one where all will be met with friendliness; everyone is welcome, no matter your age, spouse's rank, gender, how long you have been in the area, how often you are able to come, who you know or don't know, or even your religion. This is for *all* Chaplain spouses.

Because of many work schedules and sometimes Family schedules, some spouses may not be able to attend the monthly get-togethers. Try to find ways to connect with all your spouses, no matter if they are able to attend, through such methods as email or a spouse Facebook page. There are so many ways to achieve connectivity.

As the number of Army female officers increases, the number of female Chaplains is increasing as well. Our male Chaplain spouses bring a new dimension to our Chaplain spouse community, and often become integral parts of FRGs, military units, and volunteer organizations. They are a vital part of our Chaplain Corps Family and we always want to make them feel comfortable and welcome.

The spouse of the Chaplain who works for the most senior commander on a post is *usually* responsible for leading the spouse group. When there are several senior spouses, it is recommended that they combine their efforts to support *all* Chaplain spouses. Often, the senior spouses meet together to plan the best way to meet the needs of their group. They may elect, for example, to have all spouses meet together on even months and then meet with their own unit (division, garrison, etc.) the other months. A good practice, of course, is to ask your group members their expectations and the types of gatherings and activities they prefer.

If you are in the position to lead a Chaplains' spouses' group (remember this is voluntary), but prefer to bow out for whatever reason, please be honest and find the appropriate person to take your place. The group is very important to many spouses, so you want the group to remain strong and serve their needs. Do what you can to ensure the group is able to continue.

When you leave, hand off any information, including rosters, to the spouse following you. Inform the incoming spouse what the group has done, what worked and didn't work.

All in all, you have a remarkable opportunity to serve your fellow Chaplain spouses. Your time and effort will be felt and appreciated on so many levels as you make a difference with each and every Chaplain's spouse in your care.

Enjoy, serve, connect!

Some Thoughts from Our Chaplain Spouses about Chaplain Spouses

Differences between a Pastor's Spouse and an Army Chaplain's Spouse

Sara: Our church felt like a very close-knit Family. In Army life, the people we minister to are a much larger, more mobile Family. I feel like I have loved ones all over the world now!

Constance: A Chaplain's spouse is exposed to secular lifestyles more than a pastor's spouse. Chaplains' spouses have an all-inclusive ministry that extends to people from all walks of life, lifestyles, and religious beliefs, as opposed to those whose ministry remains primarily within the confines of a church.

Sherry: I feel less pressure and expectations on me as a Chaplain's wife. I feel more freedom to do what God is calling me to do for ministry to the military *without having to do* what the previous pastor's wife did in the local church. I can use my gifts the way God wants to use me uniquely at each duty station.

Dixie: The "fishbowl effect": I love being one of many rather than *one*. It's easier to be who I am; not as many expectations. I love the diversity of being an Army Chaplain's spouse! Change is something I enjoy rather than feeling stuck in one place all the time.

Supporting Your Chaplain Assistant's Spouse

Jennifer: When my husband's Assistant was a female, I did not go to great effort with her husband, but remained cordial the few times I saw him. I did not feel it was appropriate to have coffee, get to know, or make phone calls as I would have done if he had a male Assistant. With a female spouse, I will do the above if she is open to it. Practice kindness. We all want it.

Sarah: I treat the spouse of my husband's Assistant as another military friend. She can call me as needed, and we laugh about the challenges that our husbands face together.

Renee: I have always tried to create a relationship with our Assistant's Family by having them to dinner, inviting them to events, and praying for them. I have found it one of the more challenging relationships to nurture. There can be a natural resistance or hesitation on the part of the Assistant.

Adele: Oftentimes, we have invited them to our home for dinner, have tried to recognize and celebrate their achievements, and have especially tried to reach out to them and their children during special times (holidays, birthdays, etc.) when their spouses were absent.

Ann: I have always made sure I personally know my husband's Assistant and spouse and attempt personal friendship. Since the Assistant is the only armed person between the enemy and my husband, I want to keep those folks firmly in my corner! I feel like I have been successful and very blessed in turn in those friendships, particularly with the spouse.

Becci: I have tried to reach out to my spouse's Assistant's wife at each assignment. However, I have not been successful in these attempts. We are in quite different stages of life and it's been a challenge to find common ground.

Karen: Focus on the positive, give words of encouragement, acknowledge and thank them when you see or notice that a job is "well done." Tell them that we love them, are praying for them, and expect good things for them. Emphasize that they are an important part of the team.

Thoughts on Chaplains' Spouses' Groups

Debbie: It has helped to hear how others deal with the same issues I face.

Lori: A "safe place" to just be friends, get great ideas, and encouragement

Renee: These groups have been a lifeline over the years. I always say that no one understands the life of a Chaplain's spouse except another Chaplain's spouse. I have always been involved in monthly get-togethers and have encouraged younger spouses to attend. This is also a great way to avoid isolation. It is a built-in support system.

Sharon: I love the fellowship! I love to laugh, eat, and catch up with the other spouses—it refreshes me.

Emma: It's a great way to relax and just be yourself. Everyone there is a Chaplain spouse and has realistic ideas of what a Chaplain spouse should be doing. It's great to know that others understand you.

Ann: I ask for our group to be purely social, not devotional. There are more appropriate places for the devotional aspect. I know many people think this is antithetical to who we are, but our practices and belief systems can be very different and therefore potentially divisive. I want the group to be a safe place for all to come.

Thoughts on Practicing Inclusiveness

Kelli: Remembering that we are not all of the same faith group, belief system, or denomination sets a stage for inclusiveness. It seems the best gatherings have had a theme other than religion to bind us together—art, exercise, food, etc. We focus on what is common to us and not on our differences.

Sheri: I think it is very important to model inclusiveness at all Chaplains' spouse group meetings and communications. Modeling inclusive prayer, mentioning upcoming religious holidays of all faiths, making a point to spend time developing relationships, and communicating with spouses of other faith groups and getting to know more about their religious practices and traditions are important.

Penni: Everyone is welcomed. We all share the same military lifestyle and burdens and joys.

Robin: Typically I don't even ask someone their denominational background. I would start by what we have in common, assignment to a particular post, same unit, same deployment, etc. I think I usually focus on what is the same among us, not the differences.

Sandra: I truly believe that we are to love each other, differences and all, which includes differences in theology and faith.

Karen: Educating myself on the faith of each participant, being respectful to each person regardless of faith preferences, acknowledging specific holy days with complimentary greetings, focusing on what we have in common rather than our differences.

Top Challenges

Conli: You are always "on" as a Chaplain's spouse! Every social event, outing, homeschool field trip, "Girls' Night Out," becomes an opportunity to listen to someone who needs help, counseling, advice, etc. This is the way my husband has felt for years as a pastor/ Chaplain; now I understand! As a result, I am much more aware of protecting his time away from the spotlight, of making sure we take needed downtime as a Family to regroup and refuel. We love the calling, the outreach, the ministry, but it can be exhausting! We both need opportunities to be "antisocial" together, so that we can be the best versions of ourselves when out and about.

Kelly: I worry that people will not befriend me or I will be treated differently once people learn that my husband is a Chaplain. Other Army spouses don't want to open up to me in friendship because they feel that I will judge them in some way because my husband is a Chaplain. Nothing could be further from the truth. I just want others to be themselves around me!

Judy: Being content to not know everything is a challenge. I now understand and respect that some restrictions come as a result of confidentiality of counseling; some restrictions come as a result of the unit he is assigned to; some lack of information is simply a by-product of time and distance limitations. During a deployment there's just sometimes no way to share everything.

Ginger: Deployments and dealing with the aftermath of deployment are challenges. After the deployment is when everything "hits the fan" for all the Soldiers, and many situations (Family issues, suicides, etc.) require the Chaplain. It's important to realize that your Chaplain's job is not over and even though the unit is home, your Chaplain will still be gone much of the time. It may be harder to communicate with your spouse when he or she is home than during deployment.

Barbara: It revolutionized my appreciation and sympathy for my husband's work and stress level once I realized that he always wore at least three hats and had at least three bosses. His time was not mine—it was not even his own. Coming to terms with that was very challenging. (The three hats are: unit ministry, garrison obligations like funeral duty and staff duty, and chapel ministry.) But knowing it has made me a much better encourager and support for him.

CHAPTER 11

A BALANCED LIFE

Genie Brainerd and Brenda Shaw

To Arms

Signals all troops to fall under arms at designated places without delay.

The Army and the Chaplain Corps by nature are all about service, and chances are that your heart beats for others as well. As the years fly by in a blur of moving boxes and new schools, household tasks and volunteer activities, you may find yourself weary and stretched. Though it sometimes takes great effort, carving out time for self-care will allow you to go the distance and enjoy the journey.

Your Soldier is coached in the "Five Pillars of Comprehensive Soldier and Family Fitness." Soldiers are also required to build physical fitness time into each workday, which is a great bonus for them! As Family Members, we might have to work a little harder to ensure balance in our own lives, but we can learn from the Army's model and tweak it to suit our needs.

SPIRITUAL FITNESS

Because our spouses' careers literally revolve around taking care of others' spiritual needs, we might feel that this area of life is easy to maintain (or feel pressure to look like we're doing a good job of it!). Often, we are eager to come alongside our spouses and support the unit's Families, the chapel Family, and, especially, our own growing Families. As we invest in sharing the importance of our faith with those we love, it's easy to shortchange ourselves and skimp on the spiritual feeding that will strengthen our own hearts and minds. In the midst of *doing*, be encouraged to take time to just *be*. Quiet time, study, reflection, prayers, retreats, events, conferences, music, worship, and sharing in a community of faith are all ways to renew your spirit and nourish your faith.

Emotional Strength

As caregivers, we expend a great deal of emotional energy. The constant upheaval of frequent moves and realizing the harsh realities of war can take a toll even on the strongest of us. Our spouses may feel the burdens of dealing with the often very serious problems of the Soldiers in their care, and in our desire to support them, we can absorb a great deal of sadness. Stressors abound, so take care to recognize if you're feeling overwhelmed, depressed, anxious, or angry. There are many resources available to help you get through the rough patches. Of course, there are Chaplains available. Behavioral Health offers assistance, and ACS has Military Family Life Consultants who are trained to provide nonmedical counseling services geared toward short-term problem resolution. These consultants do not even keep records, so you may feel comfortable and assured that you can share what you need to share.

Stress affects almost everyone. Sometimes, it can be a good thing because it can energize us to meet new challenges or changes. But if it's not managed, stress can affect your physical and emotional health, your relationships, and your quality of life. Below you'll find tips for managing stress. The first step is learning how to become aware of it in yourself. Some common physical and emotional symptoms include:

- difficulty sleeping
- headaches
- neck or back pain or muscle tension
- stomach pain
- irritability
- anger
- depression
- mood swings

Sometimes, the best way to deal with stress is to confront it at the source. If you're worried about what your boss thinks of your performance, you could ask and find out. If you feel overwhelmed by your to-do list, you could block out some time to tackle it. But not all stresses can be handled so directly. Some sources of stress can't be eliminated. You may be the caregiver for an aging relative, or parenting a child who is having difficulty in school. To manage those kinds of stresses, you may need to use other techniques:

- Relaxation techniques are often successful. You might try deep breathing, meditation, prayer, or just sitting quietly for a few minutes each day to gather your thoughts.
- Taking care of yourself is also important. Eating a nutritious diet and getting enough rest are vital.
- Research shows that social relationships make you feel better and have a positive effect on your health. Be sure to set aside time for friends and Family.
- The old adage that "getting outside yourself" will lift your spirits is often true. Becoming involved in volunteering, serving others, and building community can go far toward augmenting your emotional health. Practicing the art of a thankful heart by thinking of and expressing thanks for a few things you are grateful for each day helps too.

THE FAMILY DIMENSION

Building and maintaining a strong Family can be a challenge when you're living in a constant state of change and are far from an extended Family support network. Investing in a strong marriage is worth every effort. If you're struggling, seek help from a wise couple who is farther down the road than you, or from a counselor. We are fortunate that counseling resources are plentiful and cost-free to military Families. Commit to forgiveness and making each other a priority. Make time to date each other—between the rigors of ministry and deployment, your spouse's time may be scarce. Flexibility might be necessary, but a strong marriage is a prize worth fighting for!

Take a cue from the kids and learn how to play. No matter where you are on the age spectrum, fun, laughter, and silliness will melt away your troubles—at least for a moment. Rediscover the joy of water balloons, practical jokes, and board game tournaments. Even when your nest is empty, cultivating a carefree spirit will keep your heart light.

Family traditions are the makings of precious memories for you and your children. The one constant in your Family's world is each other. As houses, friends, and duty stations come and go, you will weather the storms and delight in the adventures together. Build those sweet little rituals that are unique just to your Family, and watch how you all will treasure them.

Stay connected to extended Family as well. This can sometimes be a feat of creativity, but relationships will be enriched as you share your lives with those who love you, no matter where you are on the globe.

Your Family is as important a ministry as the Soldiers your Chaplain serves. Seek the balance that fits your Family best when it comes to work, volunteering, and home life.

Physical Fitness

Life's challenges to physical health and fitness can be discouraging, but there's good news. Did you know you're never too old to get in shape? That you can grow new brain cells? Did you know scientists now believe you can make some improvements on genes in your body by making some lifestyle changes? These can be as simple as learning to be flexible, using meditation and prayer, deep breathing to calm anxiety, maintaining your loving relationships, and supporting your body with better levels of physical activity and nutrition.[1]

Encourage yourself to improve your lifestyle as you're able. Reward yourself for progress. Learn what motivates you, and use it. Resources abound in the military world to help you keep strong and healthy. Preventive care screenings are part of our Army health care system. Wellness centers offer advice on healthy eating. Fitness centers and gyms are available on posts, and they are generally free. Here you may find amenities ranging from equipment to classes to onsite childcare, sometimes for up to two hours, and even more generous hours during deployments. If you prefer a non-gym type of workout, there are many choices for childcare for a reasonable fee on posts. From referrals to trained teenage babysitters, to mother's night out, to hourly care, to daycare, options are plentiful at a price Soldiers can afford. You can also exercise at home. "Way of life workouts," including cleaning, climbing stairs, chasing after a toddler, dancing, gardening, being active in the yard with kids and pets, are significant moves toward fitness.

Healthy lifestyles are important for your children, too! Youth sports leagues are active on most posts and the fees are usually less than in civilian communities. Schools of Knowledge, Inspiration, Exploration and Skills Unlimited (SKIES) offer classes for Families in areas of dance, gymnastics, and martial arts. Post websites will usually detail what's available. Even more fun is blending fitness and fellowship by engaging in activities with friends and fellow spouses. One spouse organized something she called a "Three Hour Tour" during a deployment. Once a month, the spouses got together to enjoy three different activities in a three-hour block of time. One of those activities was exercising together.

If you're not a gifted athlete or a dietician by trade, don't despair. You can easily keep up with the latest trends in healthy eating online. Moving around regularly throughout the day is key to good health. Not sitting for too long at a time is extremely important, according to recent studies. Do interrupt sitting once every hour, by standing up or walking a bit. Even people who work out for thirty minutes, five days per week, may be at greater risk for conditions leading to premature death (such as cardiovascular disease) if they sit for long stretches during the day.[2]

Social Support

The Army journey is made more beautiful by the gift of friends. Camaraderie is so valuable to your spouse and the Soldiers with whom he or she serves; the network of social contacts you create and foster will be precious to you as well. Where else but in the military might you find that the neighbor who walked over to say hello two months ago will be the same woman holding your hand in the delivery room as you birth your child while your husband is deployed?

You'll never lack for new places to explore as an Army spouse, so build some bridges instead of walls with your neighbors and new acquaintances, and get out there together. You'll be amazed at the variety of things you can do at or near every post. At Fort Drum you can tap maple trees, at Joint Base Lewis/McChord you can see a fish hatchery up close, and at other posts there are classes in everything from upholstering to quilting. There's a shop at Fort Leavenworth that sells beautiful wrought iron pieces made by the prisoners there. The USO and MWR overseas plan weekend getaways for skiing, shopping, and sightseeing.

It can feel awkward to build new friendships in transient circumstances, but you'll get better at it with time. Develop your people skills by remembering to appreciate the good qualities in your new friends, to forgive real or imagined slights quickly, and to listen attentively when others speak.

Mentors are priceless. Find one—and be one! We all have much to learn and much to teach.

Old friends, though they may not be physically present, can give you an anchor and sense of security, and the time spent to write, call, email, or chat online with them is well worth it.

Keeping our own "Five Pillars" balanced is an investment in true health. Each dimension is important and worthy, so don't hesitate to take good care of yourself!

NOTES

1. Courtesy of Dr. Dean Ornish, MD, US Army War College speaker, August 6, 2013.

2. For more details see Joseph Mercola, "What Makes Sitting so Detrimental to Your Heath?" http://fitness.mercola.com/sites/fitness/archie/2013/12/13/sitting (last accessed 29 April 2014).

CHAPTER 12

ARMY BRATS

Genie Brainerd

School Call

Signals school is about to begin.

The term *Army brats* elicits different reactions from different people. For some, it is both endearing and a badge of honor. For others, it's not at all accurate according to most people's understanding of the word. In fact it's not a word at all but actually an acronym! As with many of our military traditions, this one is rooted in British history. When a member of the British Army was stationed overseas and allowed to bring Family Members, the Family accompanied the Soldier in an administrative status called BRAT (British Regiment Attached Traveler). As time went by, the term evolved mostly to refer only to children and has been adopted worldwide. Whether we love it or hate it, it is a term that most people know and use to refer to children who grow up in military service alongside their parents. It is commonly recognized these days that our young people do indeed serve and sacrifice while their parents are employed by the military. Great military parents try to ensure that the experience is positive rather than burdensome.

> "We will also venture out and begin exploring, taking away our son's fears as he sees Mom willing to get out, make a few wrong turns, and laugh about it."
> —Jenn

Military "brats" have been observed[1] to be more able than their more geographically stationary peers to adjust to new situations—largely, the researchers determined, because they have had a lot of practice doing so. What military parents do to make those transitions as seamless as possible contributes to the children's resiliency. In the follow-up study commissioned by the Army, researchers also noted that the common threads (in coping with deployment, but applicable to all students dealing with transition) include "connectedness to the community, maintenance of routines and extracurricular activities, and the competence and confidence that comes from experience."[2] Parents doing what they can to keep these threads common in children's lives will enhance their transitional and educational experiences all the more. Spouses surveyed informally agreed that getting involved early in familiar activities helps children adjust to new communities.

> "We research activities and opportunities that may interest our children before we arrive so that our kids have new adventures to look forward to."
> —Robyn

Home

At each duty station, the location of your home helps determine how community will evolve for your children. You may be offered a choice of on- or off-post housing. Living on post with others who are accustomed to the same transitional lifestyle offers certain advantages. It is not unusual for the neighbors and their children to come over soon after the moving truck rolls in to meet their new friends and offer help. That can certainly speed up the adjustment in the new setting. The Family has to decide if that kind of togetherness is best for them or not. In a civilian neighborhood, it may take longer for the neighbors to warm up, but there may be more privacy, which may be more important to your Family. You will learn to gauge the advantages of both situations and they will vary according to the stages of your kids' lives.

> "We try lots of different things soon after arrival. We adopt the attitude of, "we may never go back, then again, we might!" I am also very proactive in inviting kids over to our home."
> —Becci

Living on post may offer some familiarity and support as you make frequent moves. Many military Families choose to live off post but stay connected through participating in garrison (on post) activities, while others try to become more connected in their local communities. The decision is personal and somewhat unique for each Family, but one that should be made fully equipped with all the knowledge of the resources available.

Child Services

Each post has a Family, Morale, Welfare, and Recreation division. Child Youth and School Services (CYSS) is a division of FMWR. Families can go to the garrison webpage to get a complete listing, but some of the offerings include daycare, after school care, hourly care, and enrichment activities such as league sports. Eligibility includes active duty, Department of Defense personnel, and reservists on active duty.

Also falling under CYSS is the School Liaison Officer (SLO). This person is the primary point of contact for school-related matters, whether Families choose home school, private school, or public school. The SLO works to forge a relationship with the local school officials and the military to assist military Families with educational issues. All installations have a SLO; additionally, School Transitions Specialists (STS) are in place in six regional offices. The STS's primary responsibility is to establish infrastructure to encourage reciprocal practices to ease educational transitions (see militaryk12partners.dodea.edu).

Special Needs

In recent years, the Army has made significant progress in serving and supporting Families with special needs. The Exceptional Family Member Program (EFMP) works with military Families with special needs to address their unique challenges throughout the assignment process and after Families have settled into their new installation. This program offers many helpful resources and tools. If you have children enrolled in this program, always connect with EFMP as soon as you arrive at your new location.

At the direction of Congress, the Defense Department has set up an Office of Community Support for Military Families with Special Needs, which helps Families navigate the maze of medical and special education services, community support, and entitlements. Other resources include information about respite care benefits, federal resources, state resources, and the service branches' programs. For more information, contact http://apps.militaryonesource.mil /MOS/f?p=EFMP_DIRECTORY:HOME:0.

Specialized Training of Military Parents (STOMP) is a federally funded Parent Training and Information (PTI) Center established to assist military Families who have children with special education or health needs. STOMP began in 1985 and is funded through a grant from the US Department of Education.

The staff of the STOMP Project are parents of children who have disabilities and have experience in raising their children in military communities and traveling with their spouses to different locations. STOMP provides information and training about laws, regulations, and resources for military Families of children with disabilities; connects Families to other Families; assists parents and professionals in developing their own community parent education/support group; and provides a voice to raise awareness of issues faced by military Families of children with disabilities.

Military Families who aren't near an installation, including those of the National Guard and Reserve, can call a Military OneSource consultant for support and to discuss special-needs concerns. Families can receive twelve free consultations per year by calling 1-800-342-9647. For more information concerning special needs, visit www.militaryonesource.mil/efmp.

Religious Opportunities

It would not make sense, in a book devoted to Chaplain spouses, to forget about the array of opportunities available through the post chapel. Check the chapel link on your garrison homepage to learn what services and programs are offered for children and youth. When surveyed, many spouses mention that getting their kids involved in chapel-related activities early on helps the children adjust to a new community.

In addition to Chaplains assigned to unit ministry, the Army has Family Life Chaplains to provide spiritual and counseling services to the entire Family—brats included. Information about Family life services can be found on the chapel websites also. Family Life Chaplains work at installation Family Life Centers. If counseling is needed in a more clinical setting, behavioral health services are available. To learn more, contact your Medical Treatment Facility (MTF).

EDUCATION

One of the challenges military Families face is educating children in the best way possible in light of frequent moves (PCSs). In years past, Families depended on the "mommy network" for support and advice in navigating these challenges. Military Families are among the best at looking for ways to take care of one another. They do a phenomenal job of passing along good information about education options and this is one of the things that is great about the Army Family community. An informal system has developed over the years, where information is passed on from those who have been "there" to those who are on the way "there." Sometimes that information can be spot-on, but sometimes there may be gaps and, unfortunately, even misinformation. All children are different, so one Family's experience may not reflect another's. Listen to the advice (especially advice given in a positive tone), and adapt it to your own Family's needs.

For Families with school-age children, it is important to start doing research as soon as a move might be on the horizon. Making contact with the SLO to find out things like basic school information is a good first step. Don't forget to pay attention to school start dates and calendars, which are determined at the local level. Parents (especially of high schoolers) should know that moving from a traditional calendar to a block calendar, and vice versa, presents challenges if the move takes place anytime during the school year. Websites such as www.militarychild.org can be helpful.

The Military Child Education Coalition (MCEC) is contracted by the Department of Defense (DoD) and their mission is "to ensure inclusive quality educational experiences for all military children affected by mobility, Family separation and transition." On more than twenty-seven installations, they have staff in place to train parents in these areas to better serve their children. MCEC came into being in the 1980s around a kitchen table with military parents who were concerned about their children's education and transitions. Education is governed at the state level and although organizations like MCEC have been successful over the years advocating ways to standardize academic requirements, such as the Military Interstate Children's Compact (www.mic3.net), transitioning Families will face different graduation requirements as they move from state to state. It is important to find out the requirements for such things as enrollment and graduation as soon as possible.

Aside from academics, many students participate in extracurricular activities. The school district's website will provide lots of information. If you need more details, a phone call will be helpful as well. Sports physical forms are usually accessible and this physical can be done before a Family moves—one less thing to do in the new place!

Many military Families are choosing to homeschool. One of the advantages of this is maintaining continuity through transitions. Today there are many more online resources than in the past to assist the homeschooling Family. Co-ops exist across the country and around the world. Home schooled students have been shown to perform academically equal to or better than their peers as a whole.[3] States do have varying requirements, with which parents will need to become familiar.

> "We are intentional on finding home school groups and church youth groups—our children have benefited socially and spiritually from them. We also try to keep them involved in some type of sport activity."
> —CeCe

Department of Defense Education Activity (DoDEA) operates school systems worldwide. DoDEA's roots can be traced back to the early 1800s when the first school was set up on post at West Point, and later in the same century when a school was started at Fort Riley. It is encouraging to note that "students educated in DoDEA schools perform at or above the national average when compared to their civilian counterparts" (National Assessment of education progress—December 2011) (www.dodea.edu/aboutDoDEA/history.cfm). You may move to an area where these schools are available to your student. They exist overseas to enable military and DoD students to continue their educational experiences in places where they might have been limited by language or culture. Students may also have the opportunity to attend host country schools when posted overseas. This is more common for preschool and elementary-age students, as the language barrier becomes more of an issue as children age. Again, checking with the SLO in the area will provide helpful information.

For Families with students looking toward postsecondary education, scholarships are available specifically for military-connected children. The Post Spouses' Clubs and many military organizations award funds each year to qualified students. There are many search engines online to aid in this research. Fastweb.com is a great place to begin looking. The service member's Post 9/11 GI Bill may be eligible for transfer to a dependent. Additional funding may be available through the Yellow Ribbon Program. Questions about these programs can be addressed at the VA's website (www.va.gov).

There are two worthy websites that are focused on the military child. The first one is www.tutor.com/MILITARY. You can get homework and studying help from a professional tutor any time you need it. It is *free* for students in Army, Navy, Air Force, Marines, National Guard, and Reserve Families. Expert tutors are online 24/7 and available to help in more than sixteen subjects, including test prep, proofreading, Math, Science, English, and Social Studies. Be sure to check it out.

The other website is http://apps.militaryonesource.mil/MOS/f?p=MYOM:HOME2:0. Military Youth on the Move (MYOM) is designed specifically for military children—kids, preteens, and teenagers—giving them the tips and advice needed to help navigate everything from moving to social life, school, and more. MYOM also includes tips and information to help parents guide their children through the challenges of not only a military lifestyle (such as when a parent deploys and saying good-bye to friends), but also everyday challenges (such as how to save money and going green). The updated content for each audience of military children includes articles and information written for specific age groups. Each article has helpful tips and cool links that encourage viewers to find additional information about the topics, to help incorporate the information into their daily lives, and to help them overcome the challenges they face. MYOM also features quotes from military children of all ages, which let viewers know there are military children and parents out there going through the same experiences, and the quotes share those experiences and give helpful advice.

"Army brats" are a unique and wonderful group of young people, who often have the privilege of growing and learning as they travel around the world. Their opportunities are unparalleled and their patriotism unmatched. They have a broad grasp of world cultures and become savvy travelers and resilient people. Though the military life is not always easy for children, most look back and feel honored to have been ambassadors for our country in their own ways.

NOTES

1. "Education of the Military Child in the 21st Century: Current Dimensions of Educational Experiences for Army Children," (a Report on the Research Conducted by the Military Child Education Coalition for the U.S. Army, 2012), http://www.militarychild.org/public/upload/images /EMC21FullReportJun2012.pdf.

2. Ibid., 10.

3. Ibid., 76.

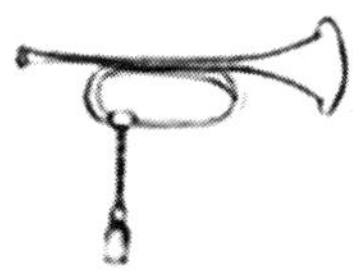

Chapter 13

Brat to Brat

Sheri Lewis

Fatigue Call

Signals all designated personnel to report for fatigue duty.

Through their unyielding support, military children increase not only their military parents' strength, but also their resilience.

—Air Force Chief of Staff Gen. Norton A. Schwartz[1]

I think that our military kids are who they are because of the hardships. Kids become who they are because of what we ask them to do and because of what they see us do [and] see their moms and dads do.

—Chairman of the Joint Chiefs of Staff Army
Gen. Martin E. Dempsey[2]

Children of Army Chaplains and the spouses of Army Chaplains who grew up as military dependents were asked to share personal reflections and responses to survey questions regarding their military life experiences. The result is a touching collection in their own words of the ups, downs, joys, and heartaches of military life as well as their words of wisdom and advice for those who follow in their footsteps.

Reflections on Life as a Chaplain's Kid—Drew, Age 25

Life as a Chaplain's kid is, above all, unique. It combines the already bizarre circumstances of both being a preacher's kid and a military brat. Being unique, of course, comes with both challenges and rewards. It certainly doesn't come easy. The Family (the entire

Family) has to be willing to work at it—and work hard. The lows are lower—deployments, repeated moves, even attending college half a world away from your Family's current duty station. The highs, though, are much higher—exploring new cultures, meeting people of various (and extremely diverse) backgrounds, and even getting to "go home to Germany" for Christmas break. The military, and especially the chapel communities, are examples of the American experiment: people from all walks of life, cultures, creeds, social backgrounds, coming together. It is the melting pot.

The struggles of the military's seemingly nomadic lifestyle are offset by the unparalleled opportunity to see the world, to be fully immersed in the context of history, to be a world citizen. The common joke is that if the Army had wanted me to have a hometown, they would have issued me one. This can make small talk rather difficult:

"Where are you from?"

"Erm . . . that's a long story."

"Well, where did you go to high school?"

"Which high school?"

Changing schools so frequently can certainly make things difficult—socially and academically—but can also yield tremendous opportunity. It can be hard to stay in touch with old friends from past duty stations, but one must never doubt the serendipitous nature of the military (for instance, a friend from when I was in second grade ended up moving to the same town as me during my senior year of high school). Keeping up with shifting curriculum is not easy, but a student will remember ancient history much better if he has been to Rome (or, in my sister's case, going with the school drama department to see *The Merchant of Venice* at the Globe Theater in London). Despite all of the ups and downs, life on the road forces military children to adapt, but in doing so, to engage their world.

More specific to the life of the Chaplain's kid is life in the chapel community. The chapel system is as diverse as the rest of the military. This means services also tend to represent a wide variety of faith traditions—for example, the Collective Protestant service, when I was in high school, included many different protestant denominations. On any given Sunday, a Collective Protestant service might feature a hymn more commonly sung in a Baptist or Presbyterian church, a Methodist communion liturgy, and a Pentecostal style sermon. The practical implication of this is that it can be very difficult for kids growing up in this environment to have any sense of denominational identity. Again, this is a challenge and a benefit. On the one hand, some Chaplains' kids find it difficult to express a strong sense of what, exactly, they believe; on the other hand, these same kids have a tremendous understanding of what it means to be part of a diverse church. And much like the educational advantages, the travel afforded by military life can be a tremendous benefit for religious development; exploring the catacombs of Rome, seeing the birthplace of the Reformation, visiting Buddhist temples, spending time in a secluded monastery, or just going to an old church down the street fundamentally changes the way we engage with our belief.

The chapel community differs from the civilian congregation in another important way: church governance. There is still a hierarchy (it is, after all, the military; rank and insignia are not just for show), and there are still the normal congregational politics. What is different, however, is the element of congregational responsibility. The congregation doesn't participate in the hiring of Chaplains because Chaplains are assigned by the Army. Nor does it decide to take on a building project. The congregation doesn't pay the Chaplain's salary. All of this means that there is a good deal more security for the Chaplain's Family; on the most basic level, it means that if congregational giving goes down, the Chaplain's salary is unaffected.

In short, being a Chaplain's kid is not easy—being a military dependent or a preacher's kid is not easy. It takes a lot of getting used to, and there is no shortage of oddities that become commonplace—showing a government-issued ID to go home, hearing cannons fire in the distance, watching military helicopters land on golf courses. There are parts of the lifestyle that nonmilitary kids will never understand. There are days when you don't realize how weird it all is and there are days when the abnormality of it all hits all at once. But it is well worth it.

Reflections on the Pros and Cons of Being a Chaplain's Kid—Audrey, Age 29

As with all walks of life, being raised as a military brat has its ups and downs, its pros and cons. Chaplains' kids face a slightly more unique set of circumstances than most children growing up in military settings. As a young adult looking back on my life, I can see how these pluses and minuses have affected my experiences and the way I view the world at large. Life as a military brat taught me to be accepting of people from various cultures, and to take the best bits of cultures and incorporate them into my own life. Learning this value helped teach me that things are not black and white; no one person or culture is all bad or all good.

I learned the importance of being responsible for my actions at an early age. I think this applies mostly to the unique world of being a Chaplain's kid. In the civilian world, if children get in trouble at school repeatedly, their parents are informed. If the police bring a teenager home for various reasons, the Family knows but that is the extent of it. In the military world, children's infractions are reported not only to the immediate Family but to the parent's commanders as well. I was always aware of how my actions outside (and inside) the home could negatively impact not only me but my father's career. It brought real-world consequences to childish behaviors that civilian children may not learn until it is sometimes too late. Additionally, in my role as a Chaplain's kid, I knew that my behavior was noticed and would reflect on my father even more so. I learned to think through how my actions could be perceived at an earlier age than most. That is not to say that I did not continue with those actions even though I knew the consequences could be bad, but at least I was aware of the responsibility I bore. I lost a bit of that awareness when living off post and even more at college when I was no longer known as the Chaplain's daughter.

Life in a military environment requires adaptability. You learn quickly to get used to new environments and people. Change is a stressor at first for everyone, but I think the military life helped me learn to deal with it and move on quickly. You have to learn to accept that there are things in life that stink and you can't fix them. Instead, you learn to figure out the best way to deal with it and then you move on.

One of the hardest lessons in adaptability came when I lost my "dependent" status. For those military children who study full-time in college, it happens when you turn twenty-three. The Army drops you like a hot potato. You go from being part of a community to being an outsider, and that is hard to accept. Having to be signed on to post when visiting always made me feel like I was no longer a part of my Family in a small way; I was the different one now even though all I had done was stay alive past twenty-three. Adult children whose Families are serving overseas are hit the hardest by this, I think. You go home one year and you live life on post like you always have; then the next year you aren't even able to make purchases at the commissary or PX. Things that never felt like privileges are suddenly taken away. It is a hard pill to swallow, but like I said, you learn to accept it and move on.

Being the young adult child of a military service member can lead to feelings of isolation, that no one understands your rather unique situation. This is especially true for college-age children. I think one of the hardest times for me as an Army brat was when my dad was in Iraq. When your parent is deployed, and you're physically with your Family and other Families of deployed Soldiers, you have a built-in support network. But when you're away at college with no direct connection to the military, and no apparent support resources, it can be quite a challenge. It was especially hard being on a college campus with a lot of people protesting the war verbally. I was so worried about my dad that it was difficult to carry on with normal life. If this happens to you, don't hesitate to seek counseling. Keep in close touch with your Family for support and to receive accurate information. Watching the news can sometimes raise your anxiety needlessly.

Growing up in military communities, I learned to bond quickly with people. You never knew how long you had with them. I think this can be both a positive and a negative. On the one hand, I learned to make friends very quickly; on the other hand, sometimes I think I can be a bit intense with a new friendship. I find myself now feeling like I am BFFs (best friends forever) with someone if we hang out a few times because when I was growing up that was all it took. Unfortunately, I let go of relationships quickly as well. Sure, it hurts like it would for anyone, but I move on quickly. This can be a positive and a negative. Sometimes I have found that I may have let go of a friendship due to distance or circumstances that separated us for a time. I then regret my hastiness when I realize that person was someone I should have held on to. You would think that being an Army brat would make me great at the distance-friendship thing, but I think it had the opposite effect on me. You grow and change so much as you move from station to station that you find that you and your old friends are no longer the same people you were. Since you didn't go through those changes together, the differences are hard to reconcile. I found it easier to just let them go, rather than working to continue the friendships. Again a blessing and a curse, as I truly miss some people that I did not hold on to even after I rejoined the civilian world.

They say hindsight is 20/20 vision. When my dad first joined the Army, I was not the biggest fan. We had to move away from our Family in Georgia. I screamed at him that I was going to kill him and that I hated him for it. To be fair, I was six and I loved my grandparents more than anything and didn't want to leave them behind. Looking back, I wish I could show that little girl how wonderful her life would be thanks to her dad's sacrifices. I have traveled throughout Europe and I have visited Asia. I learned foreign languages and I witnessed things a lot of people in the States only get to read about. Thanks for serving, Dad, thanks for giving us the opportunity to see the world, and thanks for defending the rights of the people of this country.

Transitions and Academics

One of the most difficult aspects of the military life for military dependents is moving to a new duty station. Survey participants provided suggestions for making the transition to new schools and communities:

- research the new community and school system on the Internet
- organize personal belongings and records as part of moving preparations
- be yourself
- have a good sense of humor
- greet others and introduce yourself
- join groups
- be willing to take the first step in order to establish friendships

Respondents to the survey recommend the following to aid in academics:

- support and involvement of parents is key
- establish good relationships with teachers
- ask questions
- stay after school for extra help
- keep up with homework and assignments
- take advantage of the variety of classes offered
- investigate graduation requirements ahead of time

Military kids indicate they feel more included at school when they make new friends and participate in athletics, Scouts, and extracurricular activities such as band and drama.

Here are some of the survey questions and answers:

How do you plan for a move to a new place and/or school?

Ashley: You say good-bye to old friends. Start doing research on where you will be moving. Try to get to the new location early enough to try out for after-school activities if possible. Know that with every move you can reinvent yourself!! At first I hated moving and then I realized everyone wants to get to know me: the new girl!

Austin: If I know someone who goes there, I get in contact with him or her. Otherwise I do a bit of Google search and go to the school's website to see the classes, clubs, and activities they offer so I know what to expect and what opportunities I will be presented with.

David: I like to look on the Internet and find information about the area/school that I will be moving to.

Marjorie: We always sat as a Family to select our top five places (which we never got, so that became funny). We also visited each place before moving (except overseas transitions). Whenever we moved from a house, we had certain rituals, which included going from room to room after packing day and sharing our fondest memories associated there.

What has helped you make friends quickly?

Andrew: What has helped me to make friends is being me and being funny.

Alexandra: By being nice to people.

Austin: Being outgoing and open is a huge help, but if you're the quiet type, just being involved. Being willing to speak up during class or help out someone when in need is always helpful. Putting yourself out there and being in conversations or relating to others helps you get planted on your feet right after arriving.

Crystal: You just need to get involved. Joining groups or activities is the quickest way to get to know other people. Be ready to invite people over, as well as to accept invitations.

Isabel: I dress nice and I express my bubbly attitude and people like that.

Jennifer: I find someone who seems to have the same interests and likes as me and then I ask them to be my friend.

Joshua: Do not concern yourself too much on who you hang out with at the start. Your starting off friends are not the same as your final friends. It's a big new place so hang out with people and see who you eventually click with.

Rebekah: Being outgoing and asking people questions to get to know them. Being willing to step out of my comfort zone.

What helps you be included in activities in a new school?

Abigail: When I was younger, it was a lot easier. Being at schools where all the other students were military brats made the students a lot more welcoming and open to making a new friend, but now if I really want to be a part of something I have to put myself out there and make myself known.

Alexandra: The student ministries (Club Beyond and Cadence) really helped me meet new people and get involved. I was a pretty shy kid growing up. I wouldn't have survived middle school if it hadn't been for Julie, the youth pastor who worked for Club and came to lunch at school every week.

Crystal: You just have to go for it. If you see something you are interested in, show up. Don't worry that it might be something that you've never done before.

David: Find a friend before you start attending the new school. A friend helps to introduce you to other peers and makes you feel comfortable.

Joshua: Sign up for some sports, preferably ones you are at least mediocre at. You're new and are going to have a lot of free time; you might want to fill it up so you don't get focused on your old friends.

What helps you be academically successful as you move from school to school?

Bob: Parents being involved in homework. Sometimes there are holes in education due to school curriculum.

Caleb and Cosette: Having a consistent school to school conversation between us and the schools and making sure everything will transfer smoothly.

Joshua: It's your job to learn, you are a student. A teacher's failure to teach doesn't mean it's okay for you to fail at your job of learning. Someday all that learning matters.

Sarah: I always kept a good relationship with my teachers. Teachers always appreciate you asking questions during and after class. Before teachers can help you, you must first help yourself by asking questions when you don't fully understand the material.

Vanessa: In high school, it helped to look ahead of time at the next school's requirements for graduation and see what classes they offered/required for that year.

For homeschoolers, what are some things you do to be a part of the community?

Bob: Join a sports team for local youth.

Edward: I am in Scouts and am going to run track this year. I ride my bike around the neighborhood and meet other kids; some are Italian and some are American.

Chloe and Sarah: We attend different homeschool groups and fun activities with church and dance school. Participate in Skies Unlimited classes and camps. Attend FRG functions. Attend VBS on post and in community.

Jake, Rachel, and Titus: Sports, music, church, worship team, youth group, art, homeschool co-op.

Sarah: I was homeschooled for my middle school years. I really enjoyed it and I was involved in YMCA and a couple of other Christian organizations. Homeschoolers can also attend the local Club Beyond and meet other students that way. As a homeschooler, you have more time to volunteer at post activities, which is always a plus.

What advice would you give to those military children seeking to attend college?

Alexandra: Don't be in a rush. After spending your life moving around, this is the first time that you get to pick where you go. Take your time to figure out what you want to do and where you would like to go. Growing up in the military helped me in HUGE ways that I didn't expect when I left for college. I made friends so quickly and adapted to change faster than the nonmilitary kids in my dorm. While moving around so much is hard, it really has helped me in ways that I will always be extremely grateful for.

Ashley: Go somewhere you want to go, not because of where your parents are located at the moment. My first two years of college I was in Georgia while my parents were still in Germany. Being a military kid, this was no big deal for me; that is why phones and email are available. Your parents are bound to move and unless you plan on transferring schools every time, you're going to be stuck there (good or bad). Find a school with a major you are passionate about.

Crystal: Be excited! You have a unique opportunity to go anywhere, as your home is not dependent on one location. However, it will be beneficial to at least look at the schools in the state where you graduate from high school to attempt to get in-state tuition. Talk to admissions counselors from other places and see what they might be able to work out even if you are not necessarily from that state.

Danielle: Start looking early and don't be afraid to do community college for at least the first year. The schools start telling you about college when it is almost too late. The first year at community college is great, especially if you can live at home. It's a great way to transition into the new academic world and is also cheaper on the whole. If you take core classes like Algebra, English, History, etc. at a community college, chances are you will have better help because the classes are smaller. At a community college, the tuition will be cheaper, and living at home means you don't have to learn all about rent and living expenses while trying to figure out the registrar system.

Jacob: The GI bill is much more complicated than it needs to be, so get it dealt with. Also, look into the possibility of military kids getting in-state tuition in some states, and military scholarships.

Pros and Cons of Life as a Military Brat

Most respondents take pride in the title of *military brat* and pride in their military parent. They also enjoy the advantages of living on post: conveniences the post offers, the close proximity of the post facilities, and the feeling of protection the security provides.

Not having a place to call home, frequent moves, deployments, and the difficulty of leaving friends and making new ones were recurrent themes in responses as the most difficult aspects of military life. Leaving friends was echoed time and time again as the most difficult aspect of moving for our respondents. On the flip side of the coin, their favorite aspect of moving was seeing new places and meeting new people.

How does it feel to be a military brat?

Caleb and Cosette: It feels like I'm part of something.

Edward: BRAT—British Regimental Attached Traveler (original meaning of the acronym). It really has felt normal because that is all I know.

Isabel: Awesome! I love being proud of my dad and his decision.

Krista: Like you have one of the greatest parents in the world because they are risking their lives for the freedoms we enjoy and even if people don't always see that, it is so awesome being a part of that Family. It makes me feel like I am a part of history because I am so connected to the defense of our nation's freedoms and values.

What do you like most about living or being on an Army post?

Andrew: What I like best about living on a post is you don't have to live in bad places and there are other kids my age.

Alexandra: I like the community centers and the playgrounds while living on post.

Austin: Being on an Army post is awesome because oftentimes you will be very close to the friends you attend school with. It's also safe so the parents aren't worried about you going out at night or riding your bikes and hanging out with friends.

Anonymous: It's like a mini-town. You can walk anywhere (PX, Commissary, movie theater, bowling alley, etc.).

Caleb and Cosette: You feel like you're in the US.

Rebecca: The cheap movies!

Sarah: There are far more pros than cons living on an Army post. You live close to most of your friends and it's a lot easier to get involved and volunteer when things are close. I would recommend living on post especially if you live overseas. My brothers and I also delivered the newspapers on post, which was a lot of fun.

Vanessa: I felt safe even when most of the units were deployed. I knew that other people on post were going through similar situations. I liked having easy access to gyms, pools, and parks.

Patrick: What I like most was the sense of community and camaraderie all the Families shared. Everyone was in the same boat, which definitely eased my transition from post to post. There is without a doubt a significant difference in the civilian world and the military community. Even now having been in the civilian world for several years, I still wish I was back on post. In a nutshell the sense of belonging I had at whatever installation I was living on was dependable and a cornerstone of stability I had throughout my moves. Even though Soldiers and their Family Members were diverse in religion, ethnicity, and beliefs, everyone shared a common bond. The core values that military Families share was a kind of communal glue that held everything in place. This I have missed and have come to appreciate more and more over time.

What is the most difficult/favorite aspect of moving for you?

Alexandra: I'll miss people, I'll miss my house, I'll miss my street, and I will miss my favorite stores.

Anonymous: You get to reorganize your room; sometimes I get a bigger room. The most difficult part is leaving friends.

Crystal: The most difficult aspect of moving was leaving the people I'd come to know. I struggled with not fully engaging with people as I knew that I would be moving again. This led me to miss out on some friendships that could have become stronger. I especially remember living in Texas for one and a half years while Dad was at a school. I intentionally tried not to get close to people. However, the summer before we left, I got close to a few friends, and deeply regretted keeping my distance during most of my stay there. My favorite aspect was traveling. I loved going to different places and seeing how people live in different parts of the States and world. It has allowed me to be more willing to try new things and understanding of different cultures.

Gray: I like going to new places. But I really miss friends and people from the last place.

Hannah: The most difficult is leaving friends I have grown close to, and Family. My favorite things are getting to see new places and meet new people.

Jennifer: The hardest part of moving is saying good-bye to your friends.

Marjorie: It was always the worst to leave, which must mean that each place became the best. Looking back, I appreciate the variety of experiences it afforded me and the way it established my "normal" as a much more expansive worldview. The down side might be that it implicitly trained me to run from issues/problems by relocating, and I struggle with maintaining long-term relationships.

Patrick: The most difficult and favorite aspect of moving for me was surprisingly one and the same—being constantly surrounded by new people, cultures, traditions, values, outlooks, and opportunities. As life goes on, the valuable life lessons I acquired over the years did not come mainly from the great times but rather the difficult ones. As I was living my "Army brat" life of constant moving and starting over, I was developing the skills of making friends quickly, being a better judge of character, building self-confidence, honing my coping skills, and adapting to whatever situations came my way. As opposed to many kids growing up in a single location, I was able to take a piece of the various traditions, cultures, and lessons I accrued and use them with school, friendships, and new surroundings. I developed a great respect for different kinds of people and how they live. Many people dream of living in places that they have only read about in history books. I was able to live it. It was difficult and sometimes painful but I loved it and wouldn't want to have grown up any other way.

What do you cherish most about growing up in a military Family?

Abigail: We stay together, we get close, we become better friends with each move, and I get the opportunity to experience so many different cultures. I wouldn't trade it for the world.

Andrew: What I cherish most about growing up in a military Family is the fun of moving to different places.

Ashley: The military is its own Family. I cherish the opportunities that have been afforded to me because of the reassignments throughout my childhood. Meeting new people and being thrown into different situations, I believe that I am more able to adapt than others who have been in the same location, with the same people, with the same situations their whole life. When you get knocked down just laugh, dust off, and get back up because as military brats we know how to pick up the pieces and move forward.

Chloe: Knowing that our Family is a part of helping our country and others.

Danielle: The exposure to a different way of thinking and looking at the world. My perspective is completely different than a lot of civilian kids, and my world is sometimes large, too. I cherish the closeness it has brought to my Family because home really is where the heart is since the building always changes. It inspires me to live for more and make a difference in the world however I can.

Erika: Learning firsthand about patriotism and pride of country. Knowing that my "Family" is much more than just the people who live in my house with me. There is an instant connection with anyone who has spent time in or around the military.

Gray: Adventure and experience.

Jennifer: Growing up in a military Family makes me feel safe and stable. I learned I can always depend on my Family to be there.

Rebekah: The thing I cherish most about growing up in a military Family is that it has really shaped who I am, and I don't feel that I am as sheltered as most people who live in one place their entire lives. Being in a military Family means you have to be willing to try new things, step out of your comfort zone, and enjoy some amazing opportunities.

What is the toughest part about growing up in a military Family?

Alexandra: Deployments. I really hated it when my dad had to leave. Through my four years of high school he only got to see my junior year start to finish. He missed seeing me get crowned Royalty Queen my senior year. He missed most of my swim meets. I completely understand that it's part of his duty to his job and country, but it was very hard. I am so proud of my dad and all that he's done, but deployments definitely were the hardest part of growing up an Army brat.

Gray: Having to move all the time.

Hannah: When daddy has to leave.

Jacob: Not being able to grow up with the people you're close to.

Krista: Not having other people give Soldiers the respect they deserve and tearing up every single time I hear taps. Also having a fear that my dad would be killed in a foreign country and knowing that he could deploy at any time. But this did allow me to appreciate my time with him all the more.

Sarah: To see daddy go away, when daddy has to stay up on long nights. He doesn't get as much time with you.

Young Adult: Once I moved out of my nuclear Family and went to college, all of my new friends had somewhere they called home and a group of friends they had grown up with. I did not have that luxury, but I did have the luxury of travel and many experiences they did not.

MEMORIES, REFLECTIONS, AND ADVICE

Survey participants were asked to reflect on their favorite memories, most difficult experiences, and the transition to young adulthood and the civilian world. Respondents indicated that they have acquired valuable life skills from their experiences. They have learned to take the good with the bad, they are more accepting of others than their peers, and their adaptability allows them to roll with the changes that come their way. They treasure their memories and their Families—the ones they were born with and the military Family they have acquired along the way. Perhaps the most ringing endorsement for the positive impact the military has had: some of our respondents who grew up as military brats went on to marry military members and Chaplains!

Share a favorite experience from when you lived overseas.

Anonymous: We live on the island of Oahu, Hawaii. Most people pay a lot of money just to vacation here. We get to live here. If we do our schoolwork quickly (homeschool), we can go to the beach for the rest of the day.

Bryn: My Family lived in Germany for ten years when I was a child. I still get homesick for it. I loved traveling, and even though we had a shoestring budget we got to see a lot!

Edward: I have been able to go around and sightsee with my parents. Like one time, I went all the way up to Normandy and celebrated the 67th anniversary of the Normandy remembrance. I met some French gentlemen who fought in WWII on the beaches. I camped with over 3,000 Scouts as we had our Mediterranean Scout Jamboree and visited the American Cemetery at Normandy.

Danielle: There are so many! I loved traveling to the different countries and seeing new and exciting things. One favorite experience was traveling all around Europe in the summer when we lived in Germany. One summer we went to Switzerland, Italy, and France. It was fantastic. Another was living in Hawaii and taking Space-A flights over to Japan and Korea. The sushi is amazing, and the people are so friendly!

Jake, Rachel, and Titus: Japanese girls wanting to take our pictures because we were all blonde!

Marjorie: So many! Generally, the ability to travel and see so many new things was an adventure, but a specific thing was in Germany where we used to go every Sunday to a Gast Haus we called "Margaret's" after the proprietress. She always had German candy and let us sit at the bar since it was earlier in the afternoon. She also tried to make various kinds of "American" food for us (the most mysterious to her being corn on the cob), which was always better with the German spin.

Rebekah: When we first went to Germany, I was thirteen and I hated it. We had moved from Colorado, where I had some great friends, great school, etc. But once I realized that I had a unique opportunity, unlike most of my other friends, I started to enjoy being overseas. I started taking advantage of traveling, learning a new language, and being a part of a different culture. I am now twenty-nine years old and I look back on that time in my life and actually miss living overseas.

Share one experience that was especially difficult for you due to being a military Family Member; how you dealt with it, lessons learned, things to consider, etc.

Bob: Dating was hard because it is hard to get to know people. Lesson learned—go for it.

Edward: I had to have my dad go to war for nine months. He also missed me being born because he was deployed then, too.

Jake, Rachel, and Titus: Dad deploying—we had to get used to him being gone, and then had to get used to him being back in the home. It takes patience and time to readjust.

Vanessa: We had just moved, started going to a new church, the youth was going on a missions trip, but I was unable to go because we hadn't started attending in enough time to sign up for it.

Young Adult: I am nineteen and still do not have my license, and am finding it very hard to obtain one due to state domesticity. Additionally, it's difficult to be recognized by colleges while you're overseas for athletics, etc.

How has military life impacted you as a person?

Chloe: It has taught us to stay strong and stand up for what you believe. It has taught us to stay healthy and fit. Having to move away from friends has taught me how to sacrifice for the sake of a bigger purpose.

Bryn: Military life has taught me to climb out of my shell more often. It's often difficult to start a conversation with people I don't know, but I try to remember that others are new as well and are hoping someone will talk to them too. So just do it!

Jacob: I like to think I'm more unique, in that I've never tried just fitting in, and I adapt well.

Sarah: I have more experience with stuff, traveling and meeting new people, than I would have if I were not a military kid.

Young Adult: I like to believe I am more tolerant of different cultures and pride myself in cultural curiosity.

Every child has a different story. What is the one thing you would like to share about growing up in a military Family?

Abigail: A lot of people say, "I bet you hate having to move so much" but honestly, I consider it a blessing. I know exactly where God wants me to be, and I see how God is working across the world.

Isabel: I just remember my dad coming home and waiting for him while having donuts and hot chocolate at 4:00 in the morning. When I saw him march in, I jumped up! I was so full of excitement! It was a fun day!

Rebecca: Because you are stationed all over the place, the people you meet from place to place become your Family. Honestly for me, I have met people who are now my "aunts and uncles" who keep in touch and see me more regularly than my true blood relatives. The military community is such a small world. Wherever you go, you will meet people who know the other people you just left from another station. It's always a fun surprise when you make connections like that.

Sarah: Our Family came on active duty when I was in junior high. So I have lived in both civilian and military worlds. Each world has positive and negatives, but when your Family is close to one another, you can do anything. I must have enjoyed military life as I married a wonderful guy who is active duty Air Force! I love the adventure.

Those of you who are young adults or college students, describe your transition into the civilian world, sharing your personal insights, challenges, and feelings that will help others in the future.

Bryn: How many times have I had this conversation?

"Where are you from?"

"I grew up in the Air Force."

"Oh, so you're from all over."

I usually just leave it at that because it's too long to explain. But I grew up in a specific community—I don't feel like I'm from "all over." After marrying a man in the Army, I've come to realize that the military is my community.

Erika: I went away from home to college during my father's last year in the Army. I was nowhere close to a military installation so there were very few people who had any idea what the military lifestyle was about. Most of my friends had lived in the same house or at least the same town for all of their lives. I couldn't relate as I had lived in thirteen homes before graduating from high school. But one thing that helped a lot was finding a group of "TCK"s (Third Culture Kids). Most of these college students were missionary kids but we had something in common. We were Americans but had grown up in a different "culture" and had become a third "culture."

I recommend the book *Third Culture Kids: The Experience of Growing Up among Worlds* by David C. Pollock and Ruth E. Van Reken. They give great advice about understanding ourselves and on making the transition into the civilian world as well as transitions while growing up in the military. I was only able to stay away from the Army for ten years, however. My husband (also an Army brat and son of a retired Chaplain) felt called to join the Army and serve as a Chaplain. We are more "home" in the Army than we were in the civilian world. It's just in our blood!

Sarah: The most challenging part of transitioning to college/civilian life is being able to communicate with and visit your Family. In college, it was difficult during breaks when my Family was abroad because I couldn't go home for breaks. I either stayed at school or went home with friends. Post college, it was very difficult to communicate with my Family, as there was a six-hour time difference. If I wanted to speak to my Family on the phone, I had to either call them before work or during my lunch break (they were asleep after work). Taking advantage of technology has helped us stay better connected. During the weekends, we Skype and during the week we either speak on the phone (if possible) or send emails. Utilizing social media has also helped us feel more connected as we can post updates, pictures, and send messages.

Anything else you would like to share that you think will be helpful to other military kids?

Erika: Allow yourself to grieve each move you go through. It might not be a death per se, but it is a loss. If you acknowledge the fact that you are losing things, people, places, etc., you will be better able to go to the next place with anticipation of new friends, a house, new experiences. Take pictures of people, places, and things that meant the most to you and then you can take the memories with you.

Hannah: Times can be tough but it always gets better!

Krista: Just remember that above all else, your parent loves you. Even if they have to miss the recital, game, birthday, Christmas, or Fourth of July, they love you so very much. Also, no matter what, know they have one of the most important jobs in the United States. We couldn't be the United States without our armed forces, so be proud when you say "I'm an Army brat!" no matter what people say. Lastly, don't watch the news when your parent is deployed—it will just give you panic attacks! Please listen to me on that!

Rebecca: Being a military kid doesn't define you, but it's a part of you. Don't try to hide it or be embarrassed. I'm proud to be the daughter of an Army Chaplain. We get to see firsthand the ministry God is doing in our military, and I get to see my dad doing what he loves. Any move, any deployment is worth that. Make the most out of what is given to you. Instead of complaining about another move, try to get excited about it. Start researching your new area and finding cool things to see around there. Yes, it's going to be rough at times, but you were made for this. Strive to be the best wherever you go and get involved as much as you can.

Sarah: Appreciate the adventurous nature of living in the military community. Except for visiting my parents, I really don't have any more ties to the military community, so I no longer move every few years. While the moves presented certain challenges as a child, you're also moving around the world and meeting various types of people. The military life is very adventurous and life can be a bit boring as a civilian.

ACKNOWLEDGMENTS

Thank you to the following survey participants who took the time to thoughtfully and candidly respond to the questionnaire:

Abigail (age 16)
Alexandra (age 11)
Alexandra (age 23)
Andrew (age 11)
Anonymous
Ashley (age 24)
Austin
Bob
Bryn (Air Force Brat/Chaplain's Spouse)
Caleb (age 13)
Chloe (age 12)
Cosette (age 19)
Crystal (age 25)
Danielle (age 24)
David (age 13)
Edward (age 10)
Erika (Army Brat/Chaplain's Spouse)
Gray (age 14)
Hannah (age 12)
Isabel (age 13)
Jacob (age 19)
Jake (age 17)
Jennifer (age 10)
Joshua
Krista (age 20)
Marjorie (age 37)
Patrick (age 26)
Rachel (age 15)
Rebecca (age 20)
Rebekah (age 29)
Sarah 1 (age 9)
Sarah 2 (age 26)
Sarah 3 (age 27)
Titus (age 13)
Vanessa (age 25)
Young Adult (age 19)

NOTES

1. Sanchez, Elaine, "Senior Leaders Honor Military Children of the Year," American Forces Press Service, April 6, 2012, http://www.defense.gov/News/NewsArticle.aspx?ID=67849, May 25, 2013.

2. Ibid.

Chapter 14

The Big World of Army Benefits

Lori Jeffries

To the Color

"To the Color" is a bugle call to render honors to the nation. It is used when no band is available to render honors or in ceremonies requiring honors to the nation more than once. "To the Color" commands all the same courtesies as the National Anthem.

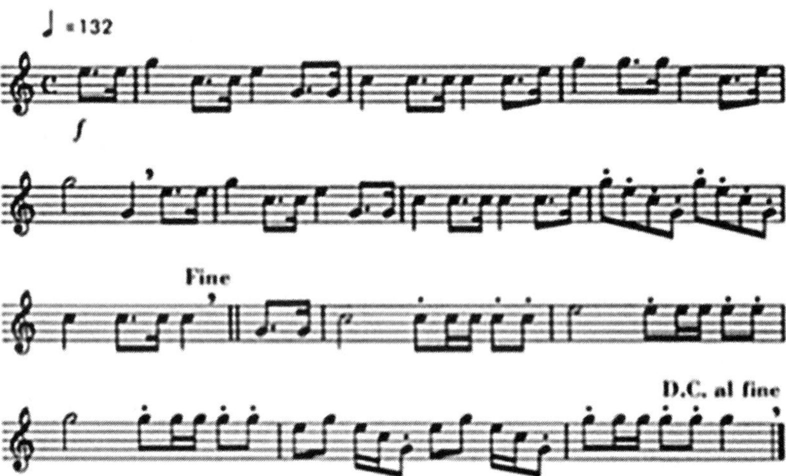

As part of the Department of Defense (DoD) Family, your Soldier is entitled to many benefits designed to support his or her service and enhance the quality of life for your Family. Additionally, there are countless perks you never even imagined, just waiting to be discovered! Benefits do constantly change and evolve. Don't assume you will automatically be informed of any benefit changes that may occur. Keeping up-to-date on the latest benefit information is your responsibility. It is imperative to always check with the organization about current policies and regulations. Stay vigilant to ensure you receive your full benefits.

Medical insurance is a primary concern to all of us. As of this writing, health coverage is provided by TRICARE. TRICARE is a regionally managed health care program for active duty, Activated Guard and Reserves, retired members of the uniformed services, their Families, and survivors. TRICARE brings together the health care resources of the Army, Navy, and Air Force, and supplements them with networks of civilian health care professionals to provide better access and high-quality service while maintaining the capability to support military operations. Active duty and Guard and Reserve service members are automatically enrolled in TRICARE Prime. However, military dependents and retirees must choose the TRICARE option that best suits their needs. Eligibility for TRICARE is determined by information in the Defense Enrollment Eligibility Reporting System (DEERS). It is important for sponsors to keep DEERS records up-to-date. For eligibility, enrollment, cost, and coverage details, visit www.tricare.mil or contact your regional contractor.

TRICARE Program Options

Depending on your beneficiary category and location, you may be eligible for different program options. Use the chart below to determine your options. Additional program details are listed below the chart. Your options may change if you move, if your sponsor changes location or status, or if you have a life event such as getting married or becoming entitled to Medicare Part A.

Beneficiary Types	Program Options[1]
Active duty service members (includes National Guard and Reserve members[2] activated for more than 30 consecutive days)	-TRICARE Prime -TRICARE Prime Remote -TRICARE Active Duty Dental Program
Active duty Family Members (ADFMs) (includes Family Members of National Guard and Reserve members[2] activated for more than 30 consecutive days and certain survivors)	-TRICARE Prime -TRICARE Prime Remote for Active Duty Family Members -TRICARE Standard and TRICARE Extra -TRICARE For Life (TFL) (ADFMs must have Medicare Part A and Medicare Part B to participate in TFL.)[3] -US Family Health Plan -TRICARE Dental Program (TDP)
Retired service members and eligible Family Members, survivors, Medal of Honor recipients, qualified former spouses, and others	-TRICARE Prime -TRICARE Standard and TRICARE Extra -TFL (If entitled to premium-free Medicare Part A based on age, disability, or end-stage renal disease, the beneficiary must have Medicare Part B to keep TRICARE eligibility.)

Beneficiary Types	Program Options[1]
National Guard and Reserve members[2] and their Family Members (qualified, non-active duty members of the Selected Reserve of the Ready Reserve, Retired Reserve, and certain members of the Individual Ready Reserve)	-TRICARE Reserve Select (members of the Selected Reserve) -TRICARE Retired Reserve (members of the Retired Reserve who have not reached age 60) -TDP -TRDP

[1]Qualified adult-age dependents may purchase coverage through the TRICARE Young Adult (TYA) program.
[2]The National Guard and Reserve includes the Army National Guard, Army Reserve, Navy Reserve, Marine Corps Reserve, Air National Guard, Air Force Reserve, and US Coast Guard Reserve. For more information about benefits for the National Guard and Reserve, visit http://ra.defense.gov.
[3]ADFMs who have Medicare Part A are **not** required to have Medicare Part B to remain eligible for TRICARE. Once the sponsor reaches age sixty-five, Medicare Part B must be in effect no later than the sponsor's retirement date to avoid a break in TRICARE coverage.

TRICARE Prime

TRICARE Prime is a managed care option offering the most affordable and comprehensive coverage. Enrollment is required. Beneficiaries who may enroll in TRICARE Prime include:

- Active duty service members and their Families
- Retired service members and their Families*
- Activated National Guard/Reserve members and their Families
- Non-activated National Guard/Reserve members and their Families who qualify for care under the Transitional Assistance Management Program

- Retired National Guard/Reserve members (age sixty and receiving retired pay) and their Families*
- Survivors
- Medal of Honor recipients and their Families
- Qualified former spouses

*Note: When retired service members and their Families become eligible for TRICARE For Life, they are no longer able to enroll in TRICARE Prime.

When enrolled, you'll also enjoy enhanced preventive care and vision benefits. With TRICARE Prime you have an assigned primary care manager (PCM), either at a military hospital or clinic or from the TRICARE network, who provides most of your care. Your PCM will refer you to a specialist for care he or she cannot provide and coordinate with your regional contractor, who will provide for authorization, find a specialist in the network, and file claims on your behalf. You have certain time and distance standards for care including wait times for urgent, routine, and specialty care. Active duty service members and their Families have no out-of-pocket costs for any type of care as long as care is received from the PCM or with a referral. All other beneficiaries pay annual enrollment fees and network copayments.

- Active duty service members and activated Guard/Reserve members must enroll in TRICARE Prime.
- All other eligible beneficiaries have the option to enroll or use TRICARE Standard and Extra.

TRICARE Prime offers fewer out-of-pocket costs than TRICARE Standard and Extra, but less freedom of choice for providers as you must select a provider from the network. So, you should look at your options closely.

TRICARE Standard and Extra

TRICARE Standard and Extra is a fee-for-service plan available to all beneficiaries (except active duty service members and activated Guard/Reserve members) throughout the United States. Enrollment is not required. Coverage is automatic as long as you are registered in the Defense Enrollment Eligibility Reporting System. TRICARE Standard and Extra provide comprehensive health coverage.

Schedule an appointment with any TRICARE-authorized provider, network, or non-network. You will never need a referral for any type of care (routine, urgent, or specialty) but you may need to have prior authorization from your regional contractor for some types of services. If you visit a non-network provider with the Standard option, you will pay more out of pocket (5 percent) and may have to file your own health care claims. If you visit a network provider, you're using the Extra option. You'll pay less out of pocket and the provider will file health care claims on your behalf. Costs vary based on the sponsor's military status. After you've met an annual deductible, you're responsible to pay a cost share (or percentage). Remember, active duty service members (including activated National Guard/Reserve members) may not use TRICARE Standard and Extra, but Family Members can. TRICARE Standard and Extra may be the right choice for you if you have a provider who is not in the TRICARE network and you don't want to change providers; or if you live in an area where TRICARE Prime is not available, TRICARE Standard and Extra may be your only option.

TRICARE Prime Overseas

TRICARE Prime Overseas is a managed care option for active duty service members and their command-sponsored Family Members living together in non-remote overseas locations, providing comprehensive health coverage. Enrollment is required. Retirees and their Families may not enroll in TRICARE Prime Overseas.

The following beneficiaries may enroll in TRICARE Prime Overseas:

- Active duty service members
- Command-sponsored active duty Family Members
- Activated National Guard/Reserve members
- Command-sponsored Family Members of activated National Guard/Reserve members

When enrolled, you have an assigned primary care manager (PCM) at a military hospital or clinic who provides most of your care. Your PCM will refer you to a specialist for care he or she cannot provide, and coordinate with the overseas contractor when needed. There are no enrollment fees and no out-of-pocket costs for any type of care as long as care is received from your PCM or with a referral. Care received without a referral is subject to point-of-service fees. If you are an active duty service member or an activated Guard or Reserve member stationed in a non-remote overseas location, you must enroll in TRICARE Prime Overseas. Family Members must be command-sponsored to enroll or they have the option to use TRICARE Standard Overseas. TRICARE Prime Remote Overseas is a managed care option in designated remote overseas locations (Eurasia-Africa, Latin America, Canada, and the Pacific).

TRICARE Reserve Select

TRICARE Reserve Select is a premium-based plan that qualified Selected Reserve members of the Ready Reserve and their Families can purchase. TRICARE Reserve Select is available to the selected reserve members of the Ready Reserve (and their Families) who meet the following qualifications:

- Not on active duty orders
- Not covered under the Transitional Assistance Management Program

- Not eligible for or enrolled in the Federal Employees Health Benefits (FEHB) program (as defined in Chapter 89 of Title 5 U.S.C.) or currently covered under FEHB, either under their own eligibility or through a Family Member

Certain members of the Selected Reserve who are covered by TRICARE Reserve Select and involuntarily separated under other than adverse conditions, may have access to extended TRICARE Reserve Select coverage up to 180 days. For more information, contact your service personnel department. You may schedule an appointment with any TRICARE-authorized provider, network, or non-network. You will never need a referral for any type of care (routine, urgent, or specialty), but you may need to have prior authorization from your regional contractor for some types of services. If you visit a non-network provider, you'll pay more out of pocket (5 percent) and may have to file your own health care claims. If you visit a network provider, you'll pay less out of pocket and the provider will file health care claims on your behalf.

You are required to pay the monthly premiums and cost shares if you decide to enroll in TRICARE Reserve Select. The plan provides comprehensive health care coverage when you're not activated and covered by active duty TRICARE benefits. And, because you can see any provider, you don't have to change providers if you already have one.

US Family Health Plan

The US Family Health Plan is an additional TRICARE Prime option available through networks of community-based, not-for-profit health care systems in six areas of the United States. The US Family Health Plan is available to the following beneficiaries who live in a designated US Family Health Plan area:

- Active duty Family Members
- Retired service members and their Families*

- Family Members of Activated National Guard/Reserve members
- Non-activated National Guard/Reserve members and their Families who qualify for care under the Transitional Assistance Management Program
- Retired National Guard/Reserve members (age sixty and receiving retired pay) and their Families*
- Survivors
- Medal of Honor recipients and their Families
- Qualified former spouses

* Before October 1, 2012, the US Family Health Plan was also available to all Medicare-eligible beneficiaries age sixty-five and older. On October 1, 2012, this rule changed for all *new* US Family Health Plan enrollees, but existing enrollees are not affected.

You must live in one of the designated US Family Health Plan service areas to enroll:

1. Designated Area: Maryland, Washington, DC, parts of Pennsylvania, Virginia, Delaware, and West Virginia

Provider: Johns Hopkins Medicine

2. Designated Area: Maine, New Hampshire, Vermont, Upstate and Western New York, Northern Tier of Pennsylvania

Provider: Martin's Point Health Care

3. Designated Area: Massachusetts, including Cape Cod, Rhode Island, Northern Connecticut

Provider: Brighton Marine Health Center

4. Designated Area: New York City, Long Island, Southern Connecticut, New Jersey, Philadelphia and area suburbs

Provider: St. Vincent Catholic Medical Centers

5. Designated Area: Southeast Texas, Southwest Louisiana

Provider: CHRISTUS Health

6. Designated Area: Puget Sound area of Washington state

Provider: Pacific Medical Centers (Pacmed Clinics)

When you enroll in the US Family Health Plan, you will not access Medicare providers, military hospitals and clinics, or TRICARE network providers, but instead receive your care (including prescription drug coverage) from a primary care physician that you select from a network of private physicians affiliated with one of the not-for-profit health care systems offering the plan. Your primary care physician assists you in getting appointments with specialists in the area and coordinates your care.

Active duty Family Members pay no enrollment fees and no out-of-pocket costs for any type of care as long as care is received from the US Family Health Plan provider. All other beneficiaries pay annual enrollment fees and network copayments. If you live in one of the six designated areas, you may want to consider the US Family Health Plan. It is a robust Prime option that even offers enhanced coverage at each location. Visit www.usfhp.com for more information. You may enroll in the US Family Health Plan at any time during the year by completing an application for the plan in your area.

TRICARE Young Adult

TRICARE Young Adult is a plan that qualified adult children can purchase after eligibility for "regular" TRICARE coverage ends at age twenty-one (or twenty-three if enrolled in college).

You may qualify to purchase TRICARE Young Adult if you are:

- An unmarried, adult child of an eligible sponsor. Eligible sponsors include:
    - Active duty service members
    - Retired service members
    - Activated Guard/Reserve members
    - Non-activated Guard/Reserve members using TRICARE Reserve Select
    - Retired Guard/Reserve members using TRICARE Retired Reserve
- At least age twenty-one but not yet twenty-six years old.
- If you are enrolled in a full course of study at an approved institution of higher learning and your sponsor provides more than 50 percent of your financial support, your eligibility may not begin until age twenty-three or upon graduation, whichever comes first.
- Not eligible to enroll in an employer-sponsored health plan based on your own employment
- Not otherwise eligible for TRICARE coverage

TRICARE Young Adult provides medical and pharmacy benefits, but dental coverage is excluded. TRICARE Young Adult costs are based on three things:

- The option you select when you enroll: Prime or Standard
- Your sponsor's military status
- Where the care is received

- To participate, you're required to pay monthly premiums. Your plan option and sponsor's military status will determine what you pay out of pocket for care.

TRICARE Young Adult is an option for unmarried, adult children who have "aged out" of regular TRICARE coverage. The plan provides comprehensive medical and pharmacy benefits through two different health plan options. You should review all of your health plan options (military or commercial) before deciding if TRICARE Young Adult is the right plan for you.

Transitional Assistance Management Program

The Transitional Assistance Management Program (TAMP) provides 180 days of premium-free transitional health care benefits after regular TRICARE benefits end. Sponsors and eligible Family Members may be covered by TAMP if the sponsor is:

- Involuntarily separating from active duty under honorable conditions
- A National Guard or Reserve member separating from a period of more than thirty consecutive days of active duty served in support of a contingency operation
- Separating from active duty following involuntary retention (stop-loss) in support of a contingency operation
- Separating from active duty following a voluntary agreement to stay on active duty for less than one year in support of a contingency operation
- Receiving a sole survivorship discharge
- Separating from regular active duty service and agree to become a member of the Selected Reserve of a Reserve Component. The service member must become a Selected Reservist the day immediately following release from regular active duty service to qualify.

TAMP eligibility is determined by the Services and documented in the Defense Enrollment Eligibility Reporting System. Service members should check with their Service personnel departments for information or assistance with TAMP eligibility.

Continued Health Care Benefit Program

The Continued Health Care Benefit Program (CHCBP) is a premium-based health care program available to former TRICARE-eligible members and their eligible Family Members, former spouses who have not remarried, emancipated children, and unmarried children by adoption or legal custody. CHCBP offers transitional coverage for up to eighteen months for former service members and their Family Members, and up to thirty-six months for former spouses who have not remarried and adult dependents after TRICARE eligibility ends. If you qualify, you can purchase CHCBP within sixty days of losing TRICARE or Transitional Assistance Management Program eligibility. CHCBP benefits and rules are similar to those under TRICARE Standard, but you must pay quarterly premiums. For more information, contact the CHCBP administrator, Humana Military, at 1-800-444-5445 or visit Humana-Military.com. **Note:** CHCBP enrollees are not legally entitled to space-available care at military treatment facilities.

Healthcare Communications

Relay Health is the online healthcare communications network that provides connectivity, enabling all participants in the delivery of health care to communicate with each other more efficiently. Some benefits are:

- Secure connection to healthcare providers for routine communications
- Access to lab and other diagnostic test results
- Consultations for non-urgent health matters

- Access to view health care account information and pay bills
- Setup and management of Personal Health Records (PHR)
- Prescription renewal
- Personal health record management
- Delivery of lab results
- Referral requests
- Access to medically reviewed information

See more at: www.relayhealth.com/patients#sthash.YLmlN5GI .dpuf.

VISION

TRICARE offers a limited vision benefit based on your health plan option. Ophthalmic services, which may include an eye exam and other specialized services, are covered in connection with the medical or surgical treatment of a covered illness or injury. Generally, TRICARE covers:

- Routine eye exams every year for active duty service members and active duty Family Members
- Routine eye exams every two years for all other beneficiaries enrolled in TRICARE Prime (e.g., retired service members, their Families, and so on)
- Routine eye exams every year for diabetic patients enrolled in TRICARE Prime
- Eye exams under the Well-child Care benefit
- Ophthalmic services when needed

A routine eye exam is an assessment of your vision and the health of your eyes performed by either an optometrist or ophthalmologist.

You will get a prescription for glasses. Contact lens exams carry an additional charge. TRICARE covers the cost of contact lenses and/or eyeglasses only in the treatment of a few cases. Eye exams through TRICARE's Well-child Care benefit are routine eye exams that may be given every two years between the ages of three and six that also include screening for amblyopia (lazy eye) and strabismus (crossed eyes). These eye exams are provided by an optometrist or ophthalmologist.

TRICARE Dental Options

This section highlights your dental program options and costs when using the TRICARE Active Duty Dental Program (ADDP), the TRICARE Dental Program (TDP), or the TRICARE Retiree Dental Program (TRDP). These dental options are separate from TRICARE health care options. Your out-of-pocket expenses for any of the costs listed in this section are not applied to the TRICARE catastrophic cap. The TRICARE Dental Program and TRICARE Retiree Dental Program are voluntary and require you to enroll for coverage. The TRICARE Active Duty Dental Program augments services provided at military dental treatment facilities for active duty service members.

Dental Program Options	Beneficiary Types	Description of Program Options
TRICARE Active Duty Dental Program (ADDP)	-Active duty service members (ADSMs) -ADSMs enrolled in TRICARE Prime -Remote -National Guard and Reserve members active for a period of more than 30 consecutive days	-Benefit administered by United Concordia Companies, Inc. -For ADSMs who are either referred for care by a military dental treatment facility (DTF) to a civilian dentist or have a duty location and live greater than 50 miles from a DTF

TRICARE Dental Program (TDP)[1]	-Eligible active duty Family Members -Survivors -National Guard and Reserve members and their Family Members -Individual Ready Reserve members and their Family Members	-Benefit administered by MetLife -Voluntary enrollment and worldwide, portable coverage -Single and Family plans with monthly premiums -Lower specialty care cost-shares for E-1 through E-4 pay grades -Comprehensive coverage for most dental services -100% coverage for most preventive and diagnostic services
TRICARE Retiree Dental Program (TRDP)	-Retirees and their eligible Family Members worldwide -National Guard and Reserve retirees until reaching age 60	-Benefit administered by Delta Dental of California -Voluntary enrollment and worldwide, portable coverage -Single, dual, and Family plans -Monthly premiums vary regionally by ZIP code; deductible and cost-shares apply -Comprehensive coverage for most dental services; visit any dentist within the TRDP service area -100% coverage for most preventive and diagnostic services

[1]The TDP is divided into two geographical service areas: CONUS and OCONUS. The TDP CONUS service area includes the 50 United States, the District of

Columbia, Puerto Rico, Guam, and the US Virgin Islands. The TDP OCONUS service area includes areas not in the CONUS service area and covered services provided on a ship or vessel outside the territorial waters of the CONUS service area, regardless of the dentist's office address.

Active Duty Dental Program

The TRICARE Active Duty Dental Program provides civilian dental care to the following beneficiaries:

Active duty service members and National Guard and Reserve members who are

- called or ordered to active duty for more than thirty consecutive days
- covered by the Transitional Assistance Management Program (TAMP) after serving on active duty for more than thirty consecutive days in support of a contingency operation

The TRICARE Active Duty Dental Program provides coverage in the US, US Virgin Islands, Guam, Puerto Rico, American Samoa, and Northern Mariana Islands. In all other overseas areas, dental care is provided by military dental treatment facilities. For active duty service members in remote overseas locations, dental care is coordinated through the TRICARE Overseas Program contractor.

TRICARE Dental Program

The TRICARE Dental Program is a voluntary, premium-based dental insurance plan for:

- Family Members of active duty service members
- Family Members of National Guard/Reserve members
- National Guard/Reserve Members who are not on active duty or covered by the Transitional Assistance Manage-

ment Program (TAMP) after serving on active duty for more than thirty consecutive days in support of a contingency operation.

Note: National Guard/Reserve members who are on active duty or covered by TAMP use the TRICARE Active Duty Dental Program.

Guard and Reserve Dental Care

As a National Guard or Reserve member, how you receive dental care will change depending on whether your Soldier is on active duty. Here's a summary of how your dental care works.

When not on active duty, the Soldier and Family Members are eligible for the premium-based TRICARE Dental Program. The TRICARE Dental Program requires a twelve-month minimum enrollment period, so you must have twelve months remaining on your service commitment to enroll. The Soldier can enroll at any time and will pay monthly premiums based on military status.

If Family Members wish to enroll in the TRICARE Dental Program, they can at any time. They will also pay monthly premiums, but their enrollment will be separate from the Soldier's.

This way, if and when the Soldier is called to active duty, the Family Members' enrollment in the TRICARE Dental Program continues without interruption. The Soldier's enrollment, however, will change.

When called to active duty for more than thirty consecutive days, the Soldier's dental care will fall under that of an active duty service member, receiving dental care at either a military dental treatment facility, through the TRICARE Active Duty Dental Program or through the TRICARE Overseas Program Regional Call Center. You pay no premiums for dental care as an active duty service member and there is no minimum enrollment.

If the Soldier is enrolled in the TRICARE Dental Program when activated, enrollment is automatically suspended. Monthly premium charges also stop for the duration of active duty service.

Your Family's enrollment in the TRICARE Dental Program will continue when the Soldier is activated. However, you will enjoy reduced monthly premiums because you are considered active duty Family Members during that time.

Soldiers who qualify for the Transitional Assistance Management Program (TAMP) based on active duty service in support of a contingency operation will remain covered by active duty dental benefits during the 180-day TAMP period, continuing to receive dental care at military dental facilities and through the TRICARE Active Duty Dental Program. All orthodontics, implants, and certain complex treatments must be completed within the TAMP period.

At the end of the TAMP period, Soldiers may enroll in the TRICARE Dental Program. If enrolled in the TRICARE Dental Program before activation, TRICARE Dental Program coverage will automatically resume when TAMP ends, and you'll start paying your monthly premiums again.

If the Soldier qualifies for TAMP for any other reason than leaving active duty service in support of a contingency operation, or does not qualify for TAMP coverage at all, he or she may enroll in the TRICARE Dental Program upon deactivation. If enrolled in the TRICARE Dental Program before activation, TRICARE Dental Program coverage will automatically resume, and you'll start paying your monthly premiums again. If the Soldier was not previously enrolled in the TRICARE Dental Program, he or she can enroll at any time. Your Family's enrollment in the TRICARE Dental Program will continue uninterrupted, however, their premiums will return to the pre-activation rates.

TRICARE Special Programs

TRICARE offers supplemental programs tailored specifically to beneficiary health concerns or conditions. Some have specific eligibility requirements based on beneficiary category, plan, or status, and some are for specific beneficiary populations, while others offer services for specific health conditions. Some are limited to a certain number of participants or a certain geographic location. Examples are: clinical cancer trials, chiropractic health care programs, and WIC Overseas. If your Family has any special needs, be sure to ask TRICARE if there is a program that might assist you.

Life Insurance

Service Member's Group Life Insurance, or SGLI, is a program of low-cost group life insurance for service members on active duty, ready reservists, members of the National Guard, members of the Commissioned Corps of the National Oceanic and Atmospheric Administration and the Public Health Service, cadets and midshipmen of the four service academies, and members of the Reserve Officer Training Corps. SGLI coverage is available in increments of $50,000 to a maximum of $400,000. SGLI premiums are currently $.065 per $1,000 of insurance, regardless of the member's age.

Family Service Members' Group Life Insurance (FSGLI) is a program provided by the Department of Veterans Affairs for the spouses and dependent children of members insured under the Service Members Group Life Insurance (SGLI) program. It provides up to a maximum of $100,000 of insurance coverage for spouses and $10,000 for dependent children. More information can be found at http://myarmybenefits.us.army.mil/Home.html.

Death Benefits

The death gratuity is a one-time non-taxable payment to help survivors deal with the financial hardships that accompany the loss of a service member. The service member must designate the beneficiary of this gratuity on form DD93.

The benefit is a payment of $100,000 for survivors of those whose deaths occurred under the following conditions:

- a member of an armed force who dies while on active duty or while performing authorized travel to or from active duty

- a Reserve member of an armed force who dies while on inactive duty training (with exceptions)
- any Reserve member of an armed force who assumed an obligation to perform active duty for training, or inactive duty training (with exceptions) and who dies while traveling directly to or from that active duty for training or inactive duty training
- any member of a reserve officers' training corps who dies while performing annual training duty under orders for a period of more than thirteen days, or while performing authorized travel to or from that annual training duty; or any applicant for membership in a reserve officers' training corps who dies while attending field training or a practice cruise or while performing authorized travel to or from the place where the training or cruise is conducted; or
- a person who dies while traveling to or from or while at a place for final acceptance, or for entry upon active duty (other than for training), in an armed force, who has been ordered or directed to go to that place, and who has been provisionally accepted for that duty or has been selected for service in that armed force.

Dependency and Indemnity Compensation (DIC)

DIC is a tax-free monetary benefit paid to eligible survivors of military service members who died in the line of duty or eligible survivors of veterans whose death resulted from a service-related injury or disease.

If your Soldier dies while on active duty, you and your children will still receive your current medical benefits for three years at no cost, and then will pay the retiree rate for medical insurance indefinitely unless you remarry. Additionally, the Family of an active duty deceased Soldier may receive the Survivor's Benefit Plan (SBP) from the DoD, which is equal to 55 percent of your Soldier's retirement pay. This benefit is offset by the Dependency Indemnity Compensation (DIC) from the Veteran's Administration. Your survivor outreach specialist will guide you through the complicated formulas. Note that the SBP, while automatic during active duty, must be elected and paid for upon retirement. Spouses and eligible Family Members of active duty Soldiers will need to get new ID Cards, but will still have access to all on-post privileges, such as the PX and Commissary.

Post-9/11 GI Bill

The Post-9/11 GI Bill is an education benefit program specifically for military members who served on active duty on or after September 11, 2001. Depending on an individual's situation, provisions may include coverage of tuition and fees, a monthly housing allowance, a books and supplies stipend, Yellow Ribbon payments, rural benefit payments, and transferability to eligible immediate Family Members (spouse and children).

Active duty Soldiers who served at least ninety aggregate days on active duty after September 10, 2001, or served thirty continuous days on active duty after September 10, 2001, or were honorably discharged for a service-connected disability, are eligible for the Post-9/11 GI Bill. Active-duty service time required by graduates of a Service Academy or ROTC does *not* count toward the three years necessary to qualify for benefits.

The Post-9/11 GI Bill provides different percentage levels of education benefit depending on an individual's length of active duty service following September 10, 2001. Soldiers are eligible for up to thirty-six months of entitlement. Benefits are available for up to fifteen years from a Soldier's last period of active duty of at least ninety consecutive days. Soldiers released from active duty due to a service-connected disability after thirty days or more of continuous service are also eligible for benefits for fifteen years. This education benefit, unlike previous GI Bill versions, can be transferred to immediate

Family Members. The VA began accepting Post-9/11 GI Bill applications on August 1, 2009.

Approved training under the Post-9/11 GI Bill includes both undergraduate and graduate degrees, vocational/technical training, on-the-job training, flight training, correspondence training, licensing and national testing program, entrepreneurship training, and tutorial assistance. All training programs must be approved for GI Bill benefits.

Individuals who serve between ninety days and less than thirty-six months of aggregate active duty service are eligible for a percentage of the maximum benefit. For those Soldiers, the percentage level ranges from 40 to 90 percent of the basic benefit depending on length of service during the qualifying period. Those with service between ninety days and less than six months receive a 40 percent benefit; thirty to thirty-six months of service qualify for 90 percent.

Example: A Soldier with five months of qualifying service (at least ninety days, but less than six months) could receive 40 percent of the tuition benefit, 40 percent of the monthly housing allowance, and a maximum of $400 of the books and supplies stipend.

Benefit Earned Based on Qualifying Active Duty Service

Individuals serving an aggregate period of active duty after September 10, 2001, of:	**Includes entry level and skill training?**	**Percentage of Maximum Benefit**
At least 36 months	Yes	100
At least 30 continuous days on active duty (discharged due to service-connected disability)	Yes	100
At least 30 months, but less than 36 months	Yes	90
At least 24 months, but less than 30 months	Yes	80

Individuals serving an aggregate period of active duty after September 10, 2001, of:	Includes entry level and skill training?	Percentage of Maximum Benefit
At least 18 months, but less than 24 months	No	70
At least 12 months, but less than 18 months	No	60
At least 6 months, but less than 12 months	No	50
At least 90 days, but less than 6 months	No	40

Transfer of Benefits to Family Members

Any member of the Armed Forces (active duty or Selected Reserve, officer or enlisted), who is eligible for the Post-9/11 GI Bill and who meets the requirements listed below may elect to transfer the education benefits to a Family Member.

1. Has at least six years of service in the Armed Forces (active duty and/or Selected Reserve) on the date of approval and agrees to serve four additional years in the Armed Forces from the date of election.

2. Has at least ten years of service in the Armed Forces (active duty and/or Selected Reserve) on the date of approval, is precluded by either standard policy (Service or DoD) or statute from committing to four additional years, and agrees to serve for the maximum amount of time allowed by such policy or statute.

3. Is or becomes retirement eligible and agrees to serve an additional four years of service on or after August 1, 2012. A service member is considered to be retire-

ment eligible if he or she has completed twenty years of active Federal service or twenty qualifying years as computed pursuant to section 12732 of title 10 U.S.C.

4. Such transfer must be requested and approved while the member is in the Armed Forces.

Visit the VA website for more details about the Post-9/11 GI Bill and transferability to Family Members.

More VA Benefits

Soldiers who die while on active duty and veterans discharged under conditions other than dishonorable may be eligible for the following Department of Veterans Affairs (VA) burial benefits: burial in a VA national cemetery; government-furnished headstone or marker; Presidential Memorial Certificate; burial flag; and in some cases, reimbursement of certain burial expenses. The Soldier's surviving spouse, dependent children, and, under certain conditions, unmarried adult children, may be eligible for burial in a national cemetery. Additionally, many states have established state veterans cemeteries. Eligibility is similar to Department of Veterans Affairs (VA) national cemeteries but may include residency requirements. Even though they may have been established or improved with Government funds through VA's Veterans Cemetery Grants Program, state veterans cemeteries are run solely by the states. Visit http://www.cem.va.gov/grants/veterans_cemeteries.asp for more information.

The Veterans Administration Home Loan Program helps service members, veterans, and eligible surviving spouses become homeowners. For VA housing loan purposes, the term *veteran* includes certain members of the Army National Guard, the Army Reserve, Regular Army, and certain categories of spouses.

The VA also provides a home loan guaranty benefit and other housing-related programs to help you buy, build, repair, retain, or adapt a home for your own personal occupancy.

VA Home Loans are provided by private lenders, such as banks and mortgage companies. VA guarantees a portion of the loan, enabling the lender to provide you with more favorable terms.

Purchase Loans help you purchase a home at a competitive interest rate, often without requiring a down payment or private mortgage insurance. The length of your service or service commitment and/or duty status may determine your eligibility for specific home loan benefits. VA-guaranteed loans are available for homes for your own personal occupancy. To be eligible, you must have a good credit score, sufficient income, a valid Certificate of Eligibility (COE), and meet certain service requirements.

THRIFT SAVINGS PLAN (TSP)

This is the military version of a retirement savings plan and is optional. You must choose to participate. There are rules governing participation, how and when you can withdraw from participation. It functions much like a civilian-company based retirement savings plan. You are offered a variety of investment options from which you can choose. You may find more information concerning participation at www.tsp.gov/index.shtml.

THE LEGAL ASSISTANCE OFFICE

The Legal Assistance Office is there to help you with legal matters such as leases (rent), wills, powers of attorney (POA), and occasions where you have legal questions. The preparation of wills and powers of attorney are probably the two most-used services in the Legal Assistance Office. Keep these two items up-to-date and available at all times. Please be advised that although the Legal Assistance Office serves the entire Family, if the occasion should arise where you need legal advice in an action against your service member, such as separation or divorce, you may need to seek outside representation.

The Seasonal Tax Office

This office is available to help you prepare and file your taxes at no cost. Most of these offices open in late January. Each post is different, so please check with your installation as to location and times of service. Check your post newspaper for details. Many off-post tax services will also offer online simple tax preparation for service members at no charge. Whether you prefer to meet with someone face-to-face or you prefer to file by yourself, there are options available at little to no cost. Many of the online options can be found at www.militaryonesource.com (this site also provides information on many other benefits and services available to you).

Other Benefits

On-post housing is also a benefit available for military Families. As you receive your assignment, you can search for on-post housing. The military is increasingly relying on privatized housing, meaning the housing on post is managed by a private company. You can call the management company (or housing office) and they will give you an idea of what the wait time is like and what their procedures are. Policies differ from post to post as to when and how you can be placed on the wait list.

Space Available (Space-A) Travel—On a lighter note, for service members and their Families, traveling Space-A on military flights can be a great benefit, but you have to be flexible. Military planes (and planes contracted by the military) have mission assignments throughout the world and often offer empty seats to eligible passengers. Military flights are unpredictable and subject to delays and cancellations. You'll need to be prepared both financially and emotionally to change your plans at a moment's notice. But for many Space-A passengers, traveling to places like Hawaii, Alaska, Germany, Italy, or Japan at no or very low cost is worth the effort. In order to fly Space-A, eligible passengers must register (sign up) at the military passenger terminal from which they want to depart. Registration can be very competitive at some busy terminals, so be sure to sign up as early as you can. You can sign up on the terminal's register up to sixty days in advance. Some terminals accept fax or email sign up, but procedures vary by terminal. When you get to your destination, be sure to register for a return flight.

Available seats are offered to service members, retirees, certain DoD employees, and their eligible Family Members. Guard and Reserve members may also travel Space-A, but with restrictions. Eligible Family Members can travel without their active duty sponsor under certain circumstances, such as Environmental and Morale Leave or when their service member is deployed for more than 120 days. Traveling requires a bit more research and is, as the name suggests, based on space available. Information on Space-A Travel can be found at www.amc.af.mil/amctravel/index.asp and www.militaryonesource.mil/mwr?content_id=268596. The best thing to bring to Space-A Travel is a good attitude and patience.

Closer to home, you'll have the privilege of shopping for both your groceries and household items at your local commissary and PX. Both of these are constantly expanding their services to our Families, and often their prices can't be beat. Be sure to check out http://www.commissaries.com/click2go/index.cfm and http://shop.aafes.com/shop/.

Both offer tax-free shopping, but they do have a surcharge. You can bring visitors into the shopping centers, but only the ID card holder may make purchases.

No post would be complete without Family, Morale, Welfare, and Recreation (FMWR). Recreation and leisure programs include everything from sporting activities to music and theater programs, arts and crafts shops, tour and travel offices, and libraries. Profits from Army, Air Force Exchange Services (your PX) help support FMWR and fund a lot of the recreation areas on post as well as the concerts and tours.

Off post, you will find that a variety of businesses may offer military discounts. Many movie theaters, stores, and restaurants give discounts to Military ID Card holders. Some of these are advertised and some are not. Don't be afraid to ask if discounts are given to the military. Military.com is a good source that provides information about discounts offered to military service members and their Families.

As you may conclude, the subject of Army benefits is indeed a big world. This quick overview is just the tip of the iceberg regarding all the wonderful perks that come from joining the Army Family.

Helpful Websites

http://projects.militarytimes.com/benefits-handbook/
www.benefits.va.gov/benefits/
www.military.com/benefits
myarmybenefits.us.army.mil
www.militaryonesource.mil

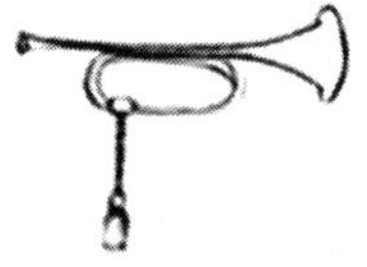

Chapter 15

The Next Chapter: Retirement

Sonia Lindsay

Retreat

Signals the end of the official day.

Is there life after the Army? Of course there is! Your Soldier served faithfully for twenty or thirty years and now it is time to write your Family's next chapter. The season of Army housing, stacks of moving boxes, serving units and chapels, and living in sometimes exotic (and sometimes really not-exotic) places is coming to a close. There is much to reminisce about, and much to prepare. Transitioning to retirement life is a great challenge for some, and for others a welcome relief. This major step requires prior planning for all involved, and an understanding of rules and regulations in order to navigate through mounds of paperwork and mandatory briefing sessions.

Will you become a Subject Matter Expert (SME) upon completion? No, but resources are presented to assist in understanding terminology and the transition process. Before proceeding, let's take a brief look into the past.

The Big Picture: Retirement Then and Now

When did the actual retirement plan come into existence? In 1900, Soldiers were approved privileges such as medical care and a percentage of basic pay as they left active duty service. Additionally, other benefits, such as commissary and exchange privileges, were offered.

Today, service members who remain on active duty for twenty or more years are eligible for military retirement pay and benefits. Retirees also retain other privileges, like the right to use post facilities such as the commissary and gym. The Military Retired Handbook (http://www.militaryhandbooks.com) is an excellent resource and guide that covers information from retirement pay, transition assistance, and life insurance to dependents, survivors, education, and training.

Getting Started—A To-Do List for Your Soldier

Reserve Component

For Reserve/COMPO2/COMPO3 Soldiers, the Point of Contact (POC) for retirement is in Human Resources Command (HRC), Fort Knox. You may contact the Human Resource Command (HRC) at Fort Knox, Kentucky, at 1-888-ARMYHRC (276-9472) or Human Resources Cmd, 1600 Spearhead Div Ave, AHRC-PD, Fort Knox, KY 40122-5400. You will also be required to contact the Soldier for Life Transition Assistance Program. The Army has created a Retirement Guide just for Army Reserve Soldiers and their Families. The twenty-six-page *Army Reserve Nonregular Retirement Information Guide* was written specifically to cover the unique circumstances of Reserve retirement. This guide helps the Reserve-component Soldiers understand the chronological steps they need to take before their actual retirement. The guide is intended to be distributed through the Reserve, but it can also be found online on both the Army G-1 Retirement Services homepage at http://www.armyg1.army.mil/rso/, under the "What's New" tab and on the special Army Knowledge Online site for Army Retirees at www.us.army.mil/suite/page/559734.

Active Duty

First, contact the human resources specialist at your personnel office to find out the exact date you will retire. Next, contact your Retirement Services Officer (RSO) on post for information on retirement benefits and entitlements, retired pay, the Survivor Benefit Plan

(SBP), health benefits, and for the pre-retirement briefing schedule. RSOs are listed at www.armyg1.army.mil/rso/rso.asp.

Also, contact your Soldier for Life Transition Assistance Program (SFL TAP), formerly known as the Army Career and Alumni Program (ACAP) or www.acap.army.mil.

Contact your local MTF for information about scheduling your pre-retirement physical. Don't delay; it can take a long time to get this appointment.

Retirement Services Officer

The installation Retirement Services Officer (RSO) is the source for information for retiring and retired Soldiers, their Families, and, ultimately, surviving spouses. Before retirement, go to your RSO for your **pre-retirement** and **Survivor Benefit Plan (SBP)** briefing. A Soldier and Family Members should attend the pre-retirement briefing twelve to twenty-four months before planned retirement. There is no prohibition against attending a briefing long before a retirement application is submitted and another shortly before an actual retirement date. After retirement, your RSO is your point of contact for assistance and for things like the installation retiree council, the annual Retiree Appreciation Day, and installation retiree newsletter.

Soldier for Life Transition Assistance Program

There are fifty-three locations serving Active and Reserve Component Soldiers worldwide, to include a Virtual Center, which is operational 24/7. Counselors provide extensive transition support to separating and retiring Soldiers, Department of Army Civilians, *and* their Family Members. Spouses are included in many of the services offered. Don't miss out! This is a valuable source of information and has programs tailored toward the unique needs of Active Component Soldiers, Reserve Component Soldiers, Army Wounded Warriors, Surviving Spouses, Caregivers, Army Military Retirees, Army

Veterans, Army Civilians, Army Family Members, and Employers. A Soldier can initiate available SFL TAP services two years prior to actual retirement date. SFL TAP provides the following services at all of its offices:

- Pre-separation Counseling. (Recorded on DD Form 2648, Pre-separation Counseling Checklist.) Soldiers are informed about transition services and benefits that are available to them. They are also offered assistance in developing an Individual Transition Plan (ITP) from highly qualified counselors. Public law mandates that Soldiers must receive Pre-Separation Counseling a minimum of ninety days prior to separation or retirement date.

- TAP Employment Workshops. These workshops are facilitated by Department of Labor staff members. The workshop provides attendees with the basic knowledge and skills to execute a successful job search. This includes the selection of a job search objective, résumé and cover letter preparation, networking, identification of job opportunities, interviewing, and salary/benefit negotiations. In order to enhance the participants' experience from this class, SFL TAP counselors provide various employment assistance seminars on private and federal employment opportunities.

- Individual Employment Counseling. Counselors assist clients in identifying a career objective, finalizing résumés and cover letters, completing employment applications, finding job opportunities, preparing for interviews and job fairs, dressing for success, and negotiating salary and benefits.

- Job Search Resources and Tools. Clients have the opportunity to use automated employer listings and tools to assist in writing résumé and cover letters and to complete online applications for federal employment. They can also participate in job fairs, career days, and use an extensive SFL TAP Reference Library.

- VA Benefits Briefings. These four-hour-long briefings are conducted by qualified VA counselors and are highly recommended for all separating and retiring Soldiers. The briefings cover all VA services and benefits available to veterans. Spouses are highly encouraged to attend with their service members and both the spouse and service member may attend these briefings more than once.

- Disability Transition Assistance Program (DTAP) Briefings. These two-hour long briefings are facilitated by VA Vocational Rehabilitation staff and should be attended by Soldiers who have or who are filing for disability due to their military service.

- The SFL TAP/ACAP Virtual Center is an immersive, three-dimensional, online environment where Soldiers can receive all the transition and education services that they would normally receive at a bricks-and-mortar SFL TAP Center. This can be accessed at www.acap.army.mil.

- Services after Retirement. Retired Soldiers and their ID card-carrying Family Members are eligible for SFL TAP services on a space-available basis for the rest of their lives.

Retirement Physical

Your Soldier's retirement physical (not applicable to Reservists unless on active duty) is required and should be obtained no more than four months and no less than one month before the retirement date or the start of transition leave. Contact your local Military Treatment Facility (MTF) for details and appointments.

If the Soldier is a Gulf War veteran, he or she is eligible for medical evaluation either through DoD's Comprehensive Clinical Evaluation Program (CCEP) or the Department of Veterans Affairs (VA)

Gulf War Registry (GWR). Consult the VA for more information on these programs online at www.va.gov; or by phone at 1-800-827-1000. OIF/OEF veterans qualify for special combat veteran eligibility for up to two years after their discharge from service.

For more information regarding services available to returning active duty, National Guard, and Reserve service members of Operations Enduring Freedom and Iraqi Freedom visit www.oefoif.va.gov/.

The Benefits Delivery at Discharge (BDD) Program is also available to those who need to apply for disability from the Department of Veterans Affairs (VA). BDD will accelerate receipt of VA disability benefits, since it allows a service member to apply for disability prior to retirement. It is a time-sensitive process and must be started 60-180 days prior to retirement to allow sufficient time to complete the application and medical examination. To learn more about BDD, contact your local Transition Assistance Office, SFL TAP Center, or call the VA at 1-800-827-1000.

Subjects to Study

1. **Combat-Related Special Compensation (CRSC).** A special payment for retirees with combat-related disabilities whose retired pay is reduced by disability pay received from the Department of Veterans Affairs (VA). https://www.hrc.army.mil/TAGD/CRSC.

2. **Concurrent Retirement and Disability Payments (CRDP).** A special payment for retirees rated by the VA as at least 50 percent disabled whose retired pay is reduced by VA disability pay. http://www.military.com/benefits/military-pay/concurrent-retirement-and-disability-pay-crdp-overview.html

3. **Dental Insurance.** The TRICARE Retiree Dental Program (TRDP) is a fee-for-service plan, funded entirely by enrollee-paid premiums. http://www.trdp.org/retirees/

4. **Dependency and Indemnity Compensation (DIC).** A VA tax-free benefit paid to surviving spouses and children of veterans who die of a service-connected disability. http://www.va.gov/opa/persona/dependent_survivor.asp

5. **Home of Selection.** The location to which household goods will be shipped at government cost upon your retirement. http://www.powershow.com/view/3b81be-YTI1M/Army_Preretirement_Briefing_powerpoint_ppt_presentation

6. **Retired Pay.** Payable during the retiree's lifetime; calculated by length of service, pay grade, and amount of active duty pay. http://www.dfas.mil/

7. **Survivor Benefit Plan (SBP).** An option for a retiree to elect to receive reduced retired pay so that payments can go to surviving spouse and/or children after the retiree's death. www.armyg1.army.mil/rso/sbp.asp

8. **TRICARE.** A three-option healthcare program available to eligible beneficiaries who are not yet Medicare eligible. www.tricare.mil

9. **TRICARE for Life (TFL).** A combination of TRICARE and Medicare coverage for Medicare-eligible, uniformed services beneficiaries. www.tricare.mil/tfl

10. **Veterans Benefits.** The Department of Veterans Affairs (VA) is your source for information on a host of programs including home loans and education. www.va.gov

11. **VA Disability Compensation.** Tax-free compensation from the VA, based on service-connected disability. http://www.benefits.va.gov/compensation/

12. **Veterans Group Life Insurance (VGLI)**. A life insurance policy available to those who had SGLI while on active duty. http://www.benefits.va.gov/insurance/resources_handbook_ins.asp

13. **Uniformed Services Family Health Plan (USFHP)**. A plan that serves enrolled retirees and Families in areas around former Public Health hospitals. www.usfhp.com

14. **Uniformed Services Former Spouses' Protection Act (USFSPA)**. A law pertaining to division of retired pay and election of SBP as determined by state courts. www.armyg1.army.mil/rso/docs/FSPA/usfspa.doc

Active Duty Retirement Pay—A Guide for Your Soldier

There are many factors that determine exactly how much your pension will be. Over the past twenty-five years, the government has made some significant changes to the military retirement system.

If you entered the service:

Prior to September 1980 you are eligible for the **Final Pay** retirement system.

Between September 8, 1980, and August 1986 you are eligible for the **High 36** system.

After August 1986 you are under the **REDUX** system, which means you have the option to choose either the **High 36** retirement system, or the **Career Status Bonus/REDUX (CSB)** retirement system. If you decline to make a choice you will automatically receive the High 36 retirement plan.

The Similarities

All of these retirement systems have a common thread: if you stay in the armed forces for twenty or more years, you are eligible to receive a pension based on a percentage of your basic pay, and if you stay in for forty years, you are eligible for 100 percent of your basic pay. But that's where the similarities end and the confusion really begins, because each of these systems determines your amount of pension differently.

The Differences

There are four major differences between the retirement systems. If you joined the military after August of 1986 you especially need to thoroughly understand these differences, because when you reach the fifteen-year mark in your military career, you will have to make a choice of a lifetime about which plan you want for yourself. The major differences are the basis for determining your highest earnings, the multiplier, the Cost of Living Adjustment, and the Career Status Bonus.

The Basis for Calculating Your Basic Pay

Although you have no choice in the basis for calculating your basic pay, it is a very important detail. For instance the **Final Pay** retirement system bases the amount of pension on a member's last month of pay. For example, if you retired at twenty years of service on the Final Pay retirement system, you received 50 percent of your final month's pay as your pension, and that percentage increases by 2.5 percent for each additional year of service.

Under the **High 36** and **CSB/REDUX** systems, a member's pension is based on the average of the highest thirty-six months' base pay. So if you retire at twenty years under these systems, you would get a percentage of the average of thirty-six months (three years) of your highest basic pay, and like the Final Pay system you would get an increase of 2.5 percent for every year that you stay in (past twenty years of service).

The Multiplier

The multiplier is the percentage of your base pay you receive for each year of service. For the **Final Pay and High 36** systems, you earn 2.5 percent per year of service. That means you get 50 percent for twenty years of service up to a maximum of 100 percent for forty years.

The multiplier for the **CSB/REDUX** system is 2 percent per year for the first twenty years, but you get an increase to 3.5 percent for each additional year past twenty. That means you get 40 percent for twenty years, but up to 100 percent for forty years.

The Cost of Living Adjustment (COLA)

All three retirement systems have an annual cost of living adjustment. This is a subtle, yet very important detail. Over the lifetime of your retirement, the cost of living adjustment could more than double your retirement check.

The COLA for the **Final Pay and High 36** systems is determined each year by the national Consumer Price Index. But the COLA for the CSB/REDUX retirement system is the Consumer Price Index minus 1 percent.

For Example: A retiree under the High 36 may have seen a COLA increase in his or her retirement check of 3.5 percent in 2007, while a retiree under the CSB/REDUX plan would have received a COLA increase of only 2.5 percent.

Note: There is one more twist to the COLA for the CSB/REDUX retiree. At age sixty-two, the COLAs and multiplier are readjusted so that the High 36 and CSB retirees get the same monthly pay.

The Bonus and the BIG Decision

Now the **CSB/REDUX** system gets a bit more complicated. Under this latest system, when you reach your fifteenth year of service, you **must** choose between taking the "CSB/REDUX" with a $30,000 cash bonus (approximately $21,000 after taxes) and a 40 percent pension check upon retirement at twenty years, or the High

36 retirement system with no bonus and a 50 percent pension check upon retirement at twenty years. This is a huge decision and cannot be made without some serious consideration and a clear understanding of the details. The following table gives a quick summary to help understand the differences between the retirement systems:

Retirement System	Basis	Multiplier	COLA	Bonus
Final Pay	Last Month's Basic Pay	2.5% for each Year of Service	CPI	No
High 36	Average of the Highest 36 Months Basic Pay	2.5% for each Year of Service	CPI	No
CSB REDUX	Average of the Highest 36 Months Basic Pay	3.5% for each Year over 20	CPI—1%	Yes

Reserve Retirement Pay

Reserve retirement is sometimes called nonregular retirement. Members who accumulate twenty or more years of qualifying service are eligible for Reserve retirement when they reach age sixty or, in some cases, a lesser qualifying age. There are two nondisability retirement plans currently in effect for Reserve qualified retirees. These are Final Pay plan and High 36 Month Average plan. There is no REDUX retirement plan under nonregular (Reserve) retirement.

The basic retirement formula is: Retired Pay Base x Multiplier percent.

Final Pay Plan

The retired pay base for a qualified Reserve retirement under the Final Pay plan is the monthly basic pay determined at the rates applicable on the day of retirement at the highest grade satisfactorily held during service. In other words, it is the rate of pay for the member's pay grade and years of service taken from the pay table in effect on the date that retired pay begins, regardless of when the member stopped participation.

The Final Pay plan uses a multiplier percentage that is two and a half times the years of creditable service. The creditable years of service for a Reserve retirement calculation is determined by the sum of all accumulated reserve points divided by 360.

High 36 Plan

The retired pay base for a qualified Reserve retirement under the High 36 retirement plan is the total amount of monthly basic pay to which the member was entitled during the member's high thirty-six months divided by thirty-six. This includes months to which the member would have been entitled if the member had served on active duty during the entire period. Usually this will be the average of the thirty-six months for the member's pay grade and years of service taken from the pay tables in effect for the thirty-six months immediately preceding the date that retired pay begins, regardless of when the member stopped participation.

The High 36 retirement plan uses a multiplier percentage that is the same as the Final Pay plan.

Years of Service

There are three categories for determining years of creditable service that have applicability to the computation of Reserve (nonregular) retired pay: one for determining when an individual is entitled to retired pay, one for determining the applicable active duty base pay upon which to compute retired pay, and one for determining the retired pay percentage multiplier. For Reserve retirements, these are generally different.

The first category we shall call "Years of Service for Retirement Entitlement." This category of years of service includes each one-year period in which the person has been credited with at least fifty points, as follows:

one point for each day of active service
one point for each attendance at a drill period
one point for each day of performing funeral honors duty
fifteen points for each year of membership in a Reserve component

Generally, a member retiring with a Reserve (nonregular) retirement must have twenty years of service for entitlement and he or she will receive a letter from the Service advising when this criteria has been met.

The second category we shall call "Years of Service for Pay Base." When combined with pay grade, YOS for pay base determines the active duty pay entitlement by defining the appropriate pay table cell, for example, E-4 over six years of service. This category of years of service includes all periods of active service and all periods of Reserve or National Guard service counted day for day. A unique feature of Reserve retirement is that the pay base is determined as though the Reserve member were serving on active duty immediately prior to retirement, thus the years of service continue to accumulate even after the member has entered the retired Reserve and continue until he or she actually begins receiving such pay (usually age sixty).

The third category we shall call "Years of Service for Retired Pay Percentage Multiple." YOS for retirement percentage multiple determines the years of service for computing the retired pay multiplier. This category of years of service includes all periods of active service (counted as one point for each day) plus all points earned through qualifying Reserve duty, not exceeding annual limits, divided by 360.

Retirement Age

A member is generally not eligible for Reserve (nonregular) retired pay until age sixty. However, any member of the Ready Reserve who is recalled to active duty or, in response to a national emergency, is called to certain active service after January 28, 2008, shall have the age sixty requirement reduced by three months for each cumulative period of ninety days so performed in any fiscal year after that date.

Application

Members eligible for Reserve retirement must request retired pay from the military department in which they last served. **Payment is not made until requested.**

SURVIVOR BENEFIT PLAN (SBP)

All retirees may choose to participate in the Survivor Benefit Plan or the Reserve Components Survivor Benefit Plan. These plans protect a Family financially in the event of the Soldier's death. Once a Soldier reaches sixty-two years of age, Social Security will likely provide additional benefits. Part of your Soldier's preretirement checklist will include an SBP Election appointment. It is important for you as a spouse to attend this particular counseling so you and your Soldier understand your options completely.

This program is designed to continue to provide up to 55 percent of the Soldier's retirement compensation to the spouse and/or children when the Soldier passes away. There is a premium for this program that can be deducted from retirement pay. The premium is based on the amount of retirement compensation received. If this coverage is not elected, all retirement pay will cease when the Soldier dies. Coverage can be provided at the maximum of 55 percent or a reduced rate. The Soldier cannot deny this coverage without consent of the possible beneficiary (typically the current spouse).

Participation in SBP is not a subject to be taken lightly. There are six election categories: (1) spouse; (2) spouse and children; (3) children only; (4) former spouse; (5) former spouse and children; and (6) natural person with an insurable interest. The decision you and your spouse make could greatly impact your Family's financial future and is likely the most important retirement-related decision you'll make. Your election is generally permanent and irrevocable. It was designed to provide a monthly annuity to eligible survivors after a retired Soldier's death. *Retired pay stops with the death of the retired Soldier.* If the retired Soldier declined SBP coverage, no continuing benefits are payable to the surviving Family Members. In short, SBP provides income protection for survivors of retired Soldiers. SBP is a cost-sharing program between the government and the retired Soldier, with the government subsidizing the cost. Please note, SBP *is income protection; it is not life insurance;* it is not a savings plan; it is not an investment program; and it is not available through a commercial or private company. It does not replace life insurance but could be supplemented by life insurance. Each individual's financial situation is different. Remember that SBP is government-subsidized and inflation-protected. SBP costs are not based on your age, your state of health, or on economic forecasts. SBP is the sole means by which survivors can receive a portion of military retired pay. It provides a tax shelter since the premiums are deducted from retired pay before income taxes are calculated. SBP is guaranteed by the US government and it is payable for the lifetime of the surviving spouse. **The election for SBP must be done prior to retirement. There is a one-year window between the twenty-fifth and thirty-sixth month following commencement of retired pay to terminate SBP participation, with spouse consent.**

Military Records

Soldiers and Families should obtain copies of their medical and dental records prior to retiring; this includes all outpatient care at Army military treatment facilities, civilian providers, and treatment received while deployed. Keep copies for yourself as these records will be turned in when your Soldier processes out. Once they leave your possession it may be difficult to obtain copies. It is also advisable to retain any paper and electronic copies of military personnel records you have. These could be difficult to obtain once they have been forwarded to the personnel records center.

Identification Cards

The Soldier and all eligible Family Members will be required to obtain new ID cards upon retirement to reflect your new duty status.

Use of Facilities

Retired Soldiers and Family Members are authorized to use facilities on military installations when adequate space is available. The capability to accommodate retired Soldiers varies at each military installation. The Installation Commander determines whether retired personnel may use the facilities. Generally, retired personnel are accommodated providing their use of the facilities does not present any hardship on active duty Soldiers.

Your Soldier's Retirement Timetable

Following is a suggested timetable for accomplishing some of your retirement out-processing tasks. Your installation RSO or your military personnel officer can provide a more detailed checklist that addresses local installation requirements. SFL TAP offers a detailed preparation timeline starting at twelve to twenty-four months from your retirement date. Be sure to get yours and use it!

Time Frame	**Action**
ASAP after decision	Contact the installation Retirement Services Officer (RSO) to arrange a retirement and Survivor Benefit Plan (SBP) briefing.
ASAP after decision	Contact the Soldier for Life Transition Assistance Program (SFL TAP) Office for job transition/résumé help.

4 months prior to	Initiate retirement physical prior to transition leave or retirement.
3 months prior to	Study medical and dental care options for retirees; consider purchasing a TRICARE supplement if needed.
3 months prior to	Make an appointment with the Staff Judge Advocate to update your will.
2 months prior to	Contact transportation for household goods shipment; must have orders.
2 months prior to	Complete DD Form 2656, Data for Payment of Retired Personnel (includes SBP election). A DD Form 2656-1 is needed if a former spouse SBP election is being made.
2 months prior to	Complete VA Form 21-526, Application for Compensation from Department of Veterans Affairs.
2 months prior to	Complete DD Form 2860, Application for Combat-Related Special Compensation (CRSC), if applicable.
1 month prior to	Obtain SF 1199A, Direct Deposit Sign-Up Form, for electronic transfer of retired pay to financial institution (needed only if changing financial institution).
1 week prior to	Initiate action to obtain retired ID cards.
Within 120 days after	Convert SGLI to VGLI (VA sends application), if desired. Consider joining military service associations and remain active in support of retiree issues.

As you can see from all the information and websites (listed at the end of the chapter), the Army offers a great deal of help to make your transition a smooth one. As you can also see, by the time you get through all the counseling, paperwork, and briefings, you will have earned a vacation. No matter how prepared you are, your new life might be an adjustment, but by now you and your Chaplain are the King and Queen of Adjustment! What a life it's been, and what a life it's going to be. Your service to God and country is appreciated.

"I can no other answer make, but, thanks, and thanks."

—William Shakespeare

Retirement Reflections from Spouses and Chaplains

From Our Chaplains

Can't say enough good about the VFW liaison person—definitely talk to them prior to starting the process.

Start early in your career to seek medical care, and have conditions documented in your official file. (Do not avoid documentation under the guise of "sucking it up and driving on.")

Start early in your retirement window with transition planning (up to two years before retirement); seek SFL TAP information and ask friends who are retiring ahead of you.

Search for either the VA or VFW retirement counselor (volunteer coordinator) and listen to his wisdom as someone who has helped scores of people navigate the difficult maze of retirement paperwork and process.

Ensure that the benefit recipient has *all* medical issues documented in writing and included in the official medical record.

From Our Spouses

Lessons Learned

Sandy: Plan, plan, plan ahead! My husband knew that he would like to continue working in ministry. It took time to see where that desire would lead. He started researching online, in magazines, and talking with people to see what was in the "civilian world" that would interest him. This process took about a year. When we separated from the Army we knew what ministries we would be involved in next. The last two or three years you are in the military, live on what you think your retirement income will be. Save, save, save the rest. You will need it. It is a huge adjustment. Get your own life insurance while you are still in good health. It is very expensive to get it when you get out/retire and so much cheaper when you are young and in good health. Save, save, save ahead! Have enough to pay off a house or purchase one and rent it out while you are in the service. It was great to have our house paid off when we retired.

Merial: I wish I had paid more attention during the retirement briefing. Because I was hospitalized two months before our leaving, I forgot to do many things—especially request my health records. With all of the moving plans and retirement ceremony requirements in addition to my health challenges, some things fell through the cracks. So my lesson learned was that even with the best advance planning, unexpected things can crop up to interrupt. Several years ago a senior Chaplain's spouse gave me a great piece of advice—never let your husband retire without a job! I watched several friends struggle with going from being a respected, senior Chaplain to someone who could not be hired. Therefore, we planned ahead and that has made our transition much smoother than many experienced.

What I Miss Most about the Army

Merial: The people and friends we made throughout our career. Because the Army is such a transient experience, I was used to moving. But I always looked forward to reconnecting to friends.

Sandy: I miss how easy it was to make friends. This was not how I felt the first couple of moves. I thought my life as I knew it would never be the same because of leaving or being left. I learned that I was given the opportunity to be a friend everywhere we were stationed. It became necessary to make friends fast when we knew we would move again in two to three years. Now, I find that no one is in a hurry to get to know me. I have had to slow down and look for opportunities to be a friend. If we had moved closer to Family, it might have been easier or it might not. I am learning to relax and take things slower.

The Actual Retirement Transition

Merial: Our last year was full of wonderful opportunities to mentor new Chaplains and their spouses. As the commandant's wife at USACHCS, I was able to interact with some of the best senior spouses and help welcome new spouses into the military life. Our first year of retirement was very busy for my husband while he learned a vocation—teaching. This was so different from his role as a Chaplain that he spent many hours mastering this new learning curve. Consequently, it didn't feel like what I had expected—a slower-paced life. Instead, I found myself thrust into a new environment without the supports I had come to know in the military.

Sandy: Our last year of service was very busy at my husband's office. He was doing four jobs as there was a shortage of personnel. That ended abruptly the last month as he was going through the retirement processing. There were others waiting to replace him, and they did not need him at the office anymore. It was not done to be mean; it is the nature of the military. It was very hard so we started cleaning out his files and shredding papers not needed anymore. We looked at the stuff we had accumulated over the years and asked ourselves what we needed in our next phase of life. We gave away or got rid of a lot of things. It is great not to be loaded down with things you do not need.

What I Love the Most about Retirement

Merial: The permanency—the knowing that I will not be moving or looking for new housing or uprooting Family again. Paradoxically, this is also one of the most challenging aspects of our new life. Because I was so used to the temporary, I find I have to relearn how to think about everything. While in the Army, I quickly unpacked and made a comfortable environment for my Family. If I was unhappy it wasn't a great problem because we would be leaving soon and I could start over. Now there are no "start overs." I find that I am taking longer to make new purchases or even hang pictures. The permanency of the experience intimidates me and makes me hesitate more than when we were active duty.

Sandy: My husband and I spent time over the years being each other's best friend. When we left the service we went on a three-month trip visiting friends and doing fun things. On a car trip you have a lot of time to talk and plan. It was great because we both like each other. Now that we are in our home, it is still fun. I am excited to see what God is doing in our lives.

And One More Bit of Retirement Wisdom

Sandy: I realized about a month after we began retirement living in our home, that my husband was experiencing, for the first time, what I experienced every time we moved. He did not have a built-in place to go every day. He had to find a new normal. I told him that he could only ask me five questions a day. For thirty years he did not care how I ran the home, and now what I did was new, and it was important to him to figure out. My life had not changed—only my location (which had happened over fifteen times in our military career). My husband's life had changed big time. During this time of adjustment, let laughter and joy be your companion, and remember that your spouse is your friend. When things get tense, take a break and do something fun. It will all come together and God is still God.

Retiree Websites

- **Army Retirement Services**—Provides information on benefits and entitlements to active duty personnel preparing for retirement. (http://www.armyg1.army.mil/rso/default.asp)

- **DFAS Online Account Access**—myPay allows management of pay information and statements. (https://mypay.dfas.mil/mypay.aspx)
- **Defense Finance and Accounting Service (DFAS)**—Home page for Retired and Annuitant pay information. (http://www.dfas.mil/retiredmilitary.html)
- **Department of Veterans Affairs**—A resource that provides information on VA programs, veterans benefits, and VA facilities worldwide. (www.va.gov)
- **TRICARE for Life**—TRICARE for Life is Medicare wraparound insurance coverage. (http://tricare.mil/Welcome/Plans/TFL.aspx)
- **The Association for Service Disabled Veterans (ASDV)**—Focuses upon opportunities for disabled veterans exploring business operations and entrepreneurial programs. (http://www.asdv.org/index2.html)
- **The Center for Women Veterans**—Wide range of information and links for women veterans. (http://www.va.gov/womenvet/)
- **The Military Officers Association of America (MOAA)**—Operates extensive transition center services, which include: weekly job bulletins, career fairs, search databases, network contacts, and worldwide transition lectures. (www.moaa.org)
- **VA Health Care**—Health information with tools for veterans and Families. (www.va.gov/health)
- **eBenefits**—DoD and VA portal that is a one-stop shop for benefits-related online tools and information. eBenefits includes a catalog of links to information on other websites about military and veteran benefits and provides a personalized My eBenefits workspace. (https://www.ebenefits.va.gov/ebenefits-portal/ebenefits.portal)

Transition Assistance Websites

- **Benefits Delivery at Discharge (BDD)**—BDD enables Soldiers to apply for Department of Veterans Affairs (VA) disability compensation benefits prior to retiring or separating from active duty. (www.benefits.va.gov /BENEFITS/factsheets.asp)
- **Soldier for Life Transition Assistance Program (SFL TAP)**—https://www.acap.army.mil/default.aspx
- **Department of Labor One-Stop Career Center**—More than three thousand One-Stop Career Centers across the nation are poised to help service members and Families with employment and training. (www.servicelocator.org)
- **National Resource Directory**—Departments of Defense (DoD), Labor (DoL), and Veterans Affairs (VA) web-based network of care coordinators, providers and support partners offering more than ten thousand medical and nonmedical services and resources for wounded, ill, and injured service members, veterans, their Families, Families of the fallen, and those who support them. https://www.nrd.gov/
- **My Health*e*Vet**—My Health*e*Vet offers veterans, active duty Soldiers, their dependents, and caregivers anywhere, anytime Internet access to VA health care information and services. (https://www.myhealth.va.gov)
- **Pre-Retirement Counseling Guide**—The sixty-page pamphlet provides comprehensive military service retirement information. http://army.com/sites/army.com/files /HandbookforRetiringSoldiersandFamilies2009.pdf
- **Soldiers' Benefits Services (SBS)**—The Army's official one-stop, web-based resource for all benefits information. (http://myarmybenefits.us.army.mil/)

- **Traumatic Service Members' Group Life Insurance—** Helps severely injured Soldiers through their time of need with a one-time payment. (https://www.hrc.army.mil)
- **DoDTAP Transition Assistance—**The Transition Assistance Program (TAP) provides information, tools, and training to ensure Service members and their spouses are prepared for the next step in civilian life whether pursuing additional education, finding a job in the public or private sector, or starting their own business. (https://www.dodtap.mil/)

Tool Kit

Every army spouse eventually acquires a tool kit to aid in assembling (and disassembling and reassembling) furniture, hanging pictures, filling the nail holes, and other practical tasks. Here, we offer you some *intangible* tools—resources and wisdom—to help you build a solid foundation of lifeskills for the journey ahead. We hope you will find something useful, and we encourage you to choose your favorite ideas and pass them along.

Crisis, Grief, and the Chaplain Spouse

Brenda Shaw

By virtue of being human, the experiences of crisis and grief are a part of our lives. The Army Chaplain spouse encounters those with wounds of heart while living in the realm of Soldiers and their Families. It's helpful to be aware that people may experience a significant sense of loss, and suffer under extreme emotional distress, in cases of perceived, anticipated, or actual loss from many types of difficult life changes. Separation or divorce, loss of other key relationships, empty nest or crises in parenting at any age of the child, serious mental or physical illness, significant changes in financial situations, and realization that one's life goals may never be met (as in a loss of purpose) are all situations which can cause huge upheaval. The extreme stress experienced by someone who has suffered great loss, or the threat of that loss, can for a time affect the person's mental and physical well-being. Physiological changes take place in the person as the natural response to great stress. The brain may undergo changes, resulting in inability to focus, concentrate, remember certain things, problem-solve, or make decisions (in children as well as adults, the ability to learn may be temporarily impaired).

The brain seems to set aside the not-so-essential functions to cope with the stressful or shocking situation at hand. It may feel like being in a mental fog. As part of the body's response to the increase in stress hormones, the person may suffer digestive problems (including stomachaches), poor sleep, a greater likelihood of becoming ill, and even problems in coordination—making one more accident-prone.[1]

Dr. Elisabeth Kübler-Ross's "Five Stages of Grief" theory helps us to better understand how people emotionally respond as they journey through their experience of significant loss. Since all people are individuals, each unique and complex, no two experiences of grief will be the same. Some do not experience all of the stages, and many repeat or overlap stages. Time spent in any stage is variable.[2]

1. Denial. Words like *shock*, *disbelief*, or *feeling numb* may describe feelings in this stage. The loss does not seem real. The "mental fog" of thinking may be overwhelming. Denial is not deliberate, and it is a helpful self-defense mechanism of the person's brain, to allow a more gradual comprehension of the loss, and to help "pace" the person through such a difficult journey.

2. Anger. The grieving person may lash out with words and emotion very unlike his or her usual self. Those receiving the anger may be caught off guard, and should not take this personally. The anger may be directed at other Family, friends, the Chaplain, or anyone else. It is easier, at this point, for the person to feel the angry emotions than to feel the terribly sorrowful ones. Brain changes under stress can involve temporary personality changes.[3] Anger will subside more quickly if allowed to be vented or expressed.

3. Bargaining. Bargaining may be more likely when there is an anticipated loss, such as with one's own, or a close loved one's terminal illness, or severe injury. Thoughts or questions arise, such as, "If I try to become a bet-

ter person, then maybe things will get better, turn around?" and "What if . . . ?" Guilt may become significant in this stage, as the grieving person recalls or imagines wrongs said or done.

4. Depression. This is the stage we tend to associate with the word *grief*. The mental anguish, heartache, trial, and deepest woes of sorrow prevail through this stage. The person may feel numb, again . . . may be in mental fogginess again . . . may need to be left alone, or may need *not* to be left alone. It's important to note that we shouldn't try to rush someone through grief, even with the good intention of hoping to help alleviate suffering. In sharing others' sorrow, we may try to bring cheer for our own comfort, but that is counterproductive to the person's healing. The stage of Depression is a necessary part of the grief experience, in order for healing to come.

5. Acceptance. This does not necessarily mean that the one in grief is back to normal, or doing great. Acceptance means the loss has become a reality for the person. Fresh air can be breathed in again. Maybe a fairly normal way of life has resumed in the household. There is hope again for the future. Since grief is about how one feels for the loved one who has passed on, grief will be, in a sense, with the person throughout life.

Taking into account these five stages, what kinds of things can we say to express our care and concern to the one who grieves? Author, speaker, and death and grief expert David Kessler suggests what to say and what not to say, to someone in grief. He also recommends keeping in mind:

- Context—Are you in public, where your comment may bring the one in grief to tears?

- Timing—Are you saying something to the person as if he or she should respond with a smile while he or she is very much still in depression?
- Appropriateness—If you don't know the person well, be careful not to cross personal boundaries.

Things not to say include:

- He is in a better place.
- It could be worse.
- There's a reason for everything.
- You should feel better by now.
- I know how you feel.
- Be strong.
- It was his time to go.
- Look at the good side.

Expressions of support and care:

- I'm so sorry for your loss.
- I wish I had the right words, but do know I care.
- You will be in my thoughts and prayers.
- My favorite memory of (the lost one) is . . .
- I'm just a phone call away.
- I'm here for you . . . we all need help at times like these.

- I'm usually up late/early, if you need anything.
- Speaking no words, but comforting with your presence.[4]

What Can You, as the Chaplain Spouse, Do to Help?

If the grieving person is a Chaplain spouse or a Chaplain, are you the Senior Chaplain spouse, or appropriate spouse to take the lead? If you cannot take the lead, ask the next most senior spouse if she or he would like to lead a team to serve the grieving Family. If the grieving person is part of your unit or Family Readiness Group, there may already be a designated spouse leader. Being a team player in support of those in your unit (including giving support to your commander's spouse) is always a good thing. In any case, do find out what the needs of those in grief are before making a plan to serve. Find out if a helping team of some sort is already in place. Perhaps extended Family is present, but leaving the area soon. You might join a group already serving, take over when that group leaves or finishes, or start a team—all contingent upon the grieving one wanting to be helped by you or your group of willing servers. Be sure to ask first.

Once you are cleared to serve, try to assess what the needs of the grieving person/Family are. These needs may fall under some of the following categories:

Meals

- Inquire about dietary restrictions
- Arrange a sign-up/schedule for meals (www.takethema meal.com, or at www.foodtidings.com.)
- Ask the grieving person for preferences for drop-off times, and communicate to those who will be delivering meals
- Bring foods in disposable containers if possible

- Provide foods that can be frozen and eaten later
- Try to avoid duplicating menus
- If appropriate, include child-friendly foods
- Pace deliveries so there is not too much or too little being sent

Transportation may include driving the grieving one to and from appointments, especially someone with distressed memory or focus. Do children need transportation to or from school, to or from lessons or sports, or to a house of worship?

Household tasks may include helping the person pay bills; doing house chores or laundry; helping with funeral arrangements, or with arrangements for any extended Family coming in; keeping a record of any memorials/flowers given in honor of the lost one; or running miscellaneous errands, including buying groceries.

Child Care: Does the grieving person need a break, some rest (especially if sleep overnight is difficult to get), or other help in caring for the children? Would you like to include the grieving children in activities with your own children? Do the children need regular or intermittent help with their studies/projects/homework? Is there a teen who could use an open ear?

Needs of the heart, for companionship, may already be filled by significant others. However, it may be that the grieving person is fairly new to the area, or for other reasons does not have close friends living nearby. Does the grieving one need a supportive person/companion to be physically present? How often? Would the person like to have a trustworthy friend to call to talk with, and/or cry to, especially early in the morning, or late at night? Does she need privacy, at least at this point? Sometimes a most beneficial comfort given, and easiest for the grieving one to receive, involves just sitting beside the grieving one in silence. Just being there. Or being a good listener. Encouraging with comforting words may be helpful. Showing love to his or her children may comfort. If he or she would like hugs, that physical support could be given. You may want to offer to write the thank-you notes.

If you know of others who have suffered a similar type of loss and are willing to share their hearts with the one now in grief, you could leave their names and phone numbers or emails, giving the grieving one the option/possibility of connecting with others who can relate. You could also be a liaison between the grieving one and the team of servers, be a bridge between the grieving one and the unit, or connect the extended Family with the Army community side of things. Options for serving to meet needs of the heart in interpersonal relations abound.

Problem solving can be a great help. Difficulties and unforeseen challenges will arise for the grieving Family. Offering your problem-solving skills and creative thinking can assist in overcoming these obstacles.

Spiritual comfort is a soothing balm to those who have religious faith. As Chaplain spouses, many of us see ourselves as having a vocation of encouraging others in matters of the soul. However, being sensitive and respectful to all others is very important. It is best to first determine whether your offers of spiritual support are welcome. Providing spiritual support for someone in grief or crisis, appropriate to the grieving one's faith, makes a difference for that person's physical and emotional well-being. An offer to pray for those in grief can enhance their healing and wellness.

Meeting social needs may occur naturally, as interactions with others take place over the course of the day, or week . . . or may not occur naturally (especially if the grieving one has been isolated and becomes ready to see more of others). Particularly during the Acceptance stage of grief, you may want to offer a pleasant drive in the countryside, go walking together on post, have lunch or dinner out together, or invite the grieving Family to join yours for an afternoon or evening of recreation.

Gifts: If you like to show caring with giving gifts, you could provide a gift card to a nearby restaurant for a meal out. Other ideas for gifts can include a green plant, a CD of soothing music, an item for personal physical comfort, a book of poetic or spiritual passages, or even a gift card for a massage. You'll likely think of more ideas, especially if you know the person fairly well.

Pets, gardens, and lawns are all things that need care even during seasons of grief. Practical help with all of these may be needed.

If you are able, try to attend the memorial service, ceremony, or funeral service, even if you are not personally acquainted with the Family. Your physical presence, in honor and respect for the lost one, as well as in showing care for the survivors, is an important support and comfort. Leaving a condolence card is also a kindness. Sometimes the Family knows few people in the area, so your presence means even more. With a genuine heart of love and concern, many Chaplain spouses have comforted strangers.

A note of encouragement can still be sent even at a later date—there is never a wrong time to show care for a person in grief. As time goes on, some sources of help will typically fade away, yet those who grieve may still be in the stage of Depression. Support after the storm can be very helpful.

In whatever way you serve, do remember to remain a confidential resource, unless the person in grief or crisis requests your disclosure to someone else, like the Chaplain or other professional counselor. Keep in mind, also, that the Chaplain, as an Army clergyperson, is the only DoD counselor who provides absolute confidentiality for counselees. As always, as you serve, be careful to avoid an inappropriate level or type of emotional or physical intimacy, and check with parents before hugging their children.

Is there a time when you should seek professional help for the person, especially if he or she is not already connected with a Chaplain, community religious leader, or other type of counselor? If you observe that someone in extreme grief is unable to take care of his or her own physical needs, including hygiene, or those of the children, do seek help from a professional, preferably the Chaplain of the unit, or a Chaplain the person is familiar with. The person may need professional therapeutic help and may be willing for you to make the connection with a professional at this point. If the person is not willing or agreeable for you to make the contact, but truly seems to need professional assistance (as noted above, if health is at risk), do make the contact, and the Chaplain can further evaluate the situation and make a determination.

In an acute crisis situation, in which the person is speaking of taking his or her own life (the person has answered your specific question, "Are you thinking of taking your own life?" with a yes), do get help immediately, through the on-call duty Chaplain. While awaiting that help, there are a few things you can do. Be gentle, remain calm and nonjudgmental, and listen earnestly, giving the person your full attention. Stay with the person till help arrives, or if you cannot, bring in someone else. Do not leave the person alone. The Army's acronym, ACE, stands for "Ask, Care, and Escort." Escorting could mean staying until help arrives, or taking the person to a professional. Give reassurance that he or she will be supported through this crisis.

What are some other resources the Chaplain spouse should be aware of for sharing with those in need? There are several helpful organizations either already at work, or readily available to assist, in time of need. When a Soldier is severely wounded or killed, there is a procedure in place for the notification of the primary next of kin (usually the spouse). This notification process falls under the commander's domain, and usually involves the unit's Chaplain. In some Family Readiness Groups, the commander of the unit chooses various volunteers to become specifically trained for service on a CARE (Casualty Response) Team. If a CARE Team is in place in your unit, and the spouse in crisis or grief wants the assistance of the CARE Team, the Team will serve the person or Family over the short-term, providing for any basic needs such as meals, childcare, or other service of immediate importance, until the extended Family arrives to help, or until another type of helping team is available to serve.

More Resources Include:

Gold Star Wives of America, Inc. (for widows and widowers), www.goldstarwives.org.

The Army Emergency Relief organization, which may provide financial assistance in times of financial crisis or other need, at www.aerhq.org/dnn563/, or by phone at 703-428-0000, between 0730 and 1530 Mondays through Fridays, or toll free at 866-878-6378.

The American Red Cross, which links Family Members during emergencies, and helps connect military Families with local community resources, found at www.redcross.org/what-we-do/support-military-families.

Army One Source provides a broad base of types of information, which may be of assistance, especially including what may be more geographically challenging for Army National Guard and Army Reserve Soldiers and Families, at www.myarmyonesource.com/default.aspx.

Military One Source, at www.militaryonesourceeap.org/achievesolutions/en/mos/Home.do, which gives information and/or services on managing life events, financial and legal concerns, health and relationships, and so on. If one would like a consultant in a time of crisis instead of, or in addition to, calling the Chaplain (also available 24/7), the military crisis line is available 24/7at 1-800-273-8255 (Option 1).

Army Community Services can be found online through Army One Source, or locally at most Army installations, and offers many free programs and classes for Soldiers and spouses (including Army Family Team Building [AFTB], in particular), which promote life skills for preventing or dealing with various stressors/challenges, as well as for improving skills in communication, group dynamics, and so on.

For acute crisis intervention, in the event of someone threatening suicide, a local suicide hotline number would be good to have on hand. The National Suicide Prevention Lifeline (in the USA), also called the "Military Crisis Line," is 1-800-273-8255 (TALK), press "1." Also, National Suicide Hotlines at the http://www.suicidepreventionlifeline.org/getinvolved/locator, may be helpful for finding local help with this type of crisis. The on call duty Chaplain is always available in times of crisis.

Resources that are unofficial, yet closest to us, may often be some of the most helpful. Though already mentioned, these include our fellow spouses in the Army community, especially fellow Chaplain spouses, unit or FRG spouses, specific volunteers from a chapel or house of worship, neighbors of the person in crisis or grief, and local clergy, especially our wonderfully trained and caring Chaplains.

Chaplain spouses are people of hope. We are privileged to bring comfort and help to others, through the storms of grief and crisis.

Thank you, Chaplain spouse, on behalf of all those who cannot now thank you, but someday will . . . for all you do in giving of yourself, compassionately. Your service makes an important difference. Thank you for serving your own Soldier and Family. You are a valuable member of the Chaplain Corps Family, and of the greater Army community!

COMMUNICATION

Lori Ludwig

The Army Chaplain Family will have opportunities beyond measure to interact with people from cultures across our country and across the world. We are also in a position of being observed, whether or not we are at our best. Part of presenting ourselves well involves communicating wisely and clearly.

GOOD COMMUNICATION: WHAT IS IT?

Good communication is a learned skill. Communication can be described as sharing with and receiving information from others, but is much more than that. When we communicate, we share a bit of who we are with people. If you are a new Army Chaplain's spouse, you are about to embark on a new adventure, and having good communication skills will aid you on this journey.

Have you ever participated in a conversation in which you knew the person wasn't really listening to you? How did you feel? By contrast, have you ever been part of a conversation in which you were not listening? Sometimes we get distracted and really don't pay attention.

Tips for Effective Face-to-Face Communication

Body Language: Keep good eye contact, and maintain an interested posture toward the person with whom you are communicating. Be aware of what your body is saying.

Active Listening: When the other person is speaking, pay attention by repeating what the person said to ensure that you understand correctly. This is not the time for you to be thinking of your response, though we have all been guilty of this.

Respond Thoughtfully: After you are certain you understand what the person is saying, you can respond thoughtfully and intelligently.

Ask Questions: If you have questions of that person, ask. Don't make judgments or assumptions.

Be Authentic: You have something to offer, so don't be afraid to be yourself. Genuineness inspires trust and depth in conversation.

Avoid Gossip: In ministry, people will sometimes share private information with Chaplains or Chaplain spouses. Please be respectful of this. *Chaplains pledge confidentiality; spouses should keep the same high standard, even among other Chaplain spouses.* In social situations, we should be good examples of kindness. Pass up every opportunity to gossip, and encourage those around you to do the same. Redirecting a conversation at the right time can save a lot of heartache.

THE ARMY: ARE THEY SPEAKING A DIFFERENT LANGUAGE?

Soldier: Meeting with the 1SGT and CO after the VTC to discuss FTX. I need ACUs for IG inspection and TA50 for the AO. No chow necessary; will have MRE at CP.

Spouse: I am going to check the APO and stop by ACS and USO. It is time to inspect the POV ASAP. I saw the OIC of the BDE at the PX and he is going TDY before we PCS. Do you want to do a DITY? HH6 is willing!

Soldier: Hooah!

You may think you will never understand what folks are saying around you, but sooner than you can imagine, you will be tossing around acronyms with the best of them.

As you listen to and are a part of conversations within the Army, you will find a great resource in the more experienced spouses around you. They can help you learn this new "language." It's a good idea to be aware of others' rank and position, and to address people respectfully. Use a senior person's first name only after he or she gives you permission. Military words and acronyms are constantly evolving. Don't be overwhelmed—you will be learning this language for many years!

Social Media and Email

Digital communication is easy and fast. It can be a great resource. Most of us have at least one email account and a Facebook page. Many tweet on a regular basis. Instagram, Vine, YouTube, Skype, and more give us unprecedented access to others and them to us. Though electronic media can be time-consuming, it is a great gift to Families who may be separated by deployment or duty station. Below are several tips that you may find helpful with regard to these methods of communication.

- Often units and installations will have their own Facebook pages and will post information on these sites. Checking them regularly is a good idea.
- Email is a great source of communication, so your spouse's unit and the UMT (Unit Ministry Team) will often ask for your email address to communicate with you.
- Be careful what you post on social media sites and personal blogs, especially with regard to Operational Security (OPSEC). Sometimes we want to post the who, what, when, and where of our lives, but it is not always a safe thing to do, especially during deployment. Always choose the most secure privacy settings available on social media.
- It is very difficult to convey tone in an email, so when you read something that may appear to be negative or rude,

be sensitive to intent or ask for clarification—don't just assume you understand it.

- Respect confidentiality. When someone shares a prayer request or something in confidence, it should never be posted or shared via email or Facebook without express permission from the person. Double check.

- As a Chaplain's spouse you represent your spouse and the Chaplain Corps. We all want to be free to express our personal views when it comes to politics and the news, but it is easy to get swept up in outrage or strong opinions or feelings of injustice. Try to remember that there is almost always more than one side to every story and temper your comments accordingly. Try to determine the actual facts about news before you post a public response on social media. Adding fuel to the fire of a sensitive issue doesn't help.

Relationship and Team Building: Moving Past "Hello, My Name Is . . ."

Sara Fisher, Crystal Niehoff, and Cecilia Thomas

Relationship Building

Unless you were raised in a military Family, you're going to encounter a whole new world when it comes to getting to know people. On the one hand, you're in a community in which you have a great deal in common with those around you, so the stage is set for friendships to form easily. On the other hand, it's lather, rinse, repeat every two to three years. Practice makes perfect, and you're going to get good at this. We will meet and interact with hundreds of people during our time in the military. Some will only cross our paths once; others will have a deep, lasting impact on our lives. The good news is that there are a few practical ways to improve our relationship-building skills.

Types of Relationships

Some relationships will be primarily professional, and others will develop into more personal friendships. Unlike civilian life and ministry, our lives as Chaplain spouses are in many ways impacted by the rank system and social structure of the military. We will encounter other service members and their spouses/Families, Chaplains and Chaplain Assistants and their Families, church/chapel members, and people in the local community. Some of these individuals will be in our spouse's unit and the relationship may be influenced by their rank or position. Kindness, respect, sensitivity, and tact will never fail you. If you have specific questions about military protocol or appropriateness regarding gifts or invitations, ask a senior spouse for guidance.

As Chaplains' spouses, we have the honor of representing the spiritual and religious dimensions. In addition to professional acquaintances and personal friends, there will be people in your life who are seeking advice, comfort, or support due to the fact that they see you as a part of your husband's ministry. In these situations, people may open up more to you than you will to them.

Stages of Relationships

Introductions. Relationships in the military unfold in a different way and at a much faster pace than in the civilian world. You are already connected with the common bond of the military, which may surprise you with its strength. You meet someone at a function and within that conversation, learn about the best teachers, where to go for swim lessons, and the best Scouting program. You may even set a play date for your children. Relationships form quickly and mightily. With both friends and acquaintances, you'll quickly find that if you wait until all your boxes are unpacked before inviting people over, you'll lose valuable time waiting for the "perfect" time. That being said, it all begins with the introduction.

Army Families are so good at reaching out to one another. Neighbors will pop in to welcome you and you'll do likewise. Even a "hi, new girl!" email can break the ice. Chapel Families, other Chaplain spouses, and your FRG will usually reach out to you. Whether it's a formal introduction or a casual sharing of information at the commissary, here is where relationships begin.

Welcomes. Consider hosting an event to introduce people to each other. When friends move to a new duty station, introduce them to a friend who is already there. Reach out to new people. Some move to a new area and get involved right away, while others have a hard time and need to be pulled in. Of course, many are in the middle of these two extremes. Welcome visits (or phone calls/emails) can be as simple as stopping by and introducing yourself, finding out if they need anything, or bringing a plate of brownies. Regardless of how you do it, the most important thing is that the newcomer feels welcomed.

Going Beyond. Sometimes it can be easy to meet people, but it takes nurture and involvement to propel a relationship further. Continue to keep in touch with people you have met. A simple phone call, email, or card to say "Hi, how are you?" lets the other person know you are interested in getting to know him or her better. Find out what interests a person and focus on common bonds.

- Extend hospitality—this can be in or out of your home
- Go out for coffee, lunch, etc.
- Play dates with those whose kids are near your kids' ages
- Shopping trips

- Visit local attractions such as museums, historical sites, and parks
- Go to a sporting event, theatre, music performance

For those times when you get a little stuck in conversation, here are some "back-pocket questions" to have ready!

- How did you meet your spouse?
- Where is "home"? What's that like?
- What do you enjoy doing in your free time?
- What kinds of things do you enjoy as a Family?
- Where is your favorite place you've lived and why?
- What brought you (or your spouse) into the military?
- What are your plans for this ___ (summer, fall, holiday season, etc.)?

Growing Deeper. As you continue to communicate, you discover more commonalities and develop stronger connections with select people. This requires mutual trust, and these relationships would be thought of more as friends than as acquaintances. At some duty stations, you may have many close friends; at others, you may have just one or two.

Everyone needs to tell his or her story: not just "stories," but the story of his or her life. Oftentimes we find commonalities with new acquaintances through hearing their stories. Sometimes in social settings, we tend to ask "closed" questions that can be answered in a few words. There is certainly a place for this, but we really find out about a person by asking open-ended questions. These allow the person to interpret the question however he or she wants, and answer as little or as fully as he or she desires.

Relationship Building and Social Media

In today's world, social media provides the chance to meet, build relationships, and keep in touch with friends. Some people have several friends whom they have met only once or twice in person, but their relationships grew through social media. Keep the following in mind:

- Remember who your friends are when you post. If you wouldn't want someone to know a bit of information about you the first time they meet you in person, would you want them to see it the first time they "meet" you online?
- Decide what kind of online presence you'd like to have, and act accordingly. If your page is very personal, it might not be a great idea to "friend" people with whom your relationship is primarily professional.
- You might consider having a personal page for Family and close friends, and another professional page for business or work acquaintances. You would be much freer to post personal information or thoughts on the former, while not causing offense or controversy on the latter.

Building Relationships in Person

Like it or not, you are living in a bit of a fishbowl. Don't allow this awareness to paralyze you with self-consciousness, but do consider the following tips:

- Don't burn bridges! It's a small Army, and a smaller Chaplain Corps. It is always better to err on the side of professionalism, treating others with respect.
- When people look at you, they see your spouse also. Living a public life, there might be people who recognize you, even if you don't recognize them. If you're tempted to be discourteous to a cashier at the store, remember that

the person standing behind you in the checkout line may meet you later at an FRG meeting, or is possibly getting marriage counseling from your spouse.

- As Chaplain spouses, we may be looked to as relational subject matter experts, whether we are or not. It is important to remember that we are modeling relational skills. How we interact with others not only speaks to our own character, but it is also a reflection of our spouses—for better or for worse.

Team Building

Some of the relationships we build will be as members of a variety of groups: Family Readiness Groups, Unit or Chaplain Spouse Coffee/ Social Groups, Special Interest or Service Groups (such as an Installation Spouses Club, Runners Club), School Groups, or Chapel Groups (such as Protestant Women of the Chapel, AWANA, Sunday school class). Being a member of a group involves team dynamics. Teamwork helps us share the workload with others, allowing each person to contribute through their unique strengths. We may participate solely as a member of the team or we may serve as the leader of a team.

What Is Team Building?

Team building, by definition, is motivating individuals who have a common purpose or goal to come together to form a cohesive unit. Team building is important to the overall success and unity of the group. Effectively done, it reduces tension and bickering among the individual members, helps the members to adapt more readily to changes within the group, and encourages commitment to the group, as well as to the individual members.

Tips for Team Building

1. First, as a group, determine the mission, or goal, of your group, and possibly draft a motto for your team

that is unique to that mission. Write down and make sure each team member knows and understands the group's mission (and motto if one is created).

2. Get to know your team members and the unique circumstances of their lives. Don't just limit your group interaction to the mission of the group. Plan get-togethers that promote a broadened interest in the group and its members. Work together to meet needs of the members as they arise. For example, several of the team members may need childcare during group meetings. As a team, brainstorm ideas for meeting this need. The important point to remember is that the group comes together to work out a solution that is acceptable to the team and meets the need.

3. Identify challenges that your team faces and plan team-building exercises to help the team work through an issue, improve on weaknesses, or strengthen skills.

4. It is vital that the team members see the team leader as committed not only to the group as a whole but also to them individually. Members will feel more comfortable in giving of their own time and resources when the team leader is equally, or even more, invested in the group.

5. Confidentiality is a must. Team members need to feel that when they share concerns or personal information, it is kept only between those in the conversation. Never disclose information that a member shares with you to anyone else, even to a fellow teammate—even for the purpose of prayer—without that person's specific permission to do so. Also, never participate in spreading gossip. Gossip will tear a group apart faster than just about anything else.

6. The most effective teams believe in what they're doing and take ownership of the results.

Dos and Don'ts for Team Building

- Don't make one team member feel inferior and less important than the other team members, and never show favoritism.
- Do show appreciation for the unique talents and input that each member brings to the group. Everyone is important to the team, and effective team building will make each person feel equally wanted and needed by the group.
- Do make your team members a part of the majority of group decisions. A wise team leader acts more as a moderator than a dictator, and will include the team members in as much of the decision-making process for the group as possible.
- Don't always be serious and "business only" at team meetings. Do remember to have fun. Group members are more apt to attend a meeting if they know that it will end on a positive note, regardless of how uncomfortable the subject of discussion may be.

Leadership

Kitty Thomsen

You may have opportunities to serve your military community by leading groups, activities, or projects at some time as a military spouse. Your skill sets may stretch far beyond what you ever dreamed; and at some seasons in your life, you may get the chance to lead by example. "Everybody can be great because everybody can serve. You don't have to have a college degree to serve. . . . You only need a heart full of grace, a soul generated by love."[5] Leadership can take many forms. Needs are great in schools, chapels, post communities, and neighborhoods. If you're asked to be in charge, don't fear—here are some simple suggestions to aid you.

Be Proactive. Take the initiative to learn everything you possibly can about the organization in which you are involved, including the people and their Families. When you see a need, be willing to jump in and assist. People respect a leader who is willing to stand side by side with the other members of the organization to shoulder the workload.

Set Boundaries. You may need to set limits to maintain balance for yourself, your Family, and your other responsibilities. Your resources of time and energy are not unlimited. When one area of your life begins to consume too much, other areas of your life will suffer.

Delegate. Find a way to make each person in your group a valuable part of the organization. "Teams make you better than you are, multiply your value, enable you to do what you do best, allow you to help others do their best, give you more time, provide you with companionship, help you fulfill the desires of your heart, and compound your vision and effort."[6]

Listen. It was not a mistake that God created man with one mouth and two ears. Becoming a good listener is an art that takes a lot of practice. Try to listen twice as much as you talk.

Inspire. A good leader inspires others by encouraging them to believe they can accomplish anything. A heartfelt commitment to the cause you are supporting will also energize others to share your enthusiasm. Be a good example by remaining authentic, positive, and humble.

"Nobody cares how much you know, until they know how much you care."—Theodore Roosevelt.

Be Flexible. The human body needs joints to make it flexible; without them, the body would be too rigid to function. Don't make the mistake of planning so rigidly that, when things change, you are left asking "what shall we do?" Make sure that you build "joints" into your planning so that you are prepared *when* change happens.

Enable. To enable "is to assist and advance others by allowing them to employ their own abilities in order to reach their individual potential."[7] Tune into the strengths of your team members, and assign responsibilities accordingly. You'll have more happy campers and more productivity.

Stay Connected. For an orchestra to produce a pleasant sound, each member must be carefully tuned to the others. Likewise, as a leader, you must be in tune with each member of the group to perform well. Fostering good communication and creating opportunities for the members of your group to get to know each other will help your team function better as a whole.

Cheer. Applause will produce greater returns than any motivational speech because it is both contagious and energizing. Applaud the efforts of those you lead and they will surprise you with what they can accomplish.

Leadership can be a rewarding experience if you are prepared, have a heart for those you serve, and have the ability to work well with others.

Management of Group Meetings

Here are some suggestions to help your meeting succeed:

Before a Meeting

- Set purpose of meeting, goals, and clarify needs.
- Plan course of meeting and time limits.
- Type up a meeting agenda and make copies for everyone.
- Add personal notes to agenda if necessary.
- Brief key people, such as committee chairpersons.
- Develop an opening statement and a starting question.

- Plan time, location, seating, and decide if and what refreshments to have.
- Arrange resources.
- Invite guest speakers from different agencies such as ACS, JAG, MWR, or health care.
- Arrive early to arrange refreshments, set out meeting agendas, set up visuals if using them, and greet speakers.

During a Meeting

- Begin and end the meeting on time.
- Make introductory remarks.
- Make sure all materials are present.
- Create proper atmosphere and remove any distractions (outside noise, paper shuffling).
- Have someone record the minutes for you.
- Be an active listener and be patient.
- Be careful not to agree on something just to be liked or to feel like you belong.
- Take the time necessary to make a right decision.
- Don't let anyone dominate the whole discussion.
- Remember managed conflict can be good to promote and generate ideas.
- Use positive nonverbal signals.
- Use visual aids (such as PowerPoint slides).

- Stick to decisions.
- Assign tasks with deadlines.
- Set time and place for next meeting if possible.

After a Meeting

- Reflect on positives and negatives.
- Follow up and be available.
- Encourage completion of tasks and address unfinished business.
- Have typed minutes available to meeting members.

Conflict Resolution

Lori Jeffries

Conflict is inevitable because people have different viewpoints, different backgrounds, experiences, values, and different levels of commitment. Since conflict is natural, the goal should not be to eliminate conflict, but to view it as essentially healthy. It can be healthy if it is handled and resolved constructively. Usually when conflict arises and is dealt with openly, people are energized and more willing to listen to new ideas and other possibilities.

Please remember that conflict can stimulate interest and/or curiosity. It can provide the means for problems to be heard and possibly resolved. It can also increase group cohesiveness and performance, and it can help to promote personal growth.

There are several ways of dealing with conflict. Please keep in mind that there are two parts to conflict, the feelings/emotions and the facts. K. W. Thomas and R. H. Kilmann have developed a five-choice response model that presents you with the following options when conflict occurs.[8]

1. AVOID—Simply avoid the other person or the issue. **This works if the person is someone you don't associate with very often or the issue is not that important to you.** Maybe you know that the issue will be decided by someone else shortly or is a moot point due to other factors. For example, a wife may be upset at what your spouse is asking her husband to do in the unit. You might use avoidance because you recognize it is not your place to address an issue like this. You might say, "I am sorry you are frustrated. Perhaps your husband could speak to his chain of command if he has concerns." Note that validating someone's feelings does not mean that you are directly agreeing with, addressing, or fixing the problem.

2. ACCOMMODATE—"Keep the peace." **This is effective when the relationship is more important than the conflict.** For example, your husband's Family is coming to visit, and he wants to take them all out to dinner. You prefer to avoid the expense and fix dinner at home. You decide to honor his wishes. Or, someone wants to bring food to the chapel meeting because you are starting earlier than usual. You don't want to start this as a routine practice in the group, but might say "Although we don't normally have snacks, tonight is an exception as we are starting earlier than usual. It might be a nice treat for a change."

3. COMPETE—**In this instance a person uses force or authority to end the conflict.** This may be a necessary solution in matters of safety or crisis, when time is of the essence and decisions must be made.

4. COMPROMISE—**This requires both sides to gain a little and lose a little.** For example, during an FRG meeting, the group develops a great idea for the December FRG meeting—making a holiday centerpiece. They estimate the cost at $20.00 per person. You realize that many people won't participate due to that high cost, so the group decides to do a smaller design for about half the price.

5. COLLABORATE—**Both sides find creative solutions for a win-win situation.** This is more time-consuming and not always possible to achieve, but is frequently desirable. For example, your group is planning welcome-home activities for Soldiers returning from a deployment. (Full potluck dinner for hungry troops vs. brownies and cupcakes for the troops who want to get home.) Two groups have great ideas, which they feel strongly about. You can suggest that everyone sit down and share their ideas and incorporate them into one great welcome home event. (Perhaps prewrapped cold-cut sandwiches and sodas in a lunch sack would work for both sides.)

REMEMBER

- Confrontation does not need to be ugly. It is simply problem solving.
- Conflict can often be avoided if clear, specific guidelines for behavior and/or performance standards are stated.
- By the same token, establishing, and/or redefining guidelines may resolve conflict.
- Humor can defuse many intense situations.
- Nonverbal clues, both given and received, can speak volumes.

- Your first priority is resolving the conflict, rather than being right or winning.
- Sometimes conflicts leave in their wake hurt feelings, bitterness, and loss of respect. Be the person who is willing to forgive and make amends.
- Choose your battles. Your time and energy are precious commodities, and some conflicts are just not worth the fight.

Constructive Traits for Effective Conflict Resolution

Whether conflict arises interpersonally or as part of a group dynamic, the following may smooth the path.

- The desire to find compromise and reject retribution
- The conviction that approaching conflict directly best benefits both parties
- The discipline to react and respond respectfully and calmly
- A willingness to forgive, forget, and grow beyond the conflict without clinging to resentment or anger
- The discernment to see clearly what is most important to all parties

Destructive Traits

- Impulsive, rage-filled, or resentful reactions
- Refusal to try to understand opposing points of view or refusal to compromise
- Being certain of negative results and outcomes, or operating out of fear
- Not knowing when to disengage and move on

What You Can Do

If you are involved in a one-on-one conflict, there are steps to minimize its impact and achieve resolution.

1. Always begin with yourself. Remember, the only person you can truly control is yourself. Ask, "What part did I play in this situation? Is it a misunderstanding of my words or actions? Or did I say or do something that truly caused hurt? If I am responsible, what can I do to help resolve this issue?"

2. If you are the offended party, you may elect to take the direct approach. Go to the person who has offended you and seek clarification. An opening that has worked in the past is "I think I misunderstood this statement/action. Can you please help me understand what has happened?" This lets the other party know that you are seeking understanding, not blame. Confronting others is always a delicate situation, and many will choose to move on without dealing with it directly. If you decide it is best for you to confront someone, do so with an attitude of kindness and work toward forgiveness.

3. Always, always, always handle issues as close to the source as possible. Many conflict situations are exacerbated by gossip. Remove yourself from the situation if possible; if you must deal with it, remember to "help" only when asked by the original members of the conflict. Rarely is help with conflict resolution welcome when you are not invited in.

4. If you find yourself taking offense, stop and make sure that offense was intended. If it was, do you really need to react? In some cases you may be able to effect a change in others' attitudes; in some, nothing will really help. Most people react favorably to those who approach them with grace and humbleness.

Spouse to Spouse

We all have our own journeys to live, but sometimes knowing a little about others' experiences and what they have learned can be a great help. Spouses were asked to share personal reflections and responses to survey questions regarding their army life experiences. Here are some insights shared by Chaplain spouses on the highs and lows of their Army Chaplain Family journeys.

Feeling at Home

Traci: When you arrive at a new assignment, unpack, decorate, and put up pictures as soon as possible. No matter how long or short you will be at the current assignment, it is home. Invest fully in that place and time. If it looks like "your" home, it will be home and not just a house for your Family. Do not dwell on where you came from and above all do not move mentally to your new assignment until the movers come. God has you in that place at that time; be fully there.

Sheri: Establish your own Family traditions. We almost always have Christmas in our own home. No matter where we live, our kids know that when they come home for Christmas, the house may be unfamiliar, but the routine and traditions will always be the same. Celebrating Christmas in a new place helps that house feel like home.

Robin: Cook a favorite meal that we dreamed of having all during temporary housing; getting personal space set up (i.e., bedroom, bathroom, and kitchen) as soon as possible so there is somewhere familiar to sleep, clean up, and eat.

Barbara: The very first weekend at a new place we find something fun to do that is unique to that place—visit the ocean, go to the state fair, hike in the mountains, etc.

Kelly: As the upcoming move nears, we discuss our next assignment and all the unique things about it—what there is to do, who we will know, how close we'll be to other people and things. We celebrate the move as a gift—not as a curse! Setting up the home quickly is a priority as well. We take walks in the evening around our new neighborhood so that we can get to know our neighbors.

CeCe: When we move in to quarters, I try to set the children's rooms up first. I also try to unpack the kitchen items quickly and prepare our favorite foods. If we are in transition or temporary quarters, we try to keep the children informed. Surprises can be hard to adjust to at times for the older ones.

Rita: We anticipate fun—we build the expectation of good things to come and new friends and places to see.

Sarah: We meet our neighbors as quickly as possible and try to find some playmates to connect with our children. My husband usually builds a giant welcome fort out of moving boxes on the driveway. It serves as a giant sign: "New Kids Here—Come Play!"

Karen: Get the familiar/favorite things in place as soon as possible, such as furniture, art, and meals. Immediately start looking for what is good and special about the new place and community.

Bits of Wisdom

Becci: One of the best decisions you can make as a military spouse is deciding that your house is good enough. It is clean enough, fancy enough, big enough. Stop comparing it to others' and stop being so critical yourself. This will free you to invite others over, both for you and your spouse and your children. There's no better place to get to know someone than your kitchen. Many lifelong relationships were begun simply by having someone over for coffee mid-morning or when their kids showed up for cookies after school.

Dorcas: We need each other. In the Army, most of the time, no one has Family close by. This is especially true in overseas assignments. We need to establish relationships with some people who would help us in a crisis. We need to be willing to do the same for others! It is a good idea to ask others questions about different businesses they use in the area. Offer a baby shower to a new mother who might not have anyone close by. Celebrate children's birthdays with each Family who requests your presence because you are their

Family for now. Make special holiday gatherings with your neighbors because this is your community for now.

Ginger: View every duty station as an opportunity to do something you have never done before, whether it's travel or experiencing the local culture.

Katherine: In all the moving and setting up a new home each time, our relationship with our Family Members is the most important. Don't be afraid to try new things that will benefit your Family.

Tonia: Military wives learn to jump on opportunities for friendships. "Looks like our kids are about the same age, want to do a play date?"

Sharon: I think there is a tendency to shy away from making good friends when you move to a new post. It almost seems not worth it in light of the fact that you will only be at the post one to three years. I recommend fighting this tendency and jumping in with both feet. I have found, even when we live somewhere for only a short time, that wonderful, long-lasting friendships can be made. I am still in regular contact with friends we made at our first duty station seventeen years ago. Additionally, it is not uncommon to be stationed a second time with friends made at a previous post. We have one Family that we have been stationed with three times now—we have literally watched each other's children grow up through the years. My military friendships are one of my most prized possessions.

Darcey: At any new duty station you should sightsee, but especially overseas because once you PCS from it you may never return! When you discover something you want to do or go see/investigate, do it then! Now that I'm preparing to PCS, I have this huge list on our giant chalkboard of, yes, of course PCS prep, but of other things I've wanted to purchase and take home from Korea or do/see. Now, it is crazy on the countdown for the packers, taking the car to the port, and flying out, etc.

Sandra: We have chosen to stick with TRICARE Prime, and have had generally good experiences wherever we have been. I know that many have chosen to go with different options, but I am convinced that Tricare Prime is the most economical and we have been very happy with it.

Adele: Carry your medical records with you. Connect with a home school group before you arrive to your new duty station. Do not listen to constant complainers. They are at every post. No place is perfect. You can be content and happy anywhere. A place is what you choose to make it.

Merial: I would advise to move the Family with the Soldier when possible. I know that moving children mid-school year or high school career is difficult. However, we found that the children adjusted without their friends, but adjusting without a complete Family is very difficult. We became a stronger Family through our shared ministry sacrifices.

Itsy Bits of Wisdom

- Be flexible and expect change.
- Get involved. You can't do everything, but find your niche.
- Find the good things in every place you live.
- People really just want fellowship and friendship—invite them over. Don't worry about the dirt!
- Stay organized. Don't wait until three weeks before a move.
- Do something! Put down roots quickly.
- Make his chapel your church home, and participate in unit functions whenever possible.
- Open your home to welcome people.
- You are not wearing your husband's rank.
- Make yourself available to the commander's spouse.
- When choosing your volunteer activities, you may want to discuss this with your spouse. Often, your spouse's unit

may have a need, which will provide you a sweet opportunity to support your Chaplain.

- If you are feeling down, take a meal to someone—it has never failed to lift my spirits.
- Consider planting a tree or flowers while living in quarters not only for you, but for those who come after you.
- Just be yourself . . . your very best self!

AHHH . . . FAVORITE MEMORIES

Karen: One of my very favorite memories is what happened while our son was playing a soccer game on post. The referee blew his whistle, the players stopped, the spectators rose to their feet, and everyone faced toward the sound of retreat. Retreat finished, the whistle blew, and the game resumed. Everyone knew that just for a moment, we all were to stop and honor our country. It was a great feeling and a proud moment!

Sheri: One of my first memories as a new Army spouse was driving through a basic training area at Fort Leonard Wood, Missouri. A unit was on the road and a road guard ran up to my car. The Soldier had a rifle and stood in front of my car signaling me to stop and wait for the unit to pass by. Seriously—he had a rifle in his hands; I had no intention of disobeying! It was a pretty surreal moment.

Jennifer: I think that would have to be pinning on my husband's Captain rank!

Rita: When my husband's first Assistant and his wife arrived on post, my husband brought them to our house for dinner. As we were settling in to visit, the Assistant's wife surprised me by asking "if my husband is your husband's Assistant, does that make me your Assistant?" I was shocked and smiled inside thinking how wonderful that would be (I had a four-month-old, twin eight-year-olds, and a thirteen-year-old at the time). I said "Yes, yes, it does." Then we laughed and became sisters—just like that.

Jeanne: I would have to say that my most memorable experience as a military spouse was planning and then attending the first-ever Fort Bliss Chaplain Anniversary Ball this past summer. It was wonderful working with other Chaplain spouses to design and create the floral centerpieces for the tables. We were fortunate to have CH Ray Bailey, the Deputy Chief of Chaplains, be our guest speaker. We also had John Cook, the Mayor of El Paso, give a proclamation. Seeing all the men and women dressed in their finest and proud to be part of a Regimental Chaplain Corps was something I will never forget. I think it was especially important for the newer Chaplains and Chaplain Assistants to see and realize that they do belong to a Regimental Corps. So many people had the chance to get involved and participate both in the "Grog" ceremony, the various toasts, and also in the explanation of the POW/MIA table. The Color Guard and the Posting of the Colors was also so moving to watch. We had pride in our Corps, and it showed!

Martha: The most memorable experience was the arrival of my husband's unit when he returned from Iraq. That was the end of a very uncertain year. It keeps one from taking the future for granted.

Sheri: As difficult as it was, my most memorable experiences were the memorial services for Soldiers killed in action during Operation Iraqi Freedom at Fort Stewart. The services were for the Rear Detachment and Family Members, and were held after the intense battles during the beginning phase of the war in 2003. I had attended memorial services for Soldiers in other situations, but never for Soldiers killed in action. Memorial services were held in Iraq for the units, but the Families left behind and the Rear Detachment Soldiers also needed the opportunity to grieve as a community. I don't think I have ever experienced such a strong sense of community and what the Army Family truly means.

Rachel: My most memorable experience was my first day of PWOC at Fort Bragg. We'd only been active military for about two weeks, and I was walking my daughter into childcare when this lady came up to me. She knew who I was, who my husband was, what training our husbands had done together, and she was so excited to finally meet me. It was like being attacked by a whirlwind! By the time our conversation was over, though, I knew I was going to survive and make some great friends along the way!

Robin: This one is a tearjerker for me. When my husband returned for R&R in Hawaii, we were allowed to go to the gate to meet him. They made an announcement at the gate that Soldiers were returning home on the flight. Many, many people formed two lines for the Soldiers to pass through and clapped and cheered for the Soldiers. We were already very emotional, and that put us all over the top!

Rita: My husband's chapel service was chosen by the Bush Family for their Easter morning worship time. George W. Bush sat in my spot (front pew on the right) and my husband was greeted by the elder President Bush during the welcome time. Just being in the same room with two US presidents was an amazing experience for us and our children. And it snowed in Texas that Easter Sunday—truly amazing!

Becky: As a lover of history and tradition, the first time I participated in singing "The Army Song" moved me to tears. It was one of the defining moments where I realized that we had transitioned from a civilian Family to an Army Family. We would join countless others, with heartbreak and pride, to do our part to serve our great nation.

Oops Moments

Merial: Our first formal ball was a real learning experience for me. We had been in the Army less than two months and the commander wanted my husband to say the opening prayer. This meant we sat at the head table. I would have preferred to sit at the back and observe. However, because we were front and center, I made several major protocol blunders (that I know of!). First, I stood when the Soldiers stood—I was the only woman to do so. And then I toasted the ladies—not realizing that I was in effect toasting myself! I was mortified, but learned never to do those things again!

Abigail: Before we arrived at our first duty station, we were assigned a sponsor. He welcomed us to Fort Bragg and gave us his office phone number. On my first trip to the commissary, I wrote a check. The cashier wanted me to write my sponsor's SSN and phone number on the check. Of course, I didn't know the SSN of our new Chaplain friend, but I dutifully wrote down his phone number. To my chagrin, I learned that *sponsor* has two meanings.

Preserving Memories

Kelly: We have a piece of artwork from each assignment as well as a coffee table book from that state/country/city. We also have pieces of clothing with the places represented. Dishes and favorite recipes from Japan are still on our menus. We talk about our past assignments, the positives and difficulties.

Sarah: We have a Thanksgiving tablecloth that we paint on each year, adding the year, location, and the names of all our dinner guests.

Brenda: We preserve our memories of places and people with whom we've grown some roots by collecting at least one Christmas tree ornament from each place or unit of our past, by taking many photos, by keeping letters, stories, news articles, etc., particular to those times in our Family's history. We return, as able, to former posts, even if just stopping by for an hour or two, to see what still stands and what's changed, as we are traveling cross country, PCS-ing, etc. Our first Family pet, Tootsie, a gerbil, was buried in the Fort Leonard Wood area, during my husband's first deployment. We returned for a visit, about fifteen years after moving from the area. We found Tootsie's grave, intact, with even her little popsicle-stick marker still in place! That was heartwarming for our kids, even though they were, by then, nearly adults.

Jennifer: We enjoy the culture and I love photography, so I will create photo books. Just a few weeks ago my son and I looked up a friend's daughter who we have not seen in years, but had fond memories of a vacation we all enjoyed together. We went back in time remembering that vacation, but then also looked at how they have both grown and where God has taken each of them. Photo books have allowed us to remember friends, places, trips, excursions, and ministry that we wouldn't remember if I had not taken the time to make them.

Karen: I have a large antique typesetter's drawer from Germany, and have spent the last thirty years filling each little cubby. I try to find a miniature "something" from every place we visit, from thimbles to miniature pewter landmarks. It doesn't take up much space and isn't very expensive, but it is one of my most treasured possessions full of many, many memories.

Becci: We take lots of pictures, and I put these in scrapbooks. Often the kids will take down books from prior places and look through them, retelling stories. I also have a quilt that lists each of our homes. Any pins earned or purchased at each place are pinned to that quilt.

CHILDREN, EDUCATION, HOMESCHOOLING

Ginger: Homeschooling is great, but it may not be for everyone or for every duty station. The benefits are continuity of curriculum, portability, and flexibility. The negatives are the different regulations at every duty station, being with your children 24/7 (insert smiley face here), and limitation of ministry opportunities, especially if your children are young.

Sarah: We have four children, and we have learned that we need to constantly be evaluating each child's educational needs and options. Each year (sometimes each semester!) we have to decide what seems to be the best fit. We have done private school, public school, homeschool, and online school. We try to be flexible, ready to adjust as needed.

Judy: Homeschooling and the military lifestyle partner together superbly! If you elect to homeschool, give it the same level of commitment and attention as if you were a teacher in a school building. As a full-time employed teacher, no, you can't answer your personal phone while teaching. No, you can't get involved in daytime clubs, no matter how worthy. No, you can't cook and clean, etc. Now homeschooling may have the latitude to allow for some of these things to happen, but *always* keep the image in mind that you are a professional.

Laura: There are so many homeschoolers within the military and chaplaincy. Some of the best places to find other homeschooled children are through the Chaplains' wives and PWOC. Seek out co-ops in the area and try to plug your children in there as well.

Organizational Tips

Dorcas: De-clutter before and after you move. We are always gathering clothes and belongings that we do not use and donating them. Our goal is never to need storage except what Army housing gives us. We teach the children that we have all we need but we don't need extras. Less is more!

Darcey: Paperwork—everyone's hardest task. Create files for each person for business, personal items, and medical. Teach children how to do this early on. A separate alpha accordion file for your owner's manuals is essential. I refer to it all the time to do repairs. Having them in one spot saves time and energy. Keep children's school and/artwork in accordion files. Have a child who does not want to get rid of any of his or her prized artwork? Take a picture of each piece he or she has done, then download them on a digital frame. Set it on "scroll" and you have one satisfied child. Your child would be very happy to select where the frame goes in the home; you may be surprised that the spot is in his or her very own bedroom.

Benita: We have a mobile app that stores web logins, passwords, and other critical info. The military life can be crazy and chaotic. Be proactive in the lulls (more peaceful times) so you'll be better prepared for the next crazy season.

Living Overseas

Ann: I loved living overseas. I loved that my children got to see other people and their cultures. If you are lucky enough to live overseas, I encourage you to travel as much as possible. We went the wrong way on at least one train in every country we visited and we have driven in a pedestrian park. We have camped in floods in the Alps and used bathrooms that consisted of two footprints and a hole.

But we have also seen Michelangelo's "David" and straddled a line between Germany and Austria on a mountain peak. We have seen Napoleon's tomb and Frankenstein's castle. Even if things get messed up, it's still an adventure! If it's raining, take an umbrella! Don't wait to make memories with your Family.

Constance: When my husband was to return from Afghanistan, we were stationed at Vilseck, Germany, and I traveled to Heidelberg and France with my children and another Chaplain's spouse and her children. We had such an amazing experience. Then when my husband came home from deployment, he and I traveled to London, crossed the English Channel on a ferry cruise ship to Normandy, then back to England and to Edinburgh before returning to Vilseck. That same summer, we traveled again with the same Chaplain's Family (this time husbands were there) to Berchtesgaden and Salzburg, Austria. We stayed in a lovely guest house and took hikes in the Alps, cooked our meals in the guest house suites, and had such a wonderful time. That summer was filled with many wonderful memories for us, and I am so thankful we were able to share them with another Chaplain's Family.

Jenn: We are presently stationed in Italy and there have been quite a few moments where I had to remind myself to be flexible and relax. We have learned to train ourselves to laugh at situations when they come at us due to cultural differences, lost-in-translation moments, being physically lost in a new place, and many more stressful times. Once, while doing an apparent legal and simple U-turn to avoid entering a wrong toll road near Pompeii, we were pulled over. Italians are notorious for bad driving, yet we found ourselves under great scrutiny by the Italian officers. Soon, a parking attendant who spoke amazing English came over and was our advocate for the next fifteen minutes, pleading on our behalf to drop the ticket. At one point, my broken Italian understood they wanted to keep my overseas license. That is when our sweet parking attendant truly spoke up and talked them out of it, hands waving and all. Losing any ID overseas is not a good thing. The officer told me he was not going to give me a ticket, acted like he was ripping up that imaginary ticket, and then mentioned Hollywood. We weren't sure about that last comment, but drove away feeling as if the Lord had sent us a very friendly Italian that day to help on our overseas "uh-oh" moment.

Travel

Sherry: We are currently living at our fifth overseas assignment. We have done extensive traveling. We find inexpensive options of travel and lodging to make our dollars stretch farther. We use travel/tour books (Rick Steves's books are the best) to explore areas on our own. Look at websites that provide apartments or houses for rent. You can save a bundle by not staying at a hotel. Do not let limited money keep you from exploring the area in which you live. Check out hiking trails, free concerts, free military admission to recreation and theme parks (Stateside), free historic cathedrals, and just meander through nearby towns and villages. If Stateside, always ask if they provide a military discount. Consistently staying at home can potentially make any duty station miserable. Get out and explore!

Sheri: Travel, travel, travel! While we have enjoyed seeing some of the most famous sights in the world—Rome, Paris, London, Seoul, New York City—some of our favorite travel experiences have been getting to see the local sights—exploring the "back alleys." Anyone who reads Rick Steves knows that he advocates exploring the lesser-known areas of tourist destinations.

Adele: If you should end up living in Europe and would like to travel by air, use Ryanair. They are very inexpensive and usually on time. It is a very easy way to see many places.

Deployment

Tonia: Deployment is one of the richest times of ministry, both for you and for your Chaplain. While every person, every Family, and every deployment has variables of what's right for them, staying on duty station opens doors to many other hurting spouses. Like all hard times, we would never ask for them, but God can use them. I had an intimacy with God during those days that is difficult to emulate when I'm not so desperately clinging to Him.

Sandra: During deployments it helps to get as involved as possible in something that you are interested in or believe in. It helps the time to go by much faster. I also planned activities and put them on a calendar so we had something to look forward to.

Jo: I actively engaged in every ministry opportunity available during my husband's deployment. I took up professional training opportunities and did a lot of volunteer and ministry work. That year was one of the most fruitful years in my life. I was very close to God, engaged in ministry totally, made a lot of lifelong friends, and acquired additional professional credentials that opened new career opportunities at the next installation.

Conli: The very first week of my husband's first assignment, we got word that he would be deployed to Afghanistan in less than eight weeks. I was reeling. A little more than a week later, the unit went out into the field for a three-week training period. I truly think I was in a bit of shock at all the change happening so fast around us! Then, my husband was called upon to do his first death notification to a young newlywed whose wife was killed in Iraq. He and I sought the Lord for the strength to get through this very difficult time. And God was so faithful! He gave us strength and courage. He also brought some incredible people into our lives at this time to support and pray for us. By the time my husband left, just before Thanksgiving in 2006, I was assured beyond a shadow of doubt of God's faithfulness to our Family and how He was going to walk with us through the months of separation to follow. This is a time I will absolutely never forget. So difficult, and yet, through it all, we developed a stronger, more abiding faith in our Savior and a significantly stronger bond in our marriage.

Rochelle: When the first deployment occurred in 2003, I was one of five keep-connected callers (also known as key callers) for the Aviation Brigade. We each had about twenty to twenty-five spouses to call each month so that we could provide updates and other command information to our Families. Each time we would meet, the other callers were sharing how they were able to get through their list within twenty minutes each month. I kept asking how that was possible because it was taking me two to three hours to get through my list. As soon as I would call, spouses were sharing everything. Either I had or the other wives had the gift of gab! More than likely it was me. But needless to say, I enjoyed each conversation because this was a time the wives wanted to connect and build relationships with a team who really cared. The spouses yearned to be kept informed and that was our job. If it meant that I needed to hear some stories that made you laugh and made you cry, we talked that talk together.

Pat: I have to stay focused on the home front, and not expect too much from my husband, allowing him to concentrate on the job at hand, which greatly contributes to his safety.

Dixie: My husband came home and told me and our youngest child and only son that he was going to Iraq for a year. Our son, finishing his junior year in high school, gave us both a big hug, and said, "I'm glad it's this year and not next year so you're not all alone, Mom." That is the result of being a true military brat: It brings a willingness to sacrifice, seeing how much your parents/Family have sacrificed. They see the bigger picture: The world doesn't revolve around them, but they can approach each challenge with hope and the knowledge that we'll get through this together. Our son grew up so much his senior year without his dad at home. He stepped up to the plate and made his dad and me so proud. It helped shape him into the caring, compassionate man that he is today.

Barbara: Implementing a self-care routine during a deployment is crucial. Eating balanced meals, exercising, and keeping a routine schedule as much as possible for you and your children are basic. Girlfriends are a must. It's great to have friends to pray with, laugh together, and to do things with. Girlfriends will take your kids for a couple of hours so you can have alone time. Certainly the most important is time with God and his word. He has nourished, strengthened, guided, provided, protected, and has poured "miracle grow" into my roots during deployments. Time management is essentially energy management. Self-care is worth the time.

Lori: I had two very different deployment experiences; our first deployment was while we were stationed in Germany. The whole post deployed, so it was a wonderful (as wonderful as a deployment can be) group experience. Everyone was going through the same thing at the same time. Some of my strongest friendships came from this time. The second deployment was out of Fort Benning. My husband was a Captain at the time and surprisingly, I was the senior Chaplain spouse from our Brigade and the only one who had been through a deployment. The Brigade Chaplain spouses decided to get together once a month for coffee. There were five of us. It was precious. I was in no way prepared for this. Both times I learned valuable lifelong lessons, but they were very different positions. I would tell you to be flexible enough to look at each deployment with fresh eyes. Be willing to adapt and change to what your situation calls for. I personally found staying put was helpful, but I think that was due in part to the fact that I had older children when my husband deployed. I would urge you to plan for deployments with your spouse with a lot of prayer. Do what is right for you. Being able to hear from a Soldier's perspective the direct impact my spouse had on Soldiers during a dangerous, physically and emotionally demanding deployment was a humbling experience and one I wish other spouses could have.

Kelly: When our kids were smaller, the night Daddy left for his deployments, we would make brownies. Then, just because we could, the next morning we'd eat them for breakfast and drink a Coke. Breaking the rules felt fun and it was a little way to celebrate the plans we had made while Daddy would be gone. We would also write a list of things we wanted to do—places to go, friends to visit, movies to watch, food to eat—and post it on the fridge. Crossing off our list made us feel like we'd completed something special.

To Remain at the Duty Station or Go Home to Family during Deployment

Conli: When my husband received orders to deploy, we made the decision to stay put in our home near the base. I got connected with the FRG and became a Point of Contact person, checking in on several wives once a month or more. While my Family made several trips that year to be with the children and me, I was thankful to be close to the other women in my husband's unit. When with my Family and civilian friends, I knew they couldn't possibly understand what I was going through. The other Army wives "got it" and that helped so much. I made some incredible, lasting friendships that year. I also felt connected and close to the information and news about my husband's unit by staying near to Fort Stewart.

Sandra: We chose to stay with our post. Our support group was there and friends who were going through the same things. I would do the same again. People back home just don't understand because they are not living it.

Emma: My children were preschoolers during deployment. We stayed at our duty station because we had a great support group among all the other Chaplain spouses. We had weekly get-togethers where our kids would all play together and we would sit down and have adult time. We had a lot of Family weddings and babies during my husband's deployment. I was able to travel with the kids and visit longer since we weren't on a leave schedule. Traveling with a one- and three-year-old is very overwhelming, but you feel empowered and that you can do anything and get through deployment.

Rochelle: Last year when my spouse deployed I chose to stay in the area. We thought this would be a difficult decision since the post we were assigned closed under BRAC 2011. What happened next was only from God. I received priority placement at the Army post up the road, and the UMT immediately took me in at that post. I received support from PWOC, Military Ministries, Garrison, and TRADOC. Not once did I feel excluded even though my spouse has never been assigned to this post. That same UMT has continued to support me throughout our separation, and they still keep me included in all their activities. Yes, I am glad we chose to stay right where I was acclimated. However, I do understand there are young Families who may need additional support and assistance from their Families of origin. So each situation is unique and decisions are made that suit that individual Family. But when you become a more seasoned spouse, you learn that Family is wherever you are assigned. As you grow you will be able to determine where your greatest support system is located. For me, wherever I am planted I am able to bloom!

Benita: Commit this decision to prayer. There are pros and cons to each scenario and there are so many variables that will also impact your decision. With our first two deployments, we had very young children (and our youngest, third child was born during the first deployment). I spent both these deployments "at home" near Family and friends and our home church. With the first deployment (during the invasion into Iraq) we received an incredible amount of support. During the second deployment (same setting but a few years later) support was minimal, and I really struggled during that time. With our third deployment, the kids were a bit older, and our decision was to stay connected with our military community instead of going home. We appreciated going through the deployment with our military "Family" and continuing with our lives where we were already somewhat established, although it was clear across the country from our friends and Family. Ultimately, you just need to pray for wisdom and then go forward trusting in God's provision. It will never be easy or fun, but trust that God is walking with you through it. Open your eyes to his blessings and provisions during this time, even in the little things.

Sheri: When my husband was assigned to Korea on a one year hardship (nonaccompanied) tour, he had been in the Army for less than three years. I struggled with the decision of whether to move near my parents or remain in housing at our current duty station. My children were both in elementary school at the time, and I decided to remain where we were so that their lives could continue with as little disruption as possible. It was a good decision. It is difficult to be the only one in the neighborhood whose spouse is away, but I was surrounded by friends who understood my situation. My next-door neighbor's husband was also on an unaccompanied tour at the time, and we were able to form a support system for each other. Our Families became one—I will cherish the relationship we formed forever.

Becci: During deployment, I recommend staying at the duty station. You are available to serve in many ministry capacities and also get all the information firsthand. Often, especially right at the beginning and again at the end of deployment, information changes hourly. This is much easier to handle on-site.

Kelley: When our son was three, he and I boarded a plane in Fayetteville, North Carolina, and headed to Germany (first time ever) to meet my husband for his R&R—overseas. So glad we did this. Scary at the time to travel abroad with a little person—having never done this before—but our memories are wonderful. Instead of Daddy coming home, we met in the middle. We chose to stay at the duty station for both deployments. The negative: We were far away from Family. The positive: We had a wonderful support group of other military spouses going through the same thing. I also had support from our chapel when my husband's car's battery corroded, when the lawnmower broke, when we needed a new roof, when the a/c in the house went kaput, when friends betrayed us . . . and that was just the first deployment! Yes, we would do it again. I like being around other Chaplains' wives who are going through or have been through the same thing. As a seasoned spouse with two deployments under my belt, I want to be there for the new spouses who have never gone through a deployment and let them know they are going to be all right and will make it through.

Adele: I stayed in Germany when my husband deployed. We had only been there a few months. I found that I was able to help the spouses in our unit and it encouraged them. I was able to spend time with some of the young spouses and dry a few tears. I am really glad I stayed. It also helped my daughter to be around other Families that did not have daddy home or mommy home. There is no way around it. It is tough, but I believe it was the right choice for us. My daughter and I were able to enjoy our time and traveled a bit on our own as well. We even went to Switzerland with another Chaplain's wife and her son.

Abigail: Newly empty nesters, we were assigned to Germany. I considered staying in the States with my college-age children, knowing that my husband was immediately deploying to Iraq with his unit. But listening to his comments, it became apparent to me that he had looked at the duplex we would be assigned on post and that it was important to him to depart the country with a picture of home in his mind. It was the hope of coming home to a wife who already had the household unpacked and set up that gave him hope and security and stability during the deployment.

Ann: I have advocated going home to Family. I love my Army Family, but they cannot help me like my biological Family. Growing up, I lived next door to my grandmother. My kids never had that experience, so the more often they get to see Family, the better. And in the last deployment, a month after I got home, my mom had a massive stroke. Because I was home, we were able to keep her at home until her passing. I've always felt like God was telling my husband where he was supposed to go every time we PCSed and I just went along for the ride. On this last deployment, I definitely felt God was saying, "Ann, you need to be home with mom."

Staying Connected during Deployment

Conli: One lesson my husband and I quickly learned while he was deployed was to carefully weigh our conversations and responses to one another. The limited time we had to talk by phone or by instant message needed to be encouraging, not me dumping all of my frustrations on him! We remained open and honest with one another, but steered away from negative talk and problems as a general rule for our talk time.

One fun thing we did: Early in the deployment, my husband said he was going to find the "perfect" song for our relationship. He challenged me to do the same. I spent months searching for just the right song with just the right words to encompass my feelings for him! He did the same. When he came home for block leave, one of the first things we did, while driving home from the airport, was play our songs for each other. What fun. Two songs that were perfect for us and will forever hold a great deal of meaning!

Cindy: We had Family meetings via Skype to handle big issues or discipline problems. This was great! By the time my husband moved to another location in Iraq and couldn't Skype, we had gotten all the discipline issues under control, thank God! My best advice is keep the Chaplain involved in Family decisions. We waited for my husband to weigh in before we added new activities or changed our Family rules in any way.

Sarah: We learned early in our first deployment that phone calls are very hard for my husband. He wants to hear our voices, but the experience is very emotionally difficult for him. So we try to stay in touch daily by emails and do phone calls a little less frequently. He knows that we still need to hear from him, but we also respect his need to call a little less often than we might like.

Becci: One idea for keeping the deployed parent involved with the kids is to have him or her give assignments to the kids. Since we homeschool, it fit perfectly with our lifestyle. My husband would assign a paper, or number of math pages, etc., and then check back to be sure it was completed on time. Also, if I had a discipline problem, I could still require them to "talk to Daddy" about it. They simply wrote an email and he wrote back. My kids were each assigned a personal email address during deployment in order to communicate with Daddy (since they were really too young to have their own at that time). He made silly video messages and emailed each child. This was much more effective for us than static-filled phone calls at unpredictable times.

Sandra: While my husband was deployed we chose to have a date night every Friday night via Skype. Sometimes it was a time when just my husband and I visited, and sometimes the kids would join in. We even would move the camera around the room showing him our cat or something special that was going on. We all felt this kept us very connected and the commitment to it was very important and special for my husband in particular. He said it was a time that gave him a break away from all that was going on around him.

Constance: During deployment, my spouse and I communicated through Skype often. We invested in a good phone service even though this was expensive, but it was worth the peace of mind to have him just a phone call away. Our three teen sons were all going through major changes during the time of my husband's deployment in 2010. They were fourteen, fifteen, and seventeen. There were power struggles, girlfriends, and authority issues. My frustration level stayed pretty high for most of that year. My husband suggested having our sons talk to one of the Chaplains on post that he knew well. Our sons were not open to this so he emailed to me a program that he uses to help me have a greater awareness of what they were going through. I learned a lot about raising teenage boys that year. The feelings of being overwhelmed with dealing with this task were strong but I at least felt that my husband was supportive and trying to help even though he was thousands of miles away.

Claire: To remain connected during the deployment (and have conversations about things other than house repairs and the children), we are trying to watch our way through the list of Academy Award Winners for Best Picture since the Oscars began in 1929. Kind of fun. Yeah, we're nerds!

Adele: I was very easy on my husband when he was deployed. I did not expect him to call every day and I did not put pressure on him. Many times he was traveling, and I know it helped him to know that I was praying and just trusted that he would call when he could. Sending packages was always a nice treat. We usually included homemade gifts for Daddy. As for parenting, when my daughter really was out of line, I reminded her that her daddy was still part of the parenting, and I had him talk to her about the incident on the phone. It really helped a lot. We had a daddy doll for her to sleep with. She still sleeps with it. I took care of myself just the same as I do when my husband was home. It helped me to still feel good about myself and not get down. It helps to keep you feeling normal, so to speak:

Dorcas: Before the first deployment, we purchased two miniature tape recorders and a package of tapes to fit. I kept one and my husband took the other. It was always with us! When something funny happened or we were feeling lonely without Daddy, we would talk to it. I would even ask friends and Family who were with me to talk to him on our tape. At the beginning of the war we rarely got to talk to him by phone so this was a great option. We would send the tape when we finished it and he would send us his when he finished. We still have those and know we made some great memories. I also sent mini albums of all special events of the month. He loved those!

He said he would look at them over and over. When he returned I had several weekend getaways planned. Some retreats were cost-free because he was a Chaplain. Others gave us incredible discounts because he had been deployed. Reunion was filled with fun times and a break for all of us!

Reunion Time

Rita: We spent our first night together when he came home for R&R without the children. It was wonderful to just be together—for us to reconnect and for me to have him to myself for just a little while. Then we surprised the children at our friend's house the next morning and they were so excited—they didn't know that they'd missed anything. We were glad to have made our time a priority.

Bryn: I am so glad that my parents and in-laws respected our Family time together and did not visit during R&R or right when he got home from deployment. Talk to your Family Members well ahead of time and explain that it is important for your own Family to spend this time together. Invite them to visit after your spouse gets home. You will not want to feel obligated to entertain extended Family Members while you are trying to spend time with your spouse.

Robin: I highly recommend that when the spouse returns, you set up a private time for just the two of you at a hotel or at home before joining the rest of the Family (kids). Have a friend watch the kids. You can watch hers when her husband comes back.

Tonia: Call it PTSD, call it reverse culture shock, call it whatever, it happens to Chaplains too. The months after deployment were the hardest of our marriage. White-knuckle, hold on tight. It will get better. And the other side is worth the wait.

Sarah: My husband loves being back with our kids, but he isn't accustomed to their constant noise and activity level. When I can see that they are starting to overwhelm him, I redirect the kids to something else to let my husband have a little space to adjust.

Laura: Nothing can compare to the anticipation of waiting for your husband on the parade field when he is coming home from a deployment—nothing. I have never been so excited in all of my life.

Martha: At the conclusion of the Iraqi deployment, my husband wrote a reunion survey for couples to take. We tested the survey beforehand, and we seemed to finish each other's sentences. That confirmed to us that we had stayed connected.

PERSPECTIVES

Jamie—Spouse of a Jewish Reserve Chaplain

I have the distinct honor of having a very different experience in this role than most of my peers. I'd like to share some of these different experiences with you.

My husband is a Rabbi and I am Jewish. Our house is kosher. Our Sabbath is from sundown on Friday to sundown on Saturday. The prayer said before the meal at our house is in Hebrew. For me, being the "Rabbi's wife" at the Chaplains' Spouses Group has given me the opportunity to teach and to learn. I make a point of asking questions about Christianity. I do this for several reasons. First, is to foster an atmosphere where the other spouses feel comfortable asking me about Judaism. Second, is to learn—I love to learn. Third, is to remind others that we are in a multi-faith environment and it is important for us, as it is for our spouses, to remember to honor diversity. However, there are times when being different causes me to feel like a fish out of water. I am not comfortable attending PWOC. At those times, it is helpful to have a good friend or two among the spouses to talk to.

My husband has been an activated reservist for the last nine years. My husband's orders tend to be for a year or less. We often don't know if he will get a next set of orders. We don't know if, after this set of orders, he will return to reservist status and need to find a civilian job. As an activated reservist Chaplain, my husband tends to be a Rear D Chaplain. I often meet the spouses from a Brigade right before their Soldiers deploy. I see them at Memorial Ceremonies, briefings, Hails and Farewells, and Welcome Home Ceremonies. A month or two later, I am no longer part of their Brigade. I support my commander's spouse by sitting next to her at Memorial Ceremonies. I usually don't know her very well, as we have just met. The same goes for FRG leaders, etc. Therefore, the only consistent camaraderie and support that I get is from the Chaplains' Spouses Group.

Theresa—Active Duty Soldier Who Is Also a Chaplain's Spouse

Ideas to ponder:

Understand what your spouse does as a Chaplain.

What is his or her role within the unit, responsibilities, expectations, and so on, not only as a Chaplain but Staff Officer as well?

Who does he or she work for? What is the relationship?

What does he or she do in garrison that may or may not differ from what is required during a deployment?

What relationships might he or she have with other organizations on the installations, for example, ACS, behavioral health specialist, military Family liaisons?

Take the time to learn the basics of military culture—rank, protocol, particularly at social events.

Ask your spouse to explain to you his or her professional timeline. What goals will your spouse be required to meet and at what point in the career, for example, military schools, promotion schedules, and so on? Sketch this out and overlay your Family milestones: kids in school, graduation, your own goals/objectives on top. Work out the differences to ensure your goals are met both professionally and for the Family. This will greatly help with anticipating the what-ifs as well as keep you more informed.

The most effective Chaplain is one who is attuned to the needs of the unit and makes an effort to bridge the gap in keeping with the commander's vision. The Chaplain is one of a kind in the unit and no one else can do what he or she is responsible for. This is very important to know, as other staff officers may have those who can assist at times in their absence, but the Chaplain can only rely on other Chaplains. The relationship between the Chaplain and the commander is extremely important because the Chaplain is the only one within the unit who provides the commander religious insight, guidance, and recommendations.

Understand that not all Command Teams make the Unit Ministry Team (UMT) a priority, which is unfortunate. (The UMTs are always supported but the level of internal support may vary.) I have witnessed both cases, where in one unit the entire command team was extremely supportive, and the Chaplain was included in everything; whereas on the flip side, the Chaplain was only able to participate in required events and had minimal support from the command.

I have seen Chaplains in action on the battlefield—dirty, tired, emotionally strained—while literally laying hands on wounded Soldiers. They are truly a beacon of hope and steadfast in their care. By their mere presence, they can almost instantaneously bring hope to what may seem a lost cause at the time.

It is so very important that Chaplains develop strong relationships with all, from the Commander down to the youngest Soldier, particularly during deployments. When they are uncertain, scared, wounded, Soldiers yearn for their Chaplain's attention. Grown, virile men who would never admit to such feelings to their battle buddy will seek out the Chaplain instead. Because of this, spouses need to understand that some Chaplains carry heavy emotional burdens and this may affect their personal well-being as well.

On a lighter note, Soldiers do not use profanity in front of the Chaplain. I mention this because the Chaplain is usually the single individual who can walk into a room and immediately whatever someone may have been doing that may be considered inappropriate (i.e., cussing, rude gestures, being loud, etc.) stops, often accompanied by a "Sorry, Chaplain" and a sheepish grin.

Rhonda—Spouse of a Muslim Chaplain

Have you ever seen the Middlemist Red? It is one of the rarest flowers in the world and the name can be deceiving because the name has the word *red* in it. However it is the most beautiful bright pink flower. As a Muslim convert, I often feel that my religion makes me that rare spouse with a name that says one thing and has a certain connation to it, but if one would take the time to get to know and understand me would realize that my religious title doesn't say it all.

"One of four" sounds like a statistic but the reality is that of the over 1,300 active duty Chaplains, my husband is one of four Islamic Chaplains providing religious support to Soldiers across the spectrum of the Army. We were both raised by Christian women right here in the good ole USA and are very patriotic individuals. Usually if I am walking with him in uniform we get weird stares, and most of the time I'm not sure if it is the symbol of the crescent moon he wears on his patrol cap, or his stature—he is a very big guy. Most of the time we just want to fit in and be normal, but sometimes that's a challenge. It leaves us to have to work harder in most social situations to make others around us feel comfortable.

Unlike the majority of chapel services, which are on Sundays, our services are on Friday at the end of the hour (1300 hrs), which makes it very challenging to attend for most of his congregation, to include myself, because of work hours. His Soldiers struggle with feeling comfortable and secure enough to request that time off because many of them have suffered repercussions as a result. It weighs heavy on my husband's heart. Friday is a day of worship not just for Soldiers but for their Families as well. But often these Soldiers have to worship alone due to having to return to work immediately after service, leaving no time for Family dinners after service or community conversation with the congregants.

Ramadan is much like Christmas to Muslim Soldiers and their Families. It is a thirty-day fast (sunrise to sunset) culminating with a celebration at the end of that fast. During Christmas, Thanksgiving, and sickness, most of the time the Chaplain spouses come together to help those Families around them because it is the time of giving. During Ramadan, my Family and I will fast from 4:30 a.m. to 8:35 p.m. daily. Sometimes fasting and preparing a meal is overwhelming, especially in the Texas heat! I would love for the Chaplain spouses' group to come together and prepare a meal or two for my Family during that month as we still have to continue with our daily lives of working, caring for our children, and so on. My cup would runneth over.

The Coffee Group is designed as a resource and retreat for the Chaplain spouses who participate. I remember the day like it was yesterday when I walked into my very first Chaplain Spouse Coffee Group. Earlier that day I had anticipated a joyful time meeting and getting to know these new ladies. I assumed not many spouses really knew much about the Islamic faith, which was okay because that meant it would lead to great conversation. Unfortunately, it didn't quite happen that way, and I slowly found myself secluded in a corner, feeling very uncomfortable. It seemed that I did everything I could to make everyone feel comfortable about a Muslim being in the room, but it still felt awkward. Our UMTs serve a very diverse group of Soldiers and their Families—ideally, we will always embrace that diversity internally as well. I was very fortunate that my self-esteem and self-worth were based on other aspects of my life, and walked away from the coffee wounded but not broken.

As a spouse, I volunteer in the community, I work a traditional nine-to-five serving transitioning Soldiers regardless of their religion, and I give back to my community. I am an American. Muslim spouses are *human* and we want what everyone else wants, and that is peace on earth and goodwill toward men. Our husbands joined and raised their hands to serve knowing there would be theological differences, but they serve together, and we spouses can, too.

Sandra—Spouse of a Reserve Component Chaplain

As a history teacher, I understand the importance of facts; yet, I also want to make this more personal by sharing our Army journey. My husband became an Army Chaplain having prior active duty service in the Air Force. He first served in the Army Chaplain Corps as a Chaplain Candidate in the Alabama and Guam Army National Guards (NG). On the island of Guam he continued his service in the NG as an infantry battalion Chaplain, troop command Chaplain, and Joint Forces Headquarters Chaplain. That meant monthly weekend drills and two-week annual training. After twenty years of service he entered the Individual Ready Reserve (IRR) in 2000 as we departed Guam and returned Stateside. He accepted a civilian pastoral position in Pennsylvania in August 2001—one month before 9/11. It did not take too many months before he began to be contacted through the IRR about returning to monthly training. He was able to begin serving in the Military District of Washington (MDW) at Arlington National Cemetery. As Operation Iraqi Freedom (OIF) continued, his eventual activation became a reality. He resigned his pastorate and volunteered for service.

At age fifty, he was attached to a National Guard unit from Wisconsin and served twelve months in Kuwait and Iraq. I lived in South Carolina at the time—away from any military services and support groups. Upon his return, he continued being activated one year at a time, serving in MDW. As an activated reservist, we both have medical coverage through the military. He has dental and eye coverage; I have to utilize TRICARE for both. We do not qualify for military housing, but are grateful to receive BAH. As a reservist, he does not receive his retirement and medical benefits until age sixty and at a much lower percentage than that of active duty personnel.

All of us can give testimony of our own unique journey—whether through active duty service, Reserve service, or a combination of both. Our uniqueness is what strengthens us; our diversity unifies us; and the result is that the Army Family is ARMY STRONG.

Notes

1. For more information, see Melinda Smith, Robert Segal, and Jeanne Segal, "Stress Symptoms, Signs and Causes," updated July 2013, http://www.helpguide.org/mental/stress_signs.htm (accessed August 3, 2013), and University of Maryland Medical Center, "Stress," http://www.umm.edu/health/medical/reports/articles/stress (accessed Augusts 5, 2013).

2. Elisabeth Kübler-Ross and David Kessler, "The Five Stages of Grief," http://grief.com/the-five-stages-of grief/ (accessed July 22nd, 2013). This source is used for our review of all of the five states of grief.

3. For details on the effects of stress on the brain, see "Stress," University of Maryland Medical Center, http://www.umm.edu/health/medical/reports/articles/stress (accessed August 5, 2013).

4. For other information on assisting those in grief, including regarding both "what not to," and "what to" say, see David Kessler, "10 Best Things to Say to Someone in Grief," www.healyourlife.com/author-david-kessler/2010/07 wisdom/inspiration/10-best-things-to-say-to-someone-in-grief.

5. Dr. Martin Luther King Jr., "The Drum Major Instinct" (Atlanta, GA, February 4, 1968).

6. "John Maxwell Quotes," Sources of Insight, http://sourcesofinsight.com/john-maxwell-quotes/.

7. Darrell E. Thomsen Jr., *The Propensity Principle: A Practical Approach to Positive Leadership Impact.* 2008.

8. J.D. Meier, "Five Conflict Management Styles at a Glance," Sources of Insight, March 11, 2011, http://sourcesofinsight.com/conflict-management-styles-at-a-glance/.

CONCLUSION

Dear Wonderful Spouses,

The material presented here is the result of hundreds of pages of advice, caution, encouragement, and wisdom from both seasoned and rookie Chaplains' Spouses. From entry to exit, the offerings found in these pages are designed to help spouses learn from each other's successes and challenges, to provide springboards from which more detailed information can be gleaned, and to serve as a basic one-stop resource.

I truly believe there is no better life than that of an Army Chaplain Spouse. Our lives are filled with great adventures, amazing places, strong friendships and more importantly, our own deep personal faith. And we get to share this life of service to God and Country with our best friend, our very own Army Chaplain.

If we embrace the Army lifestyle, we will become stronger, more compassionate, incredibly flexible, and more appreciative of our nation and our freedoms than we ever dreamed. As you strive to live a life of grace, dignity and faith—you touch people's lives and make the Army better for Soldiers and their Families.

It is my heartfelt hope and prayer that your seasons of life will be well lived, that you take time for yourself to keep your spirit strong, and that you are a shining light for others around you.

Your journey belongs to you. Our goal is to equip you well; you get to choose how to use these pages to help create the life you'll live . . . from Reveille to Retreat.

Sending my love and prayers to you all,

Karen Bailey

RESOURCES

The following resources are suggested by fellow Chaplain spouses.

BOOKS

Children, Parenting, Family

Dobson, Dr. James. *Parenting Isn't for Cowards*
Eckhart, Jacey. *Homefront Club: The Hardheaded Woman's Guide to Raising a Military Family*
Edick, Kathleen. *We Serve, Too!* (a children's book)
Feldhahn, Shaunti, and Lisa A. Rice. *For Parents Only: Getting Inside the Head of Your Kid*
Pollock, David C., and Ruth E. Van Reken. *Third Culture Kids*
Walsh, Froma. *Strengthening Family Resilience*

Customs and Protocol

Crossley, Ann. *The Army Wife Handbook*

Deployment, Reintegration, Reunion

Armstrong, Keith, Dr. Suzanne Best, Dr. Paula Domenici. *Courage after Fire: Coping Strategies for Troops Returning from Iraq and Afghanistan and Their Families*

Buckholtz, Alison. *Standing By: The Making of an American Military Family in a Time of War*
Green, Jocelyn. *Faith Deployed; Faith Deployed Again*
Kraft, Heidi Squier. *Rule Number Two: Lessons I Learned in a Combat Hospital*
MacFarland, Lynda. *Drowning in Lemonade*
Raddatz, Martha. *The Long Road Home: A Story of War and Family*

Grief and Bereavement

Sheeler, Jim. *Final Salute*

Leadership

Blackaby, Henry, and Richard Blackaby. *Spiritual Leadership*
Hybels, Bill. *Courageous Leadership*
Maxwell, John C. *Developing the Leader within You*

Leisure Reading

Austen, Jane. *Pride and Prejudice*
Mayer, Jack. *Life in a Jar: The Irena Sendler Project*
Roberts, Cokie. *Ladies of Liberty: The Women Who Shaped Our Nation*
Russert, Tim. *Wisdom of Our Fathers*

Marriage

Allender, Dan, and Tremper Longman. *Intimate Allies*
Chapman, Gary, and Jocelyn Green. *The 5 Love Languages Military Edition: The Secret to Love That Lasts*
Eggerichs, Dr. Emerson. *Love & Respect*
Feldhahn, Shaunti. *For Women Only: What You Need to Know about the Inner Lives of Men*
Gottman, John. *The Science of Trust: Emotional Attunement for Couples*

Gottman, John M., and Nan Silver. *The 7 Principles for Making Marriage Work*
Thomas, Gary. *Sacred Marriage*

Military/Chaplain's Spouse

Canfield, Jack. *Chicken Soup for the Military Wife's Soul*
Cline, Lydia Sloan. *Today's Military Wife*
Hightower, Kathie, and Holley Sherer. *Help! I'm a Military Spouse: I Get a Life Too! How to Craft a Life for You as You Move with the Military*
Leyva, Meredith. *Married to the Military: A Survival Guide for Military Wives, Girlfriends, and Women in Uniform*
Lovingood, Rachel, and Jennifer Landrith. *In Our Shoes: Real life Issues for Ministers' Wives*
Pace, Brenda, and Carol McGlothlin. *Medals above My Heart: The Rewards of Being a Military Wife*
Cilley, Marla. *Sink Reflections*
George, Elizabeth. *Life Management for Busy Women*
Payne, Sandee. *That Military House: Move It, Organize It, and Decorate It*
Schofield, Deniece. *Confessions of an Organized Homemaker: The Secrets of Uncluttering Your Home and Taking Control of Your Life*

Self-Care and Resiliency

Figley, Charles R. *Compassion Fatigue*
Johnson, Spencer. *The Present*
Swenson, Richard. *Margin: Restoring Emotional, Physical, Financial, and Time Reserves to Overloaded Lives*
Weight-loss Experts, Mayo Clinic. *Mayo Clinic Diet*
Wicks, Robert J. *Bounce: Living the Resilient Life*

Spiritual

Benner, David. *Sacred Companions: The Gift of Spiritual Friendship & Direction*

Blanchard, Ken, and Phil Hodges. *Lead Like Jesus*

Cordeiro, Wayne, and Bob Buford. *Leading on Empty: Refilling Your Tank and Renewing Your Passion*

Cowman, L. B., and Jim Reimann. *Streams in the Desert Daily Devotions: 366 Daily Devotional Readings*

Dillow, Linda. *Calm My Anxious Heart: A Woman's Guide to Finding Contentment*

Horn, Sara. *God Strong: The Military Wife's Spiritual Survival Guide*

Missler, Nancy, and Chuck Missler. *Be Ye Transformed Textbook: Understanding God's Truth*

Murphy, John Robin. *Be Transformed: A New Life Awaits*

Pace, Brenda, and Carol McGlothlin. *The One Year Yellow Ribbon Devotional: Take a Stand in Prayer for Our Nation and Those Who Serve*

TerKeurst, Lysa M. *Living Life on Purpose*

Zondervan Press. *Military Wives' New Testament*

Travel

Steves, Rick. *Rick Steves' Europe*

WEBSITES

Army Chaplain Corps

www.facebook.com/ArmyChaplainCorps
https://twitter.com/armychaplains
http://www.chapnet.army.mil/
http://www.usachcs.army.mil/

Army & Army Affiliated

www.myarmyonesource.com

Great source of information for the entire Family.

https://www.jointservicessupport.org/FP/Default.aspx

National Guard Family Programs

http://army.com/ako-army-knowledge-online.

Information about all things Army and access to resources.

www.army.mil

The official homepage of the US Army.

www.armytimes.com/

www.military.com/

www.armymwr.com/

http://www.redcross.org/

http://www.aafes.com/

www.operationwearehere.com

Contains a great list of organizations and websites for the military. There is a section for Chaplains, and a section for children, spouses, and civilians.

www.operationfaithfulsupport.com

Building strong and resilient Families throughout the deployment cycle. A national organization geared to keeping Families strong through local chapters at individual units that deal with all the pre-deployment, deployment, and redeployment issues on a monthly basis.

http://www.faithdeployed.com/

www.militaryinstallations.dod.mil/

http://myarmybenefits.us.army.mil

Personal

www.Flylady.net

Great organizational tips! Sign up for daily emails, get checklists on everything, such as emergencies, moving, time lines for home upkeep necessities, and so on.

www.blueletterbible.org

Travel

www.vacationstogo.com

It has a military section with tremendous discounts on cruises.

www.afvclub.com

http://www.ryanair.com/
Cheap flights throughout Europe!

APPLICATIONS

www.loseit.com
gasbuddy.com
This app finds the cheapest gas prices anywhere around you.
AroundMe
This can help you locate nearby restaurants, shopping, and other destinations.
Out of Milk
This app helps you share your shopping list with your spouse and lets you know when it has been bought or something else has been added from either party.

GLOSSARY

Language of the Chaplain Corps

AFCB—Armed Forces Chaplains Board.
C4—Chaplain Captain Career Course.
CCH—Chief of Chaplains.
CCP—Chaplain Candidate Program.
CAEP—Chaplain Advanced Education Program.
Chaplain Kit—A small case containing equipment/supplies used by Chaplains in the field or deployment to conduct worship rites/ordinances for Soldiers, such as Communion.
CH-BOLC—Chaplain Basic Officer Leadership Course.
CHAPNET—US Army Chaplain Corps website.
CPE—Clinical Pastoral Education.
CRM—Chaplain Resources Manager.
CSL—Center for Spiritual Leadership.
CTOF—Chapel Tithes and Offerings Fund.
CWR—Center for World Religion.

CWOC—Catholic Women of the Chapel. Military chapel auxiliary organization for Catholic women.
DACH—Department of the Army Chief of Chaplains.
DCCH—Deputy Chief of Chaplains.
DFGL—Distinctive Faith Group Leader.
DFRS—Distinctive Faith Religious Support.
DRE—Director of Religious Education.
Ecclesiastical Endorsement—Chaplains must be endorsed by an endorsing agent who certifies that they are trained in their respective faith group to practice as a Chaplain in the United States military.
FLC—Family Life Chaplain.
FLCTRCs—Family Life Chaplain Training and Resource Centers.
MCCW—Military Council of Catholic Women. A private, incorporated organization of Catholic women.
OCCH—Office of the Chief of Chaplains.
PMOC—Protestant Men of the Chapel.
PST—Pastoral Skills Training.
PST-CL—Pastoral Skills Training-Clinical.
PST-FL—Pastoral Skills Training-Family Life.
PWOC—Protestant Women of the Chapel.
PYOC—Protestant Youth of the Chapel.
RAC/REC—Religious Activity Center/Religious Education Center.
RO—Religious Organization.
RS—Religious Support.
RSA—Religious Support Activities.
RSCCH—Regional Support Command Chaplain.
RSO—Religious Support Operation.
RSP—Religious Support Plan.
UMT—Unit Ministry Team. Generally refers to the Chaplain and Chaplain's Assistant assigned together to a particular unit or organization.
USACHCS—United States Army Chaplain Center and School.

General Army Terms and Acronyms

AAFES (ay-fus)—Army and Air Force Exchange Service. Part of the military retail store system. Includes the Post Exchange or PX.

AC—Active Component.

ACAP (ay-cap)—Army Career and Alumni Program.

ACES—Army Continuing Education System.

ACS—Army Community Service. An organization usually found on Army posts that provides various services to Soldiers and their Families.

ACS—Advanced Civil Schooling. Fully funded graduate level schooling provided by the Army.

ACU—Army Combat Uniform. Current uniform worn by the Army, it is the successor of the BDU (Battle Dress Uniform) and the DCU (Desert Camouflage Uniform).

AD—Active Duty.

AER—Army Emergency Relief. A program that can provide limited financial assistance through loans or grants to qualifying individuals during times of emergency.

AFAP (ay-fap)—Army Family Action Plan, Armed Forces Action Plan.

AFN—American Forces Network.

AFTB—Army Family Team Building. An ACS program, usually run by volunteers, that helps educate Family Members about the Army. Online training is also available.

AG—Adjutant General.

AGR—Active Guard Reserve.

AIT—Advanced Individual Training. Training given to Soldiers, usually immediately following Basic Combat Training, that teaches them and qualifies them in a particular skill or occupational specialty. For example, Soldiers currently attend a specific AIT at Fort Jackson, South Carolina, to become qualified as Chaplain Assistants.

AMC—Army Materiel Command.

ANG—Air National Guard.

ANCOC—Advanced Non-commisioned Officer Course.

AO—Area of Operations.

APC—Armored Personnel carrier.

APF—Appropriated Funds.

APFT—Army Physical Fitness Test—also known as the PT test

APO—Army Post office.

AR—Army Regulation, or Army Reserve, or Armor.

ARC—American Red Cross.

ARCOM (r-com)—Army Commendation Medal.

Army OneSource—The single source for credible information, programs, services, and opportunities available for the entire Army Family (www.myarmyonesource.com).

ARNG—Army National Guard.

ASAP—As Soon As Possible.

AVN—Aviation.

AWOL (ay-wahl)—Absent Without Leave. The unapproved absence from the normal place of duty.

BAH—Basic Allowance for Housing. Money paid to Soldiers to help defray some of the costs of housing when the individual does not live in government provided housing. Amount is based on duty location, pay grade, and dependents.

Barracks—Living areas or dormitories where Soldiers who are not accompanied by Family Members live.

BAS—Basic Allowance for Subsistence. Money paid to Soldiers to help defray the cost of purchasing food when they are not required to eat in a government-provided dining facility.

BC—Battalion Commander.

BCT—Basic Combat Training. Training given to new enlisted Soldiers to give them basic knowledge of the Army and teach them basic Soldier skills.

BDE—Brigade.

"Be My Little General"—Mnemonic for remembering US military general ranks; Brigadier General (one star), Major General (two star), Lieutenant General (three star), General (four star).

BG—Brigadier General (rank); pay grade O-7.

BN—Battalion. A military organization usually exercising command and control of subordinate companies.

BNCOC—Basic NCO Course.

BOSS (boss)—Better Opportunities for Single Soldiers.

BSB—Base Support Battalion.

Care Team—Casualty response group tasked with helping Families deal with a death or other tragic events.

CDC—Child Development Center. A location that provides full, part-time, and hourly care for children from six weeks old to five years old.

CDR—Commander. The boss and person who is responsible for everything that does or does not happen within an organization.

CG—Commanding General. The general officer in charge of an organization.

CGSC—Command and General Staff College.

Chain of Command—A unit's leadership. This term is used to describe the level of leaders going in either direction, from the highest level leader down to the lowest or from the lowest up to the highest.

Chain of Concern—Spouse equivalent of chain of command.

CID—Criminal Investigation Division.

CINC—Commander In Chief. President of the United States.

Claim—Reimbursement requested for damages related to a military move.

Class Six—Liquor stores found on military installations. Operated by AAFES.

CO—Commanding officer. The officer in charge of an organization.

CO—Company. The designation for a unit created to provide command and control over a group of people (often made up of several subordinate platoons).

COB—Close of Business.

Coffee—In times past this was a get-together for officer's wives, and coffee, in fact, was served. Today the get-together may include spouses of all ranks and can take many forms, from traditional coffee and cake at someone's home to eating out together.

COL—Colonel (rank); pay grade O-6.

COLA (co-luh)—Cost of Living Allowance. Money paid to Soldiers to help defray some of the costs associated with higher-than-normal cost of living at certain duty stations, based on dependents, pay grade, duty location, and time in service.

Commissary—Grocery stores run by Defense Commissary Agency (DeCA), found on military installations.

CONUS (coh-nus)—Continental United States. A location inside the forty-eight contiguous United States.

CP—Command Post.

CPT—Captain (rank); pay grade O-3.

CSC—Community Spouses' Club.

CSF—Comprehensive Soldier Fitness.

CSM—Command Sergeant Major.

CY—Calendar Year.

CYSS—Child, Youth, and School Services. Army programs operated by FMWR that provide comprehensive child and youth programs for infants through twelfth grade.

DA—Department of the Army.

Dash One—OER support form "-1" (like a job report) produced by the service member and given to raters.

DCU—Desert Camouflage Uniform.

DeCA (dek-uh)—Defense Commissary Agency.

DEERS (dears)—Defense Enrollment Eligibility Reporting System. Computer database for tracking information about Soldiers and Family Members and their eligibility for access to services and benefits.

DENTAC (den-tak)—United States Army Dental Activity.

Dependent—Someone who is recognized by the Army as being a member of the immediate Family of a Soldier.

Deployment—Any travel away from the garrison that takes a Soldier either to war or training.

DPW—Director of Public Works.

DEROS (d-rohs)—Date of Estimated Rotation from Overseas Station.

DFAC (dee-fak)—Dining Facility, a.k.a. Mess Hall.

DFAS—Defense Finance and Accounting System. The payroll arm of Department of Defense.

DITY (dit-ee)—Do It Yourself (move). You may choose to move your household goods yourself and the military will reimburse you.

DLA—Dislocation Allowance. Partially reimburses a service member for the expenses incurred in relocating the household during a PCS.

DOB—Date of Birth.

DoD—Department of Defense. The branch of government responsible for all of the armed services.

DoDEA—Department of Defense Education Activity.

DoDDS (dahds)—Department of Defense Dependent Schools.

DOR—Date of Rank. The date the Army says you are officially the new rank.

DPS—Defense Personal Property System. Online system used to manage household goods shipments during a PCS.

DSN—Defense Switched Network. Worldwide defense communication system.

EFMP—Exceptional Family Member Program. A program that works with various agencies to provide services to Family Members with special needs.

EN—Enlisted.

ENG—Engineer.

EOD—Explosive Ordinance Disposal.

ERP—Employment Readiness Program. Training, education, information, and resources for those seeking employment.

ETA/ETD—Estimated Time of Arrival/Departure.

ETS—End (or Expiration) of Term of Service. The date when the Soldier's contractual obligation for duty will be complete and the Soldier can separate from the Army. Normally, only used for enlisted Soldiers but is informally used by officers at times.

EUCOM (u-com)—US European Command.

FA—Field Artillery.

FAC—Family Assistance Center.

FCC—Family Childcare. FCC providers are authorized by CYSS to provide childcare in their homes.

FLO—Family Liaison Office.

FM—Family Member.

FMWR—Family and Morale, Welfare, and Recreation. Programs and activities that provide support to Soldiers and their Family Members through such things as physical fitness facilities, libraries, sports programs, youth activities, child development programs, arts and crafts skill development, outdoor recreation and golf courses, bowling lanes, and clubs.

FORSCOM (force-com)—US Army Forces Command.

FPCON—Force Protection Condition.

Fraternization—A term used to describe associating in a familiar or intimate way with others in the service. Because of chain-of-command issues, some forms of fraternization are frowned upon or forbidden. It used to be that fraternization between enlisted Soldiers and officers was always frowned upon. Today, social interaction is allowed as long as it does not interfere with the chain of command.

FRG—Family Readiness Group. A group of people within a unit/organization who volunteer to provide support to Soldiers and Families. The FRG helps information flow among its members, the chain of command, and participating community activities.

FRSA—Family Readiness Support Assistant. Paid position responsible for administrative assistance within an FRG.

FSA—Family Separation Allowance.

FSGLI—Family Servicemembers' Group Life Insurance. Provides term life insurance coverage to the spouses and dependent children of service members insured under SGLI.

FTX—Field Training Exercise.

FY—Fiscal Year.

FYI—For Your Information.

FYSA—For Your Situational Awareness

Garrison—A military community that supports the functions of and provides the services for a military installation. A garrison commander is a lot like the mayor of a small town, supervising the services of those in his or her charge.

GBL—Government Bill of Lading. Household goods tracking and accountability paperwork associated with a PCS move.

GEN—General (rank); pay grade O-10.

GS—General Schedule. Government civilian employee pay grade.

HHC—Headquarters and Headquarters Company.

Hooah—Army slang (also used by the Air Force, though not as often) for everything except no. It might have originated as "Heard, Understood, and Acknowledged" (HUA), but that is only a theory.

HOR—Home of Record is defined as the state where the Soldier first enlisted or from where he or she received a commission from one of the branches of armed services.

Hourly Care—Childcare scheduled and provided on an hourly basis (babysitting) at on-post CYSS facilities.

HQ—Headquarters.

ID Card—A card issued by the Department of Defense that is used for personal identification and for access to programs and benefits.

IMCOM—Installation Management Command.

INF—Infantry.

IG—Inspector General.

ING—Inactive National Guard.

ILE—Intermediate Level Education. Course designed to prepare senior captains and majors for leadership positions in Army.

IRR—Individual Ready Reserve.

ITT—Information, Tours, and Travel. Offers discounted tickets to museums, parks, concerts, movies, and more.

Installation—Physical property owned by the federal government and commanded by a selected commander. May be made up of one or more sites. Are made up of one or more commands assigned to that location.

JAG (jag)—Judge Advocate General.

JMRC—Joint Multinational Readiness Center, Hohenfels, Germany.

JRTC—Joint Readiness Training Center, Fort Polk, Louisiana.

KIA—Killed in Action.

1LT—First Lieutenant (rank); pay grade O-2.

2LT—Second Lieutenant (rank); pay grade O-1.

Last 4—The last four digits of the social security number.

LES—Leave and Earnings Statement. The service member's monthly statement with pay and other helpful information including duty location, housing and subsistence allowance, dependents, insurance, leave time.

LTG—Lieutenant General (rank); pay grade O-9.

LP—Listening Post.

LTC—Lieutenant Colonel (rank); pay grade O-5.

LZ—Landing Zone.

MAC (mak)—Military Airlift Command.

MAJ—Major (rank); pay grade O-4.

MEDCOM—Army Medical Command.

MEDDAC (med-ak)—United States Army Medical Department Activity.

MEDEVAC (med-eh-vac)—Medical Evacuation.

Mess Hall—A large military cafeteria also known as Dining Facility (DFAC).

MFLC (m-flak)—Military Family Life Consultant. Licensed clinicians who provide assistance to Soldiers and their Families in solving issues resulting from deployment, reunions, reintegration, and/or other times of change.

MG—Major General (rank); pay grade O-8.

MI—Military Intelligence.

MIA—Missing in Action.

Mid-Tour Leave—Leave (approximately two weeks) given to a Soldier serving in a non-Family duty station of more than nine months' duration. Informally called R&R—Rest and Recuperation.

MOS—Military Occupational Specialty. A job classification, skill, or trade. Each has an alphanumerical representation and a title, for example, 56 is the MOS for a Chaplain, 56A for a command and unit Chaplain, 56D for a Clinical Pastoral Educator, and 56M for a Chaplain Assistant.

MP—Military Police. The Army's police force.

MRD—Mandatory Removal Date.

MRE—Meal, Ready to Eat. Complete, packaged meals that are usually provided to Soldiers in an operational (field) environment.

MTF—Military Treatment Facility. A health care facility such as a clinic or hospital.

NA—Not Applicable.

NAF—Non-Appropriated Funds (generated locally).

NATO (nay-toh)—North Atlantic Treaty Organization.

NCO—Non-commissioned Officer. An enlisted person who has been promoted to the rank of corporal or sergeant and above (E4-E9).

NCOER—Non-commissioned Officer Evaluation Report.

NCOIC—Non-commissioned Officer in Charge.

NG—National Guard.

NLT—Not Later Than.

Noncombatant—Those who do not participate in hostilities in the military; protocol I, 8 June 1977, Article 43.2 of the Geneva Conventions designates that Chaplains maintain this status.

NTC—National Training Center, Fort Irwin, California.

OCONUS (oh-coh-nuhs)—Outside Continental United States.

OER—Officer Evaluation Report.

OIC—Officer in Charge.

Operational Unit—Units designated for the practical purposes related to warfare as opposed to garrison units, which are for base support.

OSC—Officer Spouses' Club.

PAO—Public Affairs Officer.

PCS—Permanent Change of Station. The physical move from one duty location to another.

PLT—Platoon.

POA—Power of Attorney.

POC—Point of Contact.

Post 9/11 GI Bill—Education tuition bill for eligible Soldiers who served after September 10, 2001.

POV—Privately Owned Vehicle.

POW—Prisoner of War.

Protocol—This is the strict form of etiquette and diplomatic courtesy, customs of service (system of accepted social patterns and traditions accepted by the military), and common courtesies (the traits of kindness, friendliness, thoughtfulness, and consideration of others) to create order. They let us know what to expect in a given situation.

PT—Physical Training.

PTSD—Post-Traumatic Stress Disorder. A type of anxiety disorder that may occur following experiencing a traumatic event.

PX—Post Exchange. Retail stores operated by AAFES on Army and Air Force installations.

RA—Regular Army.

RC—Reserve Component.

RD—Rear Detachment.

REG—Regiment.

RFO—Request for Orders.

R&R—Rest and Relaxation/Recuperation

ROTC—Reserve Officers Training Corps.

RSVP—*Respondez S'il Vous Plait.* A French phrase translated loosely as "please reply."

SD—Staff Duty.

SFL TAP—Soldier for Life Transition Assistance Program.

SGLI—Servicemembers' Group Life Insurance. Low-cost group life insurance provided by VA to service members.

SHAPE (shape)—Supreme Headquarters Allied Powers Europe.

Shoppette—Convenience stores, also known as the Express, on Army installations operated by AAFES, often co-located with gas stations.

SITREP (sit-rep)—Situation Report.

SLO—School Liaison Officer.

SLR—State of Legal Residence. SLR is considered your permanent home, the state where you intend to live after you leave the military. This state is considered your residency for state income tax purposes. In addition, state of legal residence is used to determine qualification for in-state tuition rates, eligibility to vote for federal and state elections, and for a will to be probated.

SMI—Supplemental Medical Insurance.

SOCOM (soh-com)—Special Operations Command.

SOP—Standing (or Standard) Operating Procedure. A set of instructions for handling a particular situation or process—the normal way of doing business.

Space-A Travel (Military Hops)—Air Force planes that are taking Soldiers and/or equipment to a mission. On certain occasions, military personnel and their Families can fly on a space available basis for free. Also called Military Airlift Command (MAC) flight.

SQD—Squad. A unit within a platoon.

SSN—Social Security Number

TA-50—Common Table of Allowance #50. The list of special clothing and equipment used by Soldiers when operating in the field; includes things like helmets, ruck sacks, canteens, and so on.

TDY—Temporary Duty. Duty performed at some location other than the permanently assigned location. A single TDY trip is usually limited to 179 days or less.

TLA—Temporary Living Allowance.

TMP—Transportation Motor Pool.

TOC (tock)—Tactical Operational Center.

TRADOC (tray-dock)—Training and Doctrine Command.

TRICARE—TRICARE is the health care program serving Uniformed Service members, retirees, and their Families worldwide.

TSP—Thrift Savings Plan.

UCMJ—Uniform Code of Military Justice. The military's set of laws. Like a civilian penal code, it defines crimes and lesser offenses recognized under military law and the boundaries of punishment for each offense. It provides the right of defense for the Soldier. It provides for the manner under which each offense is brought before a commander or tried before a jury or panel.

Unit—Used to refer to the military organization a Soldier is assigned to.

USAREUR (use-a-rur)—US Army Europe.

USAR—United States Army Reserve.

USARC—United States Army Reserve Command.

USARPAC (use-er-pak)—US Army Pacific.

USO—United Services Organization.

VA—Department of Veterans Affairs (formerly Veterans Administration).

WO—Warrant Officer.

Weight Restrictions—Limits on the amount of household goods military personnel are authorized.

WIA—Wounded in Action.

XO—Executive Officer.